The Great Wines of Burgundy

The Great Wines of BURGUNDY

HUBRECHT DUIJKER

Chablis, Côte d'Or, Chalonnais, Mâconnais and Beaujolais

FOREWORD BY
Louis Latour

INTRODUCTION BY
Hugh Johnson

Photography by Peter van der Velde

CRESCENT BOOKS

Contents

Art direction: Will van Sambeek Design Associates, Amsterdam
Photography: Peter van der Velde, Amsterdam and Hubrecht Duijker
Maps: Otto van Eersel
First impression 1977

English translation by Danielle de Froidmont Associates

ISBN 0-517-418177

Printed in the Netherlands

Typeset and prepared by T&O Graphics and Taylor Jackson Designs Ltd, Lowestoft, Suffolk

First published in the U.S.A. by
Crescent Books
a division of
Crown Publishers Inc.
New York.

© 1977, 1982 by Het Spectrum B.V.
English translation © Mitchell Beazley Publishers 1983

Foreword

Clever people, expert in the stern science of modern economics, are agreed that the wine growers of Burgundy are hopelessly backward. Could there be anything more difficult to reconcile with rational business methods than Burgundy's incredible variety of *crus*, which every year are further diversified by the whims of sun and rain into an infinite range of wines, all of them different?

Harvested by thousands of growers, and sold all over the world by dozens of *négociants*, it is obvious that individually Burgundian wines do not have the volume to achieve the 'critical mass' a modern trade commodity needs if it is to imprint its name in the mind of the buying public.

To come up to date we would have to reorganize our vineyards, abolish dozens of *appellations* and make the taste of our wines more uniform. In short, we would have to bring about a thoroughgoing change in the rather untidy inheritance that our forefathers have handed down to us since the times of the Romans.

But who is more stubborn than a wine grower of Burgundy? He abhors any such all-too-easily given advice. He only knows that a particularly piece of his vineyard provides a number of vats of unforgettable wine one year, and only a few bottles of very moderate stuff another. This is the result of the remarkable and variable local 'alchemy of nature' — notwithstanding all the steadfast husbandry of the grower.

The Burgundians in fact ask themselves whether, having been behind in technological development, they are not now becoming pioneers, far ahead of their time. Today we see the consumer turning away from standardized industrial production and beginning to value the great wines, which are rare witnesses of a mode and style of life that has almost vanished.

To grasp this Burgundian truth, which is more than just a lesson in geography or economics, you have to get to the root of the vine, as it were. You have to become acquainted with the French countryside at first hand and get to know the real

Introduction

Burgundians. They are stubborn individualists, whether growers attached to their land for generations, or *négociants* — it makes little difference which, for the latter nearly all come from peasant stock and are proud to own one or more plots in the most famous vineyards.

Hubrecht Duijker has realized that the true Burgundy is that of the Burgundians themselves; and so he has frequently visited our towns and villages, for months at a time, talking with the people, looking at their cellars and tasting their wines. No one knows the hard life of the grower better than he, the joy over a successful vintage and the many phases of every wine year. This is the life of the wine grower, of the Burgundian countryside, and this is the actual subject of this remarkable book.

The reader, having enjoyed the informative and enthusiastically written text and the splendid illustrations, will without doubt be able to join the select band of connoisseurs who, all over the world, admire the great wines of Burgundy and reckon them among the best.

Louis Latour
President of the Comité Interprofessionnel de la Côte d'Or et de l'Yonne pour les Vins d'Appellation d'Origine Contrôlée de Bourgogne
Vice President of the Syndicat des Négociants en Vins Fins de Bourgogne
Member of the Comité National et Régional de l'Institut National des Appellations d'Origine

Regular visitors to the wine regions of France soon become aware that, contrary to British folk-lore, we are not the only, nor even the most active, northern investigators of these Elysian fields. Holland and Belgium, small though they are in man-power, are rich, critical and even more fanatical followers of French wine at every level.

For several years now I have been bumping into a young Dutch writer whose reception by the (often hard-boiled) French producers has impressed me. They like him. They open their bottles, estate records, and even their homes to him. I think it is his cool candour they admire: not always the easiest attitude when tasting the grower's pride under his gaze.

Hubrecht Duijker, this cool young man, has spent the greater part of the last decade in France, methodically tasting, interviewing and photographing to make the most complete album of France and its better wine growers that anyone has yet produced. The first volumes, on Bordeaux, were rapturously received by the Bordeaux growers — not the easiest fraternity to please. The two later volumes, on Burgundy, and on the trio of Alsace, Champagne and the Loire, have had the same reception. Translated into French they have sold like buns.

Hubrecht was kind enough to tell me, when we first met five years ago in Amsterdam, that my World Atlas of Wine was his first inspiration. I am very happy, having read and profited by his books, to have sparked something so thorough, so graphic, and so enjoyable. Duijker's books are the perfect armchair journey through my favourite French provinces: the ideal appetizer to their incomparable wines.

Hugh Johnson
London

Burgundy is a beautiful region of subtly changing landscapes, atmospheric little towns and fine buildings. It is a hospitable and very pleasurable region of genial people, a region of gastronomy with many good restaurants and delicious specialities.

But above all Burgundy is a wine region, one of the most famous in the world, at once extraordinarily complete and very complex. This book is about all these aspects of Burgundy, with of course great emphasis on the wine. From north to south you will learn about the districts, the communes, the vineyards and wine makers; plus some hundreds of the wines themselves, with descriptions and labels. I discovered them during long quests to some fifty *négociants* and a couple of hundred estates.

A book such as this cannot be put together by one person. Many individuals and bodies have helped me to gather information, to carry out my programme of visits, and in the preparation of the book. I thank them for all their support, advice and, frequently, hospitality. In particular I would like to mention M. Lucien Rateau of the Comité Interprofessionnel de la Côte d'Or et de l'Yonne; Raymond Cullas of the Comité Interprofessionnel de Saône et Loire pour les Vins d'A.O.C. de Bourgogne et de Mâcon; and M. G. Canard of the Union Interprofessionelle des Vins du Beaujolais. I am also very indebted to the Netherlands division of Sopexa, and to Christopher Fielden — himself the author of an excellent book on Burgundy — who helped me with practical counsel. Finally I must not forget Pieter Taselaar, a great connoisseur and lover of Burgundy, and its wines, who read my manuscript with a critic's eye.

Hubrecht Duijker

Burgundy

Burgundy is a place, a spirit, a wine — in brief — a world; and so it has been for centuries. The history of Burgundy began in the 5th century with the invasion of the Burgundii, a fairly peaceful barbarian people who originated in Scandinavia. After the fall of the Roman Empire they wandered for some time before settling in a fertile region to the east of what was then Gaul. They formed themselves into a kingdom and it was a Burgundii princess, Clotilde, who married the famous Frankish king, Clovis. Subject first to rule by the Merovingian, and then the Carolingian empire, Burgundia remained an independent kingdom until the 9th century when, under the impetus of Richard d'Autun, called the Just, it became a duchy. From kingdom to duchy might seem a demotion, but in fact, it was under the rule of these dukes that Burgundy made its mark on history.

The wine-loving duke

One of the most remarkable dukes of Burgundy was Philip the Bold, thus named because he fought so bravely in the battle of Poitiers when he was only 17 years old. Other victories followed, and other conquests, the most profitable of which was a private one — marriage to Marguerite of Flanders in 1369. She brought as a dowry the area of Europe now known as Benelux and at a stroke doubled the size of the duchy of Burgundy. For several years Philip virtually deserted Dijon and spent most of his time at his châteaux in Ghent and Bruges.
This powerful duke of Burgundy was very keen on wine-growing. It was he, for example, who forbade the growing of Gamay, a grape of which he did not approve, and ordered Beaune to be served with meals at court. It was also Philip the Bold who introduced the custom of the 'banquet', where the guests ate seated at benches round a table. In addition, he was the first host to present a menu, then called an *escriteau*, to his guests. After a life full of ostentation, pleasure and plenty, Philip the Bold died in 1404, a ruined but happy man.

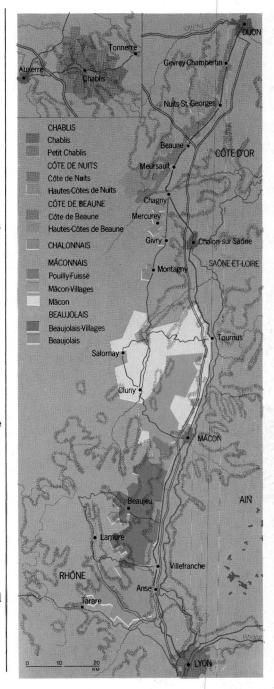

CHABLIS
Chablis
Petit Chablis
CÔTE DE NUITS
Côte de Nuits
Hautes-Côtes de Nuits
CÔTE DE BEAUNE
Côte de Beaune
Hautes-Côtes de Beaune
CHALONNAIS
MÂCONNAIS
Pouilly-Fuissé
Mâcon-Villages
Mâcon
BEAUJOLAIS
Beaujolais-Villages
Beaujolais

Burgundy becomes French

The growing power of the dukes of
Burgundy often antagonized the kings of
France, until Louis XI finally succeeded in
raising an alliance against Burgundy. In
1477, the last Duke of Valois, Charles the
Bold, was attacked by several enemies,
including Switzerland. In the course of this
war he lost not only his wealth and his lands,
but also his life. Finally, Burgundy became a
possession of the kingdom of France and
ceased to exist as a duchy. Although traces
of this glorious age are to be found all over
Burgundy, I was assured by a wine grower
that, by and large, the defeat of the Duke of
Burgundy was a good thing, 'since a victory
for Burgundy would not only have given us
the whole of Switzerland, but its wines as
well, and that would have spoiled the
wonderful unity of our own wines.'

The influence of the church

At the same time as ducal power was
increasing, Christianity was also gaining in
influence. In 910 the Benedictine order
founded the abbey at Cluny and soon became
proprietors of an enormous estate,
comprising vineyards planted and cultivated
by the monks themselves, using land they
had acquired or been given. The memory of
the monks of Cluny, renowned for their
influence and their dedication to work, still
survives in many communes in Burgundy.
After 1098, some relaxation in discipline,
compared to the austere rule of St Benedict,
led to a schism in the community. A group of
monks, determined to maintain the original
strict Benedictine regime, founded a new
abbey at Cîteaux, not far from Dijon. These
monks, the Cistercians, in turn acquired vast
estates in the area known today as le Clos de
Vougeot. The religious orders undoubtedly
gave a great boost to wine-growing in
Burgundy, not only by bringing land into
cultivation but also by transmitting their
experience and knowledge of the science of
wine-growing to growers outside the church.
It is also to the monks that Burgundy owes

its innumerable Romanesque churches, the
solid walls of which have defied the
centuries.

Five regions

Present-day Burgundy extends over five
départments: Yonne, Côte d'Or, Saône-et-
Loire, and parts of Nièvre and Ain. The wine-
growing district of Burgundy, with which we
are concerned, is different in composition to
the administrative district of Burgundy. The
former is divided into five regions: to the
north and to one side, a little away from the
others, is the area of Yonne known as
Chablis; and 75 miles from there, south of
Dijon, is the Côte d'Or, the heart of
Burgundy, with the most famous communes
and the most celebrated wines (the Côte d'Or
has given its name to the *département*). To
the south of the Côte d'Or is the Chalonnais,
smallest and narrowest of the regions, which
owes its name to the town of Chalon-sur-
Saône and belongs to the Saône-et-Loire
département. Then comes the Mâconnais,
also in the *département* of Saône-et-Loire.
Finally there is Beaujolais, the most
southerly region, part of the Rhône
département and producer of the largest
quantity of wine. Thus the wine-growing
district known as Burgundy is a long, fairly
narrow strip of land which starts to the
southeast of Paris, near Auxerre, and ends,
with a few interruptions, almost 200 miles
away, near Lyon.

Fine wines from the north

The fact that vineyards are often situated on
narrow strips of land throughout Burgundy
indicates that wine-growing is very closely
dependent on natural conditions. In the Côte
d'Or, for example, grapes yielding wine of
the highest quality occupy only a tiny part of
the *département*. In fact, the composition of
the soil determines the quality of the wine.
Together with other factors, such as hours of
sunshine and drainage, it is the soil which
encourages or inhibits plant growth. In
Burgundy, the good soils are often full of

calcium and contain marl, gravel and clay.
Occasionally, as in Beaujolais, granite is to
be found. Vines generally grow best in
barren soil, putting down deep roots to reach
rich layers of nourishment far below the
surface. It is precisely because the roots
have to thrust deeply into the subsoil to find
nourishment that the very qualities of this
soil are to be found in the vine, the grape and
ultimately the wine. The manifold subtleties
of the wine therefore reflect the complexity
of the land itself. Burgundy is the most
northerly region in the world to produce red
and white wines of such exceptional quality.
It lies at an apparently unfavourable latitude
and possesses a capricious climate (Chablis
frequently has spring frosts and hail is a
recurring hazard all over Burgundy), but
despite this the sky is often sunny, so much
so that between 1969 and 1974 no vintage
has been entirely lost.

Democracy at work

The notable feature of wine-growing in
Burgundy is that all the vineyards are
'parcelled up'. After the French Revolution,
the vast ecclesiastical and secular estates
were confiscated and sold for the benefit of
the people, and with each generation the
number of divisions multiplied. The
parcelling up of the land in this manner was
a true example of democratic action.
Approximately 100,000 acres of vineyards
which produce *appellation d'origine
contrôlée* wines are divide up between 10,000
wine growers. These figures give a
theoretical average of almost 10 acres per
grower. In the Côte d'Or the average falls to
about 5 acres. More than 94% of all
Burgundy growers cultivate less than 25
acres. Burgundy is a long succession of
vineyards, divided up into a multitude of
plots, which each owner cultivates according
to his own methods and customs. Some
growers, even those with only small
harvests, are equipped to make and bottle
the wine themselves. Often, however, the
quantity of grapes produced is too small for
the growers to make their own wine. For this

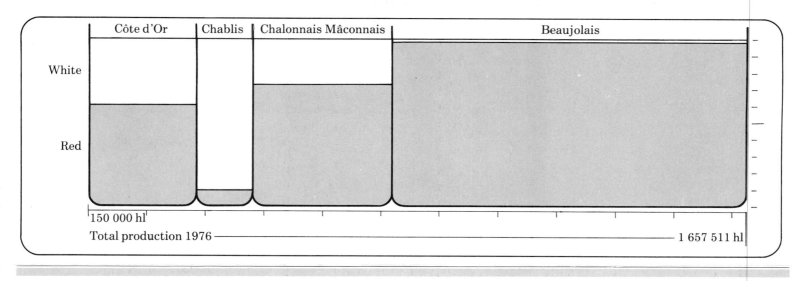

	Côte d'Or	Chablis	Chalonnais Mâconnais	Beaujolais

White

Red

150 000 hl

Total production 1976 ——————————————————— 1 657 511 hl

Burgundy

---

reason most of the actual wine-making is undertaken by the *négociants* (shippers) and, more recently, by the cooperatives, whose roles will be explained in the chapter devoted to the wine trade.

The dividing up of the vineyards into small 'parcels' gives a very individual character to the wine-making scene in Burgundy. It means, for example, that 10 or 12 proprietors of the same vineyard will produce very different wines in the same year, each grower working according to his own ability, methods and tastes, and producing a wine heavily influenced by these very personal characteristics.

Surprising discoveries

For the wine lover, the choice of a good burgundy is a particularly complicated affair; not only because of the enormous number of *appellations,* but because each one of these covers wines of such varying qualities. The strict, precise classification of Bordeaux, with its châteaux of greater or lesser importance, each making wine according to approved methods, is totally absent in Burgundy, and this apparent lack of order may discourage the consumer. How, in fact, do you find your way through this confusion? Even the importer can get lost. Furthermore, the price of burgundy is relatively higher than that of Bordeaux, and for an obvious reason: the wines of Burgundy, though a smaller area than Bordeaux, are in greater demand. How, therefore, to avoid making a bad buy? This book does not presume to give definitive guidance, but attempts to put the reader on the right track. It is worth stressing that by reason of such variety, the wines of Burgundy always hold out the possibility of new discoveries and pleasant surprises. In this region where no estate prides itself on an age-old tradition, any cellar you visit may contain treasures if you know where to look for them.

A friendly wine

The celebrated wine connoisseur, Harry Waugh, whose *Diaries of a Wine-taster* are essential reading, was once asked if he had ever managed to confuse a red burgundy with a red Bordeaux. He replied: 'Not since lunch'. In one succinct phrase he managed to summarize a world of truth, for there are many misconceptions about red burgundy. It is very often regarded as a heavy red wine, full-bodied and intoxicating, which produces a replete feeling after only a few glasses. The truth is that the finest red burgundies have great elegance, undeniable charm and only a moderate degree of alcohol. In this way they resemble, more than might be imagined, a soft, generous Bordeaux, such as a Saint-Emilion or a Pomerol. It is generally fairly easy to distinguish between a red burgundy and a red Bordeaux: the composition of the soil, the grapes and the methods of wine-making are very different. If you link them together, you find that the burgundy is fuller, rounder, more velvety, less harsh than a Bordeaux. Often these are only subtle differences, but they are precisely the characteristic qualities which make burgundy such a broadly accessible wine. Its bouquet explodes, as it were, out of the glass, full of warmth and hospitality. Bordeaux often seems severe, cold and unattainable; burgundy is always exuberant, friendly and understandable. It should be appreciated, however, that red Bordeaux often outclasses burgundy in distinction, finesse, breeding and depth. The film actor and producer Gene Wilder has described this difference admirably in *Decanter Magazine:* 'I can appreciate Bordeaux intellectually, but I am a burgundy man at heart.'

Burgundy

Bons vivants

While lovers of red Bordeaux and red burgundy may never be able to agree about the qualities of the two wines, they are completely at one on the pre-eminence of the great white burgundies. Dry and brilliant, these white wines are, without doubt, the finest in the world; and the Grand Crus of Puligny-Montrachet, Chassagne-Montrachet, Aloxe-Corton and Chablis have no equals. They outclass all other dry white wines in their richness, delicacy and subtlety. Be it red or white, however, a burgundy always testifies more or less to the character of the district from which it comes and the personality of the man who produces it. In general, Burgundians are warm, outward-going, hospitable people who seem glad to be alive and celebrate with good food and wine. But they also have a certain philosophy: they know that one bad hailstorm can destroy an entire vintage — and so they console themselves with the old adage: 'When my glass is full, I empty it; when it is empty, I fill it.'

Grape Varieties

Despite the enormous number of Burgundy appellations, the grape varieties they are made from are strictly limited. Indeed, the majority of burgundies come from only four grapes: for red wine, Pinot Noir and Gamay; for white wines, Chardonnay and Aligoté.

Pinot Noir

Pinot Noir is the noblest Burgundian grape, used to produce all the great wines of the Côte d'Or and the Chalonnais. Its history goes back at least as far as the Gauls. The grapes grow in tight clusters which look like large pine-cones and from the French word for pine-cone 'pin', comes the name 'pinot'. The grapes are small, sweet and juicy. Pinot Noir, with its colourless juice, is also grown in more than half the vineyards of Champagne. It is generally very resistant to cold winter weather, but its early growth exposes it more than any other to the particular risk of spring frosts. There are many varieties of Pinot Noir and some of the commoner, less 'well-bred' ones produce fatter bunches of grapes. The grower who goes only for the best quality, however, always prefers the small Pinot, despite its lower yield.

Gamay

The Gamay grape was introduced into Burgundy by the Chevalier du May, who brought it back from the Middle East. However, the wine it produced was of such mediocre quality that in 1395 Philip the Bold forbade the growing of these 'very wicked and very disloyal' plants (see page 127). Nowadays, Gamay is mainly grown in Beaujolais and Mâconnais, where it produces excellent results. There are several varieties of this grape but the best is known officially as Gamay Noir au jus blanc (black Gamay with white juice). Outside Beaujolais and Mâconnais some vineyards planted with Gamay produce an unpretentious wine, often sold under the *appellation* of Bourgogne Grand Ordinaire. A mixture of two-thirds Gamay to one-third Pinot Noir gives a wine with the *appellation* of Bourgogne Passetoutgrains.

Chardonnay

Chardonnay is to white burgundy what Pinot Noir is to red burgundy. From Chablis (where it is called Beaunois) to Beaujolais, this grape produces all the great white burgundies. The vine grows more slowly than Pinot Noir and its elongated grapes are less compact. Reference is very frequently made, even in Burgundy, to the Pinot-Chardonnay. This is an error, for such a vine does not exist. The grape in question may either be Pinot Blanc (though despite the fact that its cultivation is authorized this is no longer planted because it produces a wine with little perfume) or Chardonnay.

Aligoté

Like Gamay, the Aligoté is a grape of lesser quality. Because of its size, it tends to give quite a lot of wine. Bourgogne Aligoté usually has a fairly high acidity. It is pleasant as an aperitif or as an accompaniment to a simple, hearty meal. Long known in Burgundy, it often used to be mixed with Chardonnay.

Other grapes

Other grapes are used, in certain proportions, to produce the lesser burgundies. For white wines these are Pinot Blanc, Pinot Gris (or Beurot, Burot), Melon de Bourgogne, Sacy and Sauvignon; for red wines they are César and Tressot.

Making the Wine

Each year, the arrival of autumn in Burgundy heralds the start of an immense 'chess game' between nature and the wine makers, a game in which the pieces and the rules stay the same, but the moves differ. Once the harvest is gathered in, the game starts in earnest from the moment the wine-making process commences. The maker's aim is to transmit to the wine all the character potentially contained in the grape. This apparently simple task actually requires enormous experience, since the caprices of nature present different challenges every year, necessitating an immediate and effective reaction. The slightest wrong move, the smallest detail, will influence the final quality of the wine. Should the stalks be removed or not? Should this be done to all or part of the vintage? To what temperature should the must be heated? What sort of vat should be used? How long should the fermentation be left? To what temperature should the fermenting wine be allowed to go? Should the wine be stored in new or old casks? At what point should it be bottled? Should it be filtered at this point, and if so, which filter should be used? The many problems that face individual wine makers, explain why in Burgundy wines of the same vintage and the same *appellation* may often have very different characteristics.

Ancienne or nouvelle méthode

Over the years, wine-making has often been the subject of heated discussion. It is frequently said that red wine today is not what is used to be: that it is lighter, that it ages less successfully, and that its quality leaves much to be desired. It is alleged that past generations of wine makers used to produce vigorous wines, with a good colour, which aged over many years. It is certainly true that since World War II, the quality of red burgundy has not always been beyond reproach. The *négociants-éleveurs*, keen to develop their markets, have often offered large qualities of disappointing wine, lacking in character. It is also true that modern *négociants* and owners, even those who are truly quality conscious, produce a wine which seems less concentrated than those between the wars. Are the new methods of wine-making the only cause? Probably less than might be imagined, since what is called the *ancienne méthode* came into force as being rather fashionable only at the end of the 19th century. In their book, *Burgundy Vines and Wines*, Arlott and Fielden suggest that during this period the demand for burgundies had so diminished that it was once more necessary to produce wines which would take a long time to age. To this end, the traditionally short fermentation period of five to six days was abandoned; the grape stalks were left in contact with the must and the skins so as to increase appreciably the level of tannin. In this manner a full-bodied, highly coloured wine was obtained which required several years of ageing before it acquired any degree of suppleness.

The risks of over-production

Over a period of 50 years, the *ancienne méthode* has progressively been abandoned in favour of short fermentation and a partial or total removal of the grape stalks. The *négociant-éleveur* Louis Latour views the *ancienne méthode* as a bit of a myth: 'For more than 100 years we have used the same method to make our wine, as have many others. It is therefore quite absurd to attribute the fact that the wine may be less full-bodied than before solely to the wine-making process. Excessive production is the principal reason why these wines are too light'. Other *négociants-éleveurs* confirmed these opinions. Yves Thomas, of Maison Moillard, told me: 'It is well known that the quality of red wine is largely determined by the skin of the grape. If the yield is heavy, the grapes swell, the skin becomes thinner and this leads to a wine which is too light. Years ago my grandmother in Belgium used to transport grapes by train without any problem. Nowadays, those you send by train arrive rotten.'

Making the wine

Improved techniques

No one can really deny that wine-making methods have changed a great deal since the beginning of the century. At one time each maker worked according to local tradition and personal initiative, whereas the knowledge they now have at their disposal, gleaned from serious oenological study, has reduced the role of chance to a minimum. Scientific methods have replaced intuition and empirical judgments. Furthermore, there is rigorous and regular control of temperature during fermentation. However, these modern techniques do not imply a total commitment to the use of chemical products. Max Léglise, director of the research station in Beaune, commented: 'It is essential to conserve the wine's natural character, and therefore to eliminate as far as possible the use of artificial products.' Louis Latour adds: 'The greatest quality of the wine grower is patience. You must never force nature.' The new wine-making techniques meet little opposition. André Gagey, of Maison Louis Jadot (probably one of the finest *négociants* of the Côte d'Or) gave a very fair summary of the general opinion: 'From my own experience, the new wine-making methods yield very interesting results — particularly in mediocre years when they help to produce a good wine in spite of unfavourable circumstances. There are no longer any truly terrible vintages, whereas previously they were all too frequent. Furthermore, in good years these modern techniques produce a wine that is far superior to anything that could have been made under the same circumstances in the past. White wines, in particular, are much fresher and altogether better today than they were yesterday.' Thanks to the new methods, the quality of burgundy has genuinely improved, and if over-production can be curtailed, future results will be even better.

Wine Legislation and Classifications

In 1976, Burgundy produced about 22,000,000 cases of wine, of which approximately 18,400,000 cases were entitled to the term 'appellation d'origine contrôlée'. It is this wine, designated under the general term 'burgundy', with which this book is concerned. The remaining 3,500,000 or so cases are for drinking straight away, inasmuch as they are anonymous lesser wines for everyday drinking. In order to be an 'appellation d'origine contrôlée', the wine must satisfy certain legal and technical requirements concerning place of origin, grapes used, methods of cultivation, pruning, yield per hectare, minimum degree of alcohol and wine-making methods employed. Some of these conditions remain constant, such as the position of the vineyard and the way the vines are planted and cultivated; others are a question of individual know-how or of variations in climate. These latter considerations can make a considerable difference to the yield per hectare. The law takes all such factors into account when classifying a wine. Experience has shown that the quality of the wine is inversely proportional to quantity, and so legislation has been introduced which specifically limits the yield per hectare of the best quality *crus*. For the appellation of Bourgogne Rouge, for example, the law allows the production of 50 hectolitres per hectare while for Le Montrachet the authorized yield may not exceed 30 hectolitres per hectare.

Former rules

Rules designed to limit yield are very valuable if rigorously applied. Until 1974 no one was very concerned about the problem. If a grower produced, say, 60 hectolitres (650 cases) from one hectare of Chambertin, he would divide it up roughly as follows: 30 hectolitres (325 cases) of Chambertin, 5 hectolitres (55 cases) of Gevrey-Chambertin, 15 hectolitres (160 cases) of red burgundy and 10 hectolitres (110 cases) of vin rouge. Yet all these wines originated in the same vat! So the grower had to accept inferior appellations for his surplus and was

theoretically deprived of a certain margin of profit — although he stood to gain by reason of abundant quantity.

Rules enforced since 1974

The above-mentioned practices sometimes resulted in totally excessive yields per hectare, and for this reason burgundy was for a time of poor quality. Since 1974, however, things have changed. If in 1979 a vineyard yielded too much wine, the grower who produces Chambertin, for example, was faced with several alternatives:
1. To declare 30 hectolitres (325 cases) of Chambertin and send the rest to be distilled. (In 1982 the limit went up to 35 hectolitres.)
2. To request an additional 20%, i.e. 36 hectolitres (390 cases), in which case the wine has to be tasted by a special commission. If the commission's judgment is favourable, the 36 hectolitres can be sold as Chambertin; if not, the whole amount has to go for distillation. In this instance it is all or nothing.
3. Deliberately to lower the class of the wine and present it as Gevrey-Chambertin, up to the amount of 35 hectolitres per hectare.
4. To ask for Gevrey-Chambertin plus 20%, which also requires official inspection.
5. Deliberately to reclassify the wine and present it as Bourgogne Rouge, up to the amount of 50 hectolitres per hectare.
6. To ask for Bourgogne Rouge plus 20%, which also has to be officially inspected.
This new system may have its drawbacks, but by and large it is a considerable improvement over the old method. It has recently been completed by the introduction of regulations requiring all wines to be inspected. These new regulations, aiming to preserve quality, are designed, above all, to prevent over-production; others will doubtless be introduced in the future concerning such matters as the use of fertilizers and the choice of grape.

The five categories

The wines of Burgundy can be neatly divided into five categories: *Wines of regional*

appellations produced throughout the Burgundy wine-growing area, e.g: Bourgogne, Bourgogne Aligoté.
Wines of a regional appellation produced in a specific area, e.g: Beaujolais, Côte de Beaune-Villages.
Wines with the appellation of a commune or village, e.g: Pommard, Fleurie.
Premiers Crus wines, e.g: Meursault-Charmes.
Grand Crus wines, e.g: Chambertin, Musigny.
If the meaning of the first three categories is self-evident, the latter two require some explanation.
The law designates as *Premiers Crus* those wines coming from hamlets or vineyards more inclined than their neighbours to produce quality wines. There are hundreds of *Premiers Crus*, which are essentially wines from a commune, but of higher quality. A *Premier Cru* can be indicated in several ways on the label:
a) MEURSAULT-CHARMES: the size of the letters of the hamlet, in this case, Charmes, must not be greater than that of the commune name.
b) MEURSAULT-CHARMES PREMIER CRU.
c) MEURSAULT PREMIER CRU or 1ER CRU: this wine may be a mixture of several *Premiers Crus* from Meursault.
The phrase 'appellation contrôlée' or 'appellation Meursault-Charmes Contrôlée' or 'appellation Meursault 1er Cru Contrôlée'. With regard to wines from a commune, it is permitted, under certain circumstances, to add the name of a hamlet which does not have the right to the designation *Premier Cru*. The size of the letters of this hamlet must not be more than half that of the commune and it is obligatory, in this instance, to place the name of the commune between the words 'appellation' and 'contrôlée'. Subtle though this difference may be, it is important.
Grand Crus constitute the élite of Burgundy and are associated with growers of very long-standing reputation. Therefore they have their own appellation, which consists of the place-name alone, without mention of the commune, e.g: 'Chambertin, appellation contrôlée';'Montrachet, appellation contrôlée'.

Frequently used terms

Appellation: abbreviation for *appellation d'origine contrôlée,* protected name of origin.

Climat: vineyard.

Clos: A vineyard enclosed by a wall, originally as a protection against wild and domestic animals. The name 'clos' was officially registered in each vineyard in 1935; the criterion at that time demanded that the wall enclosing the vineyard be 5 feet high and 20 inches wide. Since 1935 many of the walls have disappeared but the word 'clos' still remains.

Domaine: an estate made up of vineyards and producing nothing but wine.

Égrappage: an operation to separate the stalks from the grapes.

Élevage: literally 'education', designating all the attention shown to a wine, including its ageing in casks, up to the point where it is bottled.

Fermage: renting out of a domaine or vineyard.

Feuillette: a capacity measure of a barrel of Chablis: 132 litres (175 bottles).

Finage: a commune or village.

Grand Cru: one of the finest vineyards, climats or wines of a commune which has the right to use its own name as an *appellation contrôlée.*

Métayage: renting out of a vineyard to a tenant who undertakes to cultivate the vineyard or estate on the understanding that he will share the vintage with the owner.

Monopole: a vineyard belonging to one owner, or whose wine is sold by only one *négociant.*

Négociant, négociant-éleveur; someone who buys either the grapes, for making into wine, or the wines themselves, to 'educate' and bottle them before selling them.

Phylloxera: a parasitic insect which destroyed all the vineyards in Burgundy at the end of the 19th century. This was overcome by grafting French stock onto American plants, a practice still continued today.

Pièce: in the Côte d'Or, a barrel containing 228 litres (300 bottles); in Beaujolais, Mâconnais and part of Chalonnais, a barrel of 216 litres (288 bottles).

Premier Cru: a second class of Burgundy wine, immediately below Grand Cru.

Propriétaire-récoltant: an independent wine grower.

Tastevin: a small cup used by wine tasters, often made of silver.

Vigneron: someone who works as a labourer growing vines. If he does this on his own account he is equivalent to a *viticulteur.*

Vigneronnage: is to a vineyard what a tenant famer is to an agricultural estate (this is an expression used only in Beaujolais).

Viticulteur: someone who cultivates the vineyards of which he is the owner.

Appellations

Vintages

Burgundy has a large number of *appellations d'origine* — 112 in all — which sometimes designate a red and a white wine. There is a list of all the *appellations* mentioned in this book on page 18, listed in the order in which they are subsequently discussed. The list is accompanied by a chart showing the maximum production per hectare and two charts showing the maximum and minimum quantities of the annual vintage. The *appellations* coming from hamlets are listed in alphabetical order after their commune.

In a region which extends, as the crow flies, for about 155 miles from one end to the other, the differences in soil, grapes and atmospheric conditions are very important. It is therefore impossible to describe the characteristics of a single harvest — that is to say, vintage — for the whole Burgundy wine-growing region. Many local factors influence the quality of the wine: when the grapes were harvested, the age of the vines, how and when they were pruned, etc. It is quite possible for a grower in the Chablis district to produce the best vintage of his life, while his colleague at Vaux-en-Beaujolais may have no vintage at all after

Vintages

hail has destroyed his whole crop. Finally, the wine-making methods and *élevage* play crucial roles; even the healthiest grapes can give the wines very different qualities; some will be light and delicate, some will have a good colour but be hard and slow to mature. In conclusion, no judgment of a burgundy vintage is ever more than a general opinion, which may have no bearing, in certain places, on the actual situation.

General opinions

The following opinions refer specifically to wines which are intended for laying down: wines with an *appellation communale,* Premiers Crus or Grands Crus. All white wines from before 1969, without exception, should already have been drunk.

1945 Excellent year, scarce vintage.
1946 A wine that did not keep well, now past its best.
1947 Generally great wines.
1948 Excellent, sometimes even great wines.
1949 Excellent quality.
1950 Very large quantity, variable quality, but some very good white wines.
1951 Modest vintage, modest wines.
1952 Fairly unusual, but for drinking now, not for further keeping.
1953 Reds and whites were successful: very choice wines.
1954 Abundant and acceptable, nothing more.
1955 A solid wine which keeps well.
1956 Meagre vintage, poor wines.
1957 Small vintage, great red wines, for drinking now.
1958 Fairly good vintage, especially the whites.
1959 Supple wines, uneven quality, but some very good ones.
1960 Large quantity of light wines.
1961 Very limited production of excellent wine; kept under the right conditions it can be aged still further.
1962 A fine vintage with very successful red wines, for drinking now.
1963 The most successful red wines lack a little in body and colour, but have a delicious bouquet; for drinking now; a good year for Meursault.
1964 Average vintage with some good reds and whites, for drinking now.
1965 A year to forget.
1966 The reds have improved with age; just ready for drinking now.
1967 Average year, with some elegant wines, fairly pleasant; just ready for drinking now.
1968 Thin wines.
1969 An excellent year; the greatest of the red wines should be drunk in the next few years, the whites quite soon.
1970 A supple year, lacking a little backbone, good vintage; for drinking now.
1971 Small vintage with velvety, full-bodied red wines and some good white wines; the reds may age for five to seven years.
1972 A vintage which was initially strong and acidic but has since proved very good, in fact the best for red wine between 1971 and '76. More elegant than 1971, this vintage will also keep for a long time; the good quality reds could be drunk now.
1973 Very abundant vintage; an agreeable red wine, somewhat light, developing well; the white is sometimes excellent; for drinking now.
1974 A humid year; red wine of a fairly good colour, but lacking in vigour; some good white wines.
1975 The vintage rotted because of the rain; very light red wines, without colour; some excellent white wines, especially in the Chablis area; to drink fairly quickly.
1976 An exceptionally dry summer generally gave an excellent vintage (except in Mercurey as a result of hail), for both red and white; the good red wines can be kept until the end of the 1980s, but the white should be drunk at the start.
1977 A more abundant vintage than 1976, except in the Chablis district; ordinary quality in the Côte d'Or, with some very fine whites; the red wines, lighter than those of '76, should be drunk before them.
1978 Vintage which reached only three-quarters of the 1977 quantity; excellent quality throughout Burgundy.

1979 Abundant vintage with supple wines, rather more full-bodied than those of 1973.
1980 Vintage well above average, poor quality. In spite of this, quite a few pleasant surprises, especially in the case of the whites, but also some of the reds. Select very carefully.
1981 With the exception of Beaujolais, a sadly meagre vintage. The quality is satisfactory, but uneven.
1982 Generally a big, healthy harvest; very nice whites in the Côte d'Or.

Although decanting old burgundies is not recommended, it is sometimes beneficial for a younger wine, as contact with the air will undoubtedly make it more supple.

Many burgundies have a slightly sour, sulphury smell, like that in a cheese factory. It means that the secondary — malolactic acid — fermentation has not been completed. The wine may restore itself in the course of time, but this is by no means guaranteed.

To get rid of the sediment in his quality wines, Louis Latour uses a siphon to extract it from each bottle. This operation is carried out by hand in the Aloxe-Corton cellars.

Use of a cradle is not generally recommended for mature burgundies — although one is shown in the relevant leaflet from the Comité Interprofessionnel de la Côte d'Or et de l'Yonne.

When President Pompidou was in office there was a minor scandal over a dinner to which 183 deputies and ministers of the new government were invited. Romanée-Conti 1959 was served with roast pork and lentils. Burgundians thought it a great shame that such a rare wine was not given a worthier partner. Despite protests, the government offered no explanation. The transfer to Paris not long afterwards of the government's official spokesman at Beaune was coincidental!

Serving Burgundy

How to serve burgundy, especially red burgundy, is a contentious issue among experts as well as ordinary wine lovers. Let us, for example, examine the question of the temperature. It is generally thought that burgundy should be served at room temperature, and many restaurants place their wines in the dining-room before serving them. Private individuals, too, often put their bottles of red burgundy in the dining-room before the meal, sometimes near the fireplace. But the best temperature for red burgundy is between 17° and 19°C. If this is cooler than the temperature for red Bordeaux, it is because burgundy, which is usually a more generous wine, shows to better advantage this way. The term *chambré* dates from a time when there was no central heating and when the average room temperature was lower than it is today. If burgundy as a rule, should be served at below room temperature, Beaujolais requires a lower temperature still: 15° or 16°C is usually sufficient and in its native district it is served even cooler. The great white burgundies taste best at a temperature not exceeding 12° to 14°C, but it is inadvisable to serve them too cool as this will inhibit both their bouquet and taste.

Average vintage figures	Hectolitre/hectare	Hectolitres white	Hectolitres red/rosé
REGIONAL APPELLATIONS			
Bourgogne Grand Ordinaire	60(w), 55(r)	3,800	15,000
Bourgogne Aligoté	60	43,000	
Bourgogne Aligoté Bouzeron	45		
Bourgogne Passetoutgrains	55		
Bourgogne	55/60	10,000	93,000
Crémant de Bourgogne	50	425	7,800
CHABLIS			
Petit-Chablis	50	5,100	
Chablis	50	40,000	
Chablis Premier Cru	50	22,000	
Chablis Grand Cru	45	4,700	
Sauvignon de Saint-Bris	50	3,500	
CÔTE D'OR			
Hautes-Côtes de Nuits	50	210	6,000
Hautes-Côtes de Beaune	50	150	10,700
CÔTE D'OR — CÔTE DE NUITS			
Côte de Nuits Villages	40/45		7,000
Bourgogne Rosé de Marsannay	50		1,950
Fixin	40/45		1,200
Gevrey-Chambertin	40		14,500
Chambertin	35		510
Chambertin Clos de Bèze	35		460
Chapelle-Chambertin	35		195
Charmes-Chambertin	35		1,000
Griotte-Chambertin	35		65
Latricières-Chambertin	35		235
Mazis-Chambertin	35		245
Ruchottes-Chambertin	35		83
Morey-Saint-Denis	40/45	23	2,420
Bonnes Mares	35	see Chambolle-Musigny	
Clos de la Roche	35		440
Clos Saint-Denis	35		170
Clos de Tart	35		190
Clos des Lambrays	35		
Chambolle-Musigny	40		4,600
Bonnes Mares	35		385
Musigny	35/40	6	245
Vougeot	40/45	50	440
Clos de Vougeot	35		1,430
Vosne-Romanée	40		5,100
Echézeaux	35		955
Grands Echézeaux	35		250
La Tâche	35		155
Richebourg	35		225
Romanée	35		20
Romanée-Conti	35		50
Romanée-Saint-Vivant	35		235
Nuits-Saint-Georges	40/45	20	8,740
CÔTE D'OR — CÔTE DE BEAUNE			
Aloxe-Corton	40/45	15	4,370
Corton	35/40	45	2,700
Corton-Charlemagne	40	1,250	

	Hectolitre/hectare	Hectolitres white	Hectolitres red/rosé
Ladoix-Serrigny	40/45	110	2,250
Pernand-Vergelesses	40/45	500	2,700
Savigny-lès-Beaune	40/45	285	10,130
Beaune	40/45	575	11,900
Côte de Beaune	40/45	165	128
Pommard	40		10,500
Volnay	40		7,780
Monthelie	40/45	70	3,425
Meursault	40/45	15,300	870
Blagny	40		
Auxey-Duresses	40/45	1,150	3,470
Saint-Romain	40/45	1,000	1,160
Saint-Aubin	40/45	925	2,500
Puligny-Montrachet	40/45	9,000	325
Bâtard-Montrachet	40	420	
Bienvenues-Bâtard-Montrachet	40	130	
Chevalier-Montrachet	40	180	
Montrachet	40	233	
Chassagne-Montrachet	40/45	5,300	7,550
Bâtard-Montrachet	40	see Puligny-Montrachet	
Criots-Bâtard-Montrachet	40	60	
Montrachet	40	see Puligny-Montrachet	
Santenay	40/45	165	11,490
Cheilly-les-Maranges	40/45		480
Dezize-les-Maranges	40/45		65
Sampigny-les-Maranges	40/45		30
Côte de Beaune-Villages	40		8,885
Chorey-lès-Beaune	40	15	4,120
CHALONNAIS			
Rully	40	2,250	2,475
Mercurey	40/45	815	19,100
Givry	45	435	4,300
Montagny	45	3,100	
MÂCONNAIS			
Mâcon	55/60	1,175	4,800
Mâcon Supérieur	55/60	11,120	48,850
Mâcon-Villages	55/60	89,500	4,950
Pouilly-Fuissé	50	33,600	
Pouilly-Loché	50	1,200	
Pouilly-Vinzelles	50	1,870	
Saint-Véran	55	13,530	
BEAUJOLAIS			
Beaujolais	55	4,535	495,000
Beaujolais Supérieur	55	220	16,200
Beaujolais-Villages	50/55	615	341,600
Saint-Amour	48		13,840
Juliénas	48		30,315
Chénas	48		12,480
Moulin-à-Vent	48		33,640
Fleurie	48		41,775
Chiroubles	48		17,675
Morgon	48		55,560
Brouilly	48		67,100
Côte de Brouilly	48		15,225

Opposite page:
A Meursault-Perrières, aged to a beautiful golden colour, can best be savoured in a short-stemmed balloon glass. Wine makers throughout Burgundy use this type of glass for tastings in their cellars.

Right:
In Burgundy village cafés, the more humble local wines are served in straight glasses, solid enough to withstand the firm grasp of the vineyard workers. This photograph was taken in Juliénas in Beaujolais.

Below:
The classic burgundy glass, with a long stem and a well-rounded bowl.

Serving Burgundy

Decanting drawbacks

Decanting is the act of transferring wine from a bottle into a carafe in order to let it breathe, or to separate any sediment which has accumulated over a period. It is often necessary to decant an old Bordeaux or an old Port, but this delicate operation is rarely wise for a burgundy, even an old one. Burgundy often has an expansive bouquet, but it is fragile and fleeting, and if brutally exposed to the air, there is a risk of it losing its character. Decanting an old burgundy may be fatal for its bouquet, and therefore it is not advisable to open a bottle much in advance. Decanting burgundy has another drawback: the sediment found in a burgundy is finer and lighter than that of a Bordeaux, and no matter how many precautions are taken, there is always the risk of disturbing the sediment and transferring it to the decanter.

How, therefore, do you serve the wine, while avoiding getting the sediment in the glasses? The best way to serve a burgundy is as follows: about two hours before the meal place the bottle in an upright position in a place where the temperature is just right; at the appropriate time open the bottle carefully, avoiding any abrupt movements, and if possible, pour it in one go, until the sediment appears. Glasses used for burgundy are usually larger than those used for Bordeaux so that the bouquet can develop more fully.

The Burgundy Trade

The average land holding of the 10,000 wine growers of Burgundy is, as previously mentioned, about 10 acres. In the Côte d'Or, the figure is nearer 5 acres. The small quantity of their vintages prevents many such growers undertaking their own wine-making, bottling and marketing. In other regions of France this situation has forced wine makers to form themselves into cooperatives. In Burgundy, Chablis, Beaujolais, the Mâconnais and part of the Chalonnais, there are many cooperatives which are very active, but they are rarely found in the Côte d'Or, where the role of the merchant is like that of a collector.

Traditionally, the *négociant-éleveur* buys directly from various growers; he purchases either the grapes, new wine out of the casks, or wine that has been kept for several months in barrels. These small amounts are eventually assembled by *appellation* and mixed to give a significant quantity of wine from each *appellation*.

The wine broker

Because most *négociants* prefer not to deal directly with the grower, the country agent is a key figure in the annual game of supply and demand. One *négociant* explained his point of view in this way: 'I prefer not to buy directly from the grower, as his wife, who is more greedy, always gets involved in our discussions. To avoid quarrels over price, I buy through an intermediary, a broker, and therefore anonymously. I make this decision quite freely and it does not harm my relationship with the growers.' For this service the brokers take a commission. Some *négociants*, however, do prefer to deal directly with the growers and decide prices and method of payments themselves. Furthermore, many firms have exclusive contracts which tie them to certain producers without the intervention of a broker (French *courtier*).

Different styles

Although theoretically each house uses the same grapes for the same wines, the finished products are often very different. Each firm has its own characteristic style (see the chapter devoted to *négociants*, pages 184-9) and this has a bearing on purchases. Some concerns buy only at the lowest price, whilst others disregard price and go only for quality. Almost all *négociants* are specialists in *élevage*; they are not satisfied merely with selling the wines, but are involved throughout the entire wine-making process up to the point where it is bottled. Throughout this crucial period, the wines will be developed according to the experience, outlook and final objective of the *négociant*. Does he want a light wine, soon at its peak, or a high quality wine which will last a long time? Should it have frequent racking? If he wants to improve the wine by ageing it for a time in barrels, what sort of casks should he use, and for how long should he leave it? Will he decide to pasteurize the wine, or to filter it? When and at what speed should it be bottled? What type of cork should be used? Each step and each decision will influence the quality of the wine and differentiate it from all others. Thus one firm may produce a heavy, intoxicating wine, while another will go for a light, elegant wine. Everything depends on individual attitude, competence, taste and degree of dedication.

The increasing importance of estates

Over the centuries, the *négociants-éleveurs* have been of prime importance to wine-making in Burgundy, and in the Côte d'Or, for example, until 1970, 95% of the vintage passed through their hands. This position has altered a great deal in the past few years, as the growers started to bottle and sell more of their own wine. The crisis of the 1970s, when the *négociants* bought little wine, has greatly contributed to this change, but the main reason is that the growers are becoming more experienced; they have learned to profit from advances in wine-making and *élevage* techniques. Finally, many customers have discovered that each estate produces wine of a very personal character. The *négociants*, many of whom own their own land, have long known that their best wines were almost always those from their own vineyards. The Fédération Interprofessionelle des Vins de Bourgogne has noted that estate bottling is on the increase and that in some villages on the Côte d'Or it now reaches between 35% and 40%. In the other districts this figure is between 20% and 25%. Overall, however, the *négociants* commercialize more than 70% of all burgundy produced.

Changes afoot

If lovers of new wines can take comfort from the growing importance of the estates, it is still worth pointing out that not all owners are necessarily good *éleveurs* and that some of them sell wines which are mediocre or, frankly, bad. There are other drawbacks as well. Thanks to *négociants*, the price of burgundies has long remained stable, but if the growers want to have more say, they risk making their prices even more excessive than they are at present. The 1976 vintage is one example; and that of 1978, an excellent but less plentiful one, broke all records. In the bids at the Sale at the Hospices de Beaune, the average price per barrel was already 50% higher than that of the year before, and the growers' price of the 1978 vintage twice that of the previous year. Since then, prices have risen even more over the whole of Burgundy, and especially on the Côte d'Or. Relatively poor harvests in 1980 and 1981 have further accentuated this trend. At present it is difficult to foresee the consequences of the rising importance of these estates, but it is certain that, in the future, some *négociants* are going to miss out on the good wine. Perhaps only a few of the *négociants* dealing in wine from different origins will survive, or just the smaller *négociants* who are mainly concerned with quality. Many of the *négociants*, of which there are approximately 170, may very well lose their independence in the coming years. One possibility is that the *négociant-éleveur* will become in reality a *négociant-distributeur*; at the same time, there could also be room for export agents who, working on relatively small margins, will be able to market the better wines of Burgundy in France and abroad. Time will tell.

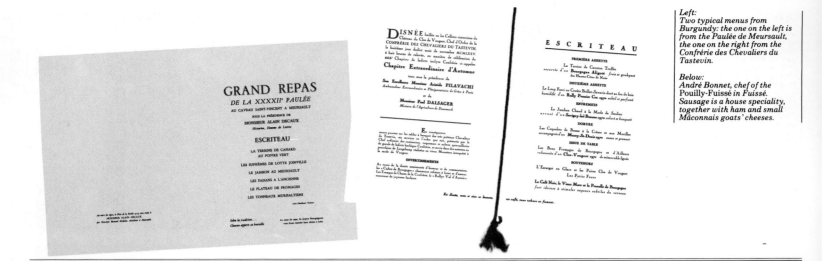

Burgundy Cuisine

The people of Burgundy love good wine, but are equally appreciative of good food, regarding a meal as one of life's greatest pleasures. It is well worth visiting Burgundy merely for its cuisine. That gastronomic expert Curnonsky justly described it as 'a gourmet's paradise'. My own notebooks are full of enthusiastic comments on the many long, leisurely meals I enjoyed during my various visits to the region.

Home cooking

The cuisine of Burgundy has for centuries been derived from family cooking, consisting of treasured recipes and culinary secrets passed down from generation to generation. It does not, therefore, claim to be either elaborate or intellectual, having always aimed basically at satisfying the hearty appetites of peasants and wine growers who needed good, solid meals washed down with plenty of wine when they returned from the fields. Happily, this fundamental tradition of family cooking still thrives in many restaurants, some modest and some prestigious, such as *Au Petit Truc* in Vignolles, near Beaune, *La Rôtisserie du Chambertin* in Gevrey-Chambertin, and *Chez Nono* in the area called La Montagne de Beaune. Often it is the sons of the family who maintain the traditional skills learned from their mothers. Wine plays an important part in this regional cuisine, being used both for actual cooking and for flavouring excellent marinades. Obviously the best wine is rarely used in cooking; it is often one which, for various reasons, has not been sold but kept back by the grower for his own use.

The Saturday market in Beaune

Nature always seems to smile in Burgundy. This region of fields and rivers, meadows and orchards, vineyards and forests, is one of the most fertile in France. This is typified by the traditional, picturesque market held every Saturday in Beaune, where you can buy food and local produce from all over Burgundy. In addition to fruit and vegetables in plenty, you will find the celebrated beef of the white Charolais cattle, cockerels for *coq au vin*, raw ham from Morvan, chickens from Bresse (with their own *appellation contrôlée* system), crayfish, freshwater fish, little Epoisses cheeses made with *marc de Bourgogne*, and countless other delicacies.

A selection of specialities

Thanks to the variety of local produce, the cooks and restaurateurs of Burgundy offer a wide range of specialities. Among the most famous are snails, known to the connoisseur as *les petits gris*. In the past, when the peasants were too poor to afford meat, they ate fattened-up snails — which are nowadays considered a delicacy. Restaurants often serve *jambon persillé*, cooked in its own jelly and seasoned, as the name suggests, with parsley, garlic and spices; this dish was once traditionally prepared and served at Easter. *Andouillettes*, a very popular local speciality, are frequently cooked according to recipes which vary from one district to another. Entrées include *oeufs à la bourguignonne* (eggs poached in red wine and served on croutons), *quenelles de brochet*, or frogs' legs (the little frogs of the Chalonnais, not those from Japan, which are too large).

Burgundy Cuisine

The main course may be an entrecôte of Charolais beef; a *coq au vin*, usually cooked in the local wine, as in *coq au Fleurie* (although not a drop of genuine Chambertin goes into *coq au Chambertin*); *boeuf à la bourguignonne* (cooked in red wine with onion, mushrooms and pieces of larding bacon); a Burgundy fondue; and saddle of hare *à la Piron* (during the vintage grapes are added to this dish). For desserts, there are delicious sorbets, often made with cassis, followed by local liqueurs, and often *pain d'épices de Dijon* as a final touch.

Some outstanding restaurants

Burgundy has so many good restaurants that it is a problem to make a choice. Among the better-known establishments offering the classic cuisine of Burgundy, though sometimes in a very refined form, are from north to south: *La Poste*, Avalon; *La Côte d'Or*, Saulieu; *La Rôtisserie du Chambertin*, Gevrey-Chambertin; *La Côte d'Or* in Nuits-Saint-Georges, the discreetly situated *Au Petit Truc* in Vignolles, where guests can enjoy an especially inventive and thoughtful regional cuisine, the *Hôtel de la Poste* in

Beaune, and *Au Chapon Fin*, Thoissey (near Beaujolais). Other restaurants and inns will be mentioned in the following sections on individual villages. In my opinion, the best restaurant in the whole area is that owned by Messieurs Lameloise, father and son, in Chagny, between the Côte d'Or and the Chalonnais. I still have wonderful memories of their *salade de haricots verts, foie gras maison, terrine de canard* (with Chagny sausage), *truite à l'Aligoté, coquelet en pâte sauce Janick, aiguillette de canard*, exquisite desserts, and other inventive dishes.

If you want to drink Ratafia de Bourgogne, a good address to know is the Maison des Hautes-Côtes in Marey-les-Fursey (in the hills behind Nuits-Saint-Georges).

One producer of excellent blackcurrant liqueur is Lucien Jacob of Echevronne (Hautes-Côtes de Nuits). In 1978 he planted 60 acres with blackcurrant bushes near the modern Kriter factory built by Patriarche close to the Autoroute du Soleil (slightly north of the exit to Beaune). The liqueur smells and tastes unusually pure.

In early spring, the blackcurrant bushes, like the vines, are pruned. By this time they are already covered with buds which, if broken open, give off a delicious fruity scent. Lucien Jacob collects these buds and sells them to the perfume industry in Grasse (Provence).

Liqueurs and Spirits

In addition to fine wines, Burgundy also specializes in liqueurs and spirits, both for cooking and for drinking. The best known regional liqueur is *crème de cassis*. As far back as the 16th century, blackcurrants were grown in Burgundy, particularly in the Côte d'Or. Doctors then prescribed them as a cure for stomach disorders, scurvy and infected bites. At the start of the 18th century a blackcurrant liqueur began to be made, and this was produced and sold on a large scale after 1840. Today, *crème de cassis* is drunk as an aperitif or *digestif*, and is also used for making desserts such as sorbets, biscuits, etc.

The aperitif *kir* is very popular: it is a mixture, according to individual taste, of *crème de cassis* and a dry, white wine, preferably an Aligoté. It owes its name to Canon Kir, legendary mayor of Dijon. A *cardinal* is a variation of *kir*, in which white wine is replaced by red, (in Beaujolais, this aperitif is sometimes called a *communiste*). Blackcurrant growing is concentrated in the area between Beaune and Dijon, partly in the plain, and partly on the Hautes-Côtes to the west of the large vineyards. Blackcurrants can withstand hard winters but suffer from spring frosts. As with vines, soil type largely determines their final character. They are harvested in July, when the sun is at its hottest, and as with grape-picking, choice of the right moment is absolutely essential: if done too early or too late, up to one-third of the crop may be lost. La Coopérative Agricole Fruitière de la Côte d'Or (CAFC) grows and sells most of the fruit, but it can also be bought through an agent from private individuals. The distilleries are the most important customers for blackcurrants, but there is also a demand from manufacturers of syrup, yoghourts, ice-cream, etc.

Natural products

To make *crème de cassis*, sugar or glucose is added to the blackcurrants and the mixture then fermented in wine spirit. In France, *crème de cassis* must contain at least 14 ounces of sugar per litre and have 15° of alcohol to be classed as a liqueur. The degree of alcohol may exceed 20° if the liqueurs are of a superior quality. When the label says *Cassis de Dijon*, the liqueur actually has to come from Dijon. The best *crème de cassis* is a totally natural liqueur, which has never been heated, coloured or 'enriched' with chemical products. Like wine, it is a living drink which can, after a time, lose its colour and fruitiness. For this reason the label of a liqueur made, for example, by Maison Trenel of Charney-lès-Mâcon, carries a vintage. Dijon is the main producer of *crème de cassis*, 80% of it being made by Maisons L'Héritier-Guyot, Gabriel Boudier and Lejay-Lagoutte; Maison Védrenne in Nuits-Saint-Georges is also a major producer. Other than *crème de cassis*, most liqueur makers in Burgundy manufacture *digestifs* from prune, cherry, strawberry or raspberry.

Fire water

The best known local *digestifs* of Burgundy are *marc* and *Fine Bourgogne*. *Marc de Bourgogne*, a veritable fire water, is produced from a distillation of the skins, pips and stems of the grapes left in the bottom of the casks after the new wine has been drained off. This drink contains nearly 40° of alcohol. It is claimed that *marc* is more supple nowadays because a larger number of grapes are de-stalked before fermentation. This *digestif* is notable for its great strength, but it becomes softer, ageing for a long time in oak casks. Les Hospices de Beaune and le Domaine de la Romanée-Conti produce *marcs* which are considered to be the best in the region.

La Fine Bourgogne is a more delicate spirit than *marc*. Theoretically, it is a derivative of burgundy wine, made somewhat in the style of Cognac or Armagnac. However, instead of distilling the actual wine, which is far too highly valued, use is made of the lees and sediment forming at the bottom of the cask during the wine's *élevage*. Unfortunately, all too little of this interesting spirit is produced.

Louis Latour softens its Vieille Eau de Vie de Marc du Château Grancey by adding one-third of distilled lees and leaving it to age for another four or five years in oak casks — an example to be followed!

Liqueurs and Spirits

Wine Fraternities

Burgundy's wine fraternities play a lively and picturesque role in the folklore of this wine-growing region. Each district has at least one such fraternity, whose members include owners, *négociants* and ordinary wine lovers. Their ceremonies are colourful theatrical events, with medieval costumes, braying trumpets, ancient documents and old drinking songs. The public takes an active part in the festivities. Following the initiation of newly-elected members and lusty singing of the *ban bourguignon*, the company settles down to a gastronomic dinner, often by candlelight, liberally supplied, of course, with wine.

Les Chevaliers du Tastevin

The most famous of these societies is La Confrérie des Chevaliers du Tastevin, founded by Georges Faiveley and Camille Rodier in 1934, with the principal aim of publicizing Burgundy wines at home and abroad, and of restoring the popularity of the traditional wine festivals. The venture was enormously successful. Today the Confrérie is a prestigious organization with almost 9,000 members, of whom about half live in France, one-fifth in the USA and the rest elsewhere. The society meets about 17 times a year in the vaults of the old Clos de Vougeot château (see page 70). The 500 or so guests are served a *disnée* of six courses, with five good wines, coffee and *digestifs*. The musical accompaniment to these festive occasions is provided by Les Cadets de Bourgogne, a jolly male-voice choir singing songs about wine.

Tastevinage

La Confrérie des Chevaliers du Tastevin also patronizes other activities, such as the festival of Saint-Vincent, held on the first Saturday after 22 January, each year in a different village, and the presentation of a prize to an author who has made a special contribution to the literature of Burgundy or good wine. The climax of the year, however, is the Tastevinage itself, a major annual wine-tasting occasion when the Confrérie label is awarded to the best wines submitted by owners and *négociants-éleveurs*. Of the 400-500 wines put forward for this Tastevinage, 40% are refused the right to use the numbered label of the Confrérie. Theoretically, wines awarded this label should be the best wines in Burgundy, but in practice many producers do not even take part, while others who go along with the selection voice criticism of the subsequent control. In their view, the labels reserved for the selected wines are not always attached to the proper bottles, so that the purchaser runs the risk of finding inferior quality wine under the Tastevinage label.

La Cousinerie de Bourgogne

La Cousinerie de Bourgogne was started in 1960 in Savigny-lès-Beaune in the Côte d'Or. There are now about 1,700 members all over the world. Their meetings, attended by some 200 people, are held four times a year.

Les Vignerons de Saint-Vincent

La Confrérie des Vignerons de Saint-Vincent is the most important in the Mâconnais and the Chalonnais. Thanks to its energetic committee, the membership has grown to over 5,000 since it was started in 1950. The principal meeting is held at the end of January in the vaulted cellars of the Château d'Aîne, several miles from Mâcon.

Wine Fraternities

Les Compagnons du Beaujolais

As befits a famous wine-growing district, Beaujolais has its own fraternity, Les Compagnons du Beaujolais. The society meets four times a year in Lacenas, about three miles from Villefranche, in a vast cellar which can hold more than 600 people. This fraternity has sections in Paris, Nice, London and Turin.

Other fraternities

In the Chablis district, La Confrérie Vineuse des Piliers Chablisiens, has since 1952 publicized its splendid wines far and wide. It holds meetings four times a year, when new members are inducted, and the proceedings end with a meal, dominated, of course, by white wines. In Saint-Bris, not far from Chablis, local wine growers belong to another fraternity, Les Trois Ceps. Founded in 1965, meetings are held twice a year, in November and January.

Other fraternities worthy of mention are: La Confrérie Saint-Vincent et Disciples de la Chante-Flûte (see page 148) and La Confrérie du G.O.S.I.E.R.S.E.C. de Clochemerle, founded in 1961 in Beaujolais.

Selecting Good Burgundy

A wine grower from Burgundy once said to me: 'Wine is always fit to drink; but with water, you never know . . .' This quip is not very helpful to someone wanting to buy a good wine. For the inexperienced wine lover bent on making a sensible choice from an enormous variety of available burgundies, it is hardly enough to describe them all as 'fit to drink', nor is there any simple advice to offer. I must repeat that no other wine-growing region of France presents such a complex picture as Burgundy. Even a specialist, familiar with every region, every village, every *appellation*, cannot absolutely guarantee the quality of what he buys. It is essential, therefore, to be knowledgeable about the suppliers, namely the *négociants* and wine growers; and this is not even a practical possibility for the majority of importers, let alone the general public. Time and inclination to explore the world of Burgundy wines are both all too often lacking.

Using labels as a guide

This book is intended to guide the wine lover, and to this end I have visited many estates and tasted the wines of the most important *négociants*. Unfortunately, I was unable to try all the good burgundies, but I hope that my selection will help the reader. I have classified the labels by village and made appraisals of some of the wines that impressed me with their character and quality. These short appreciations generally apply to several vintages and I have specified those instances where they refer only to one year. If I have referred most often to estates where wine-making is still on a small scale, it is simply because I found the best wines there. Some *négociants* are mentioned more frequently than others because of their high-quality wines. The wines described in the book are my personal choice from all those I tasted. Far too many burgundies are, unhappily, mediocre in quality.

Some guidelines

The first and foremost rule when buying a burgundy, is: never hesitate to pay for quality. This does not necessarily mean paying top prices; in the Mâconnais and the Chalonnais, for example, you can find good wines at reasonable prices. By and large, however, the best burgundies are always very expensive. The trouble is that price alone is an unreliable guideline: certain burgundies of very doubtful quality can be quite dear. I would advise you to rely principally on the reputation of the estate or *négociant-éleveur*, and secondarily on the village, the appellation or the vintage. A burgundy generally comes from one producer and you can ask for that name from the *négociant* or restaurateur from whom you are buying. Don't forget to make a note of the names of those producers whose wines you like best. I feel confident that this book will help the enthusiastic and discerning wine lover to find a way through the labyrinth of Burgundy wines, and to make some wonderful discoveries.

The Wines of Burgundy

1973 1973
Bourgogne Grand Ordinaire
Rosé d'Orches
APPELLATION BOURGOGNE GRAND ORDINAIRE CONTRÔLÉE
73 cl   CAVES DES HAUTES-CÔTES
GROUPEMENT DE PROPRIÉTAIRES-RÉCOLTANTS, ROUTE DE POMMARD, À BEAUNE (CÔTE D'OR)

Orches is a village situated on the slopes near Auxey-Duresses. Its dry-tasting rosé wine, light, simple and refreshing, goes well with outdoor meals. It is produced by La Cave Coopérative des Hautes-Côtes.

Regional Wines

In the Côtes du Rhône and Bordeaux, most of the wine produced is of inferior *appellations*, but this is not the case in Burgundy. Except when the harvest is small or of poor quality, the *appellations régionales* often account for no more than one-tenth of total production. In 1973, a very plentiful vintage, the quantity of *appellations régionales* was larger than normal — one-sixth of all the wine produced. Such an increase is possible because the maximum permitted yield per hectare is simultaneously raised to 50 hectolitres per hectare, giving a yield of 5-20 hectolitres more than for other *appellations*. Consequently, the better *appellations* are in short supply when the vintage is poor, but are freely available in better years.
Because there are relatively few *appellations régionales*, really cheap wines seldom occur in Burgundy. Consequently, the average buyer, judging burgundy to be too expensive, will rather go for a humble Côtes du Rhône, a run-of-the-mill Bordeaux, or perhaps a modest château Bordeaux. This situation presents major problems to the *négociants* in Burgundy since the *appellations régionales* ought to be among their best-selling wines. Since it is impossible to produce cheap *appellations régionales*, most firms, who sell only the more expensive *appellations* of burgundy, find it difficult to expand. *Négociants* keen on developing their businesses are obliged to sell cheaper wine from other wine-growing regions. Almost all the large firms offer wines originating from different areas. The result is that what may appear to be a genuine burgundy at a reasonable price — the label bearing the name of a *négociant* in Burgundy — may really turn out to be a wine originating outside the region. Should you be considering such an apparent bargain, make sure that the word 'Bourgogne' appears on the label. The large firms nowadays try to sell genuine burgundies at prices as low as possible, sometimes at the expense of quality. The experienced wine lover has a right to expect both!

Bourgogne Grand Ordinaire

It is generally believed that there is only one wine with an *appellation régionale*, namely Bourgogne, but this is not so. The wine with the simplest appellation is known as Bourgogne Grand Ordinaire, or very rarely, Bourgogne Ordinaire. This *appellation* applies to red, white or rosé wines; the quantities are not very significant: on average, 167,000 cases of red and rosé and 42,000 cases of white. Bourgogne and Bourgogne Passetoutgrains, other *appellations régionales*, are made in greater quantities. Bourgogne Grand Ordinaire is drunk locally and hardly exported at all, since the term 'ordinaire' even preceded by 'grand' is not appreciated by foreign buyers. The grapes that can be used for red or rosé wines are the Pinot Noir and Gamay Noir (with the César and Tressot in the Yonne *département*). Gamay is the favourite, even though, except in Beaujolais, the wines produced from this grape may be rather green and acidic. The most popular and successful rosé is the Rosé d'Orches. This Grand Ordinaire, coming from the village of Orches perched above the Côte, has all the ideal qualities of a rosé, a spring-like freshness and charming personality. It is made by the up-to-date Coopérative des Hautes-Côtes, very near to Beaune. For white Bourgogne Grand Ordinaire, the permitted grapes are the Chardonnay, Pinot Blanc, Aligoté, Melon de Bourgogne (which becomes Muscadet near Nantes) and Sacy (only in the Yonne). For some time the producers of Bourgogne Grand Ordinaire have tended to replace Gamay by the more noble Pinot Noir, and Melon by Chardonnay. If this trend continues, the simpler burgundies will become even scarcer, since Pinot Noir and Chardonnay, reserved for the better *appellations*, produce less abundant crops.

Bourgogne Aligoté

Bourgogne Aligoté, a white wine that is better known and more highly regarded than Bourgogne Grand Ordinaire, comes from the Aligoté, to which up to 15% Chardonnay may be added. 1973 was a record vintage, with nearly 830,000 cases being produced. The price fell so sharply that most wine growers subsequently replaced Aligoté with Chardonnay, thus reducing the quantity to an average of 478,000 cases and raising the price. A true Bourgogne Aligoté is generally rather acidic, but its fruitiness and *gouleyance* often compensate for this fault. The area that produces the most Bourgogne Aligoté is traditionally the Chalonnais, and I have found the wine from Bouzeron, near Chagny, to be delicious. Certain villages in the Côte d'Or, such as Pernand-Vergelesses, occasionally also produce an excellent Bourgogne Aligoté; and it can be found, too, in the Hautes-Côtes. A Bourgogne Aligoté from the slopes of Saint-Bris, in the Yonne, deserves special mention: it is of good quality, dry and faintly lively. Because of its fairly high acidity, Bourgogne Aligoté is in the region itself often mixed with a little *crème de cassis*, so producing the celebrated *kir*. Bourgogne Aligoté is also a wonderful accompaniment to Burgundian snails, so much so that they were officially 'married' during the summer of 1976. I drank a very special Aligoté with Maurice Thevenot, in the Hautes-Côtes de Nuits; this remarkably fresh wine had a slight sparkle, having been bottled *sur lie*, that is, without being racked after fermentation. This procedure, which keeps the wine at its freshest, is also used for Muscadet in the Nantes region.

Other interesting wines not mentioned in this chapter are: Grandchatel, a red Bourgogne Grand Ordinaire from Jaboulet-Vercherre; Le Cadet de Bourgogne, a Passetoutgrains from Lionel Bruck/Hasenklever; the Bourgogne Les Clefs du Roi (red and white) from Labouré-Roi; the red Bourgogne du Chapître from Jaffelin; Bourgogne Aligoté Bouzeron of the Ancien Domaine Carnot (Bouchard Père & Fils; estate of 14 acres); Bourgogne Réserve de l'Abbaye de St Martin (red) from Pierre Ponnelle; Bourgogne Aligoté from Bouthenet (Cheilly-les-Maranges); Bourgogne Aligoté from Tollot-Voarick (Chorey-lès-Beaune).

Right:
The entrance to Bouzeron, a peaceful village in the Chalonnais, near Chagny. Bouzeron produces some very good Bourgogne Aligoté. Since 1979 the law has allowed the regional appellation *labels to carry the name 'Bouzeron' in the same size letters as 'Bourgogne Aligoté'.*

Centre:
Two elderly growers enjoying a glass of wine and discussing the latest vintages.

Bottom:
Beautiful bunches of freshly picked grapes from the Mâconnais.

Up to 15% of Chardonnay grapes can be used to make Bourgogne Aligoté.

Since 1979 the name of the commune 'Bouzeron' has been allowed to be printed in the same size type as 'Bourgogne Aligoté' on the label.

Regional Wines

Bourgogne Passetoutgrains

If Bourgogne Aligoté is always white, Bourgogne Passetoutgrains is invariably red or rosé. This *appellation* is a kind of transitional stage between the Bourgogne Grand Ordinaire produced from the Gamay and the Bourgogne Rouge made from the Pinot. For Passetoutgrains, the law requires two-thirds Gamay to one-third Pinot, and because of this the wine can be regarded either as a superior Bourgogne Grand Ordinaire or as an inferior Bourgogne Rouge. The name Passetoutgrains describes a process that is typical of a region where the vineyards are very fragmented. A number of wine growers own strips of both Gamay and Pinot, neither of which produce enough grapes individually to fill an entire vat. The two types have to be mixed, therefore, in order to produce a sufficient quantity of must. Some wine growers specialize in making Passetoutgrains, and the average production is almost 590,000 cases annually. In recent years, in the Côte d'Or, the Chalonnais and the Mâconnais, the Gamay grape has been gradually replaced by the Pinot; this is bound to increase the quantity of Bourgogne Passetoutgrains at the expense of Bourgogne Grand Ordinaire, and will subsequently fall, to the advantage of Bourgogne Rouge. This is a welcome trend, for a true Bourgogne owes its quality to the Pinot Noir. The Bourgogne Passetoutgrains is somewhat nondescript, without a great deal of personality. The acidic Gamay predominates when the wine is very young, making it rather disagreeable and disappointing for anyone expecting a generous burgundy. Passetoutgrains does not acquire much colour until it has been kept for many years, when it gives the impression of having been made from the Pinot. In fact, the latter grape eventually predominates, so providing the wine with its characteristic taste and bouquet. It is usually best to allow Passetoutgrains to age for at least two or three years, and such patience is well rewarded. Incidentally, the spelling of 'Passetoutgrains' on labels may

The Bourgogne Aligoté 'Coteaux de Saint-Bris' from Regnard & Fils had a very fruity taste, somewhat green, clean and very refreshing. I have also enjoyed the Aligoté of Albert Pic, produced on the same slopes near Chablis.

Aubert de Villaine and his father are co-owners of the Domaine de la Romanée-Conti; they also have vineyards at Bouzeron, in the Chalonnais, where they make an absolutely perfect Aligoté, Bourgogne Blanc and Bourgogne Rouge.

Although the Cave Coopérative de Buxy specializes in the production of white Montagny, it also distributes a delicious Aligoté. It has a generous aroma and a fruity taste. La Tour d'Argent restaurant in Paris is a staunch customer.

The Domaine de Pérignon is situated near Crasant, a village about 12½ miles southwest of Chablis. About 90 per cent of the vineyard is planted with Pinot grapes. It produces a Passetoutgrain which usually has a fresh, pleasantly fruity taste. Bottled and sold by Chauvenet.

The Bourgogne Passetoutgrain of the Domaine Roux in Saint-Aubin has won several awards. It is usually a supple, pleasant wine, in which the Pinot Noir is incontestably dominant. Without being heavy, it is nonetheless quite fleshy and full-bodied.

At a tasting of several red burgundies, this Geisweiler got the highest marks: faultless, non-vintage wine with a pleasant bouquet and very agreeable, rather sinewy taste. The white was also delicious.

Regional Wines

vary either with or without the final 's'. The legal spelling (Passe tout grains) has the 's' but the other form is sometimes used in the interest of grammatical logic.

Bourgogne Blanc

The best of the white wines in the *appellation régionale* category is undoubtedly Bourgogne Blanc. The legal yield is fixed at 60 hectolitres per hectare, and the minimum degree of alcohol allowed is 10.5° (1° more than Bourgogne Grand Ordinaire and Bourgogne Aligoté). The slightly higher alcohol content certainly adds character and robustness to this modest wine. The grapes that are used — Pinot Blanc and, especially, Chardonnay — are all-important. The Chardonnay is a determining factor since it also produces the great white burgundies. It becomes apparent both in the taste and bouquet: Bourgogne Blanc is a fruity wine, fresh and supple, with a fine nose and a fairly full taste. The largest quantity of Bourgogne Blanc — total production of which is relatively modest, averaging just over 111,000 cases annually — is produced in the Mâconnais; an area that has traditionally specialized in white wine.

Below left:
The last rays of the sun on Chardonnay grapes.

Below right:
Vineyards near Auxey-Duresses. The harvesting machine shown here was designed and made by Bernard Roy. After de-stalking, the grapes are kept in a cylindrical tank containing carbonic gas, which keeps them fresh. This machine can hold the equivalent of half a day's harvest.

Louis Jadot markets two very good brand burgundies, red and white, under the name Couvent des Jacobins. Both are well-constituted, pure wines.

The Coopérative de Lugny-Saint Gengoux-de-Scissé produces a very pleasant Bourgogne Rouge, as well as an excellent Mâcon Rouge. Shimmering colour, pure Pinot nose, extremely supple taste.

The Cuvée Latour is a very reliable brand wine, red and white, from the house of Louis Latour. The red is usually a firm, well matured wine. The white is remarkably good with a very distinctive character.

Château Marguerite de Bourgogne (about 12 acres of vineyards) is located in the village of Couches. Its white burgundy is usually fruity, pleasant to drink, almost unctuous. Bottled and distributed by Chauvenet.

The name of Napoleon I often occurs in matters related to Burgundy. In this case, it is in the name of the Bourgogne Rouge from Dufouleur Père & Fils, négociant at Nuits-Saint-Georges. This wine usually has a good Pinot bouquet and a full, pleasant taste.

The Domaine Clair-Daü in Marsannay deliberately names its Bourgogne Blanc after the grape used. I find this wine very pleasant: strong, supple and soft, very refreshing, with a fruity taste. There are a number of other labels in addition to the one illustrated here.

Regional Wines

Bourgogne Rouge

The legal requirements for Bourgogne Rouge are less stringent than those for Bourgogne Blanc, as they allow the use of a wider range of grapes — Pinot Noir in the Côte d'Or, the Chalonnais and the Mâconnais, César and Tressot in the Chablis district and the remainder of the Yonne, Gamay in Beaujolais, but exclusively for the vineyards of the nine *crus* of that region, namely Saint-Amour, Juliénas, Chénas, Moulin-à-Vent, Fleurie, Chiroubles, Morgon, Brouilly and Côte de Brouilly. So in quality and character, this *appellation* exhibits many significant variations. Thus the Bourgogne Rouge from the north of the *département* of the Yonne (such as the wine of Irancy, see page 41), bears little resemblance to the same Bourgogne from the south of the region. Similarly, there are very obvious differences between a Bourgogne Rouge made from the Gamay and that from the Pinot. Nevertheless, the nature of the grapes and the composition of the soil are such that Bourgogne Rouge is often a wine of fairly good quality; and this is reflected in the price which, for an *appellation régionale*, is relatively high. For this reason it is important to take special care when making a choice. At first glance, a reasonable price may seem attractive; but once again, the best guarantee is the reputation of the supplier. The minimum degree of alcohol is fixed at 10° (1° more than Bourgogne Grand Ordinaire and 0.5° more than Passetoutgrains); the average annual yield is about 1,055,500 cases.

Simmonet-Febvre & Fils is the only firm in Chablis to produce sparkling burgundy: about 100,000 bottles a year, solely from the Chardonnay grape, which is evident from its nose and agreeable, lively taste.

Moingeon-Gueneau Frères is one of the two producers of sparkling wines in Nuits-Saint-Georges. It sells more than 500,000 bottles a year. Crémant 'B' is an excellent wine, fresh and supple.

Of the three producers of sparkling wine in Savigny-lès-Beaune, Parigot & Richard alone accounts for half the total production: 150,000 bottles. The Blanc de Blanc has a good nose and contains a hint of terroir.

André Delorme, in Rully, was one of the first producers of Crémant de Bourgogne. He is president of the Association des Producteurs. His own wine, with its fine, light bouquet and dry, very clean taste, is an ideal aperitif.

In the Mâconnais, the Coopérative of Lugny and of Saint-Gengoux-de-Scissé, working in close collaboration, have a potential capacity of 200,000 bottles of Crémant de Bourgogne. There is a pronounced scent of Chardonnay in the nose and the taste.

Sparkling Wines

In addition to a wide variety of red, white and rosé wines, Burgundy displays its diversity by producing, in addition, many sparkling or *mousseux* wines. Thirty firms, from Chablis to Beaujolais, nowadays make this type of burgundy, which was first produced in the early 19th century by François Hubert, a young cellar master from Avize, in Champagne. In 1820 he moved to Rully, in the Chalonnais, and discreetly began to make a sparkling burgundy. Undoubtedly he was following the example of Jules Lausseure who, two years previously, had devised the notion of producing a sparkling wine in Nuits-Saint-Georges. François Hubert's business started

to flourish when, with the assistance of some Marseilles arms dealers, he managed to sell his product to Russia — weapons and wine being shipped together. Other growers imitated his example. Production of Bourgogne Mousseux very quickly rose to a million bottles a year and new markets opened up in the United States, Britain and Germany. Around 1870 sparkling red burgundy was introduced abroad; although not taken very seriously, it became a great success. Despite the fact that true wine lovers and Burgundians themselves shudder at the thought of sparkling red burgundy, it is still popular in the United States, Britain, West Germany, Sweden and Norway.

Méthode champenoise

Sparkling burgundies are classified into several different categories, according to the way they are made. The most popular system is the *méthode champenoise*, which, as its name indicates, originated in the Champagne district. It entails a second, more thorough, fermentation after the wine has been bottled. The carbonic gas cannot escape and, at several atmospheres of pressure, remains trapped in the bottle, so producing the precious bubbles. The *méthode champenoise* is complex and requires careful handling, as the second fermentation produces a sediment which has

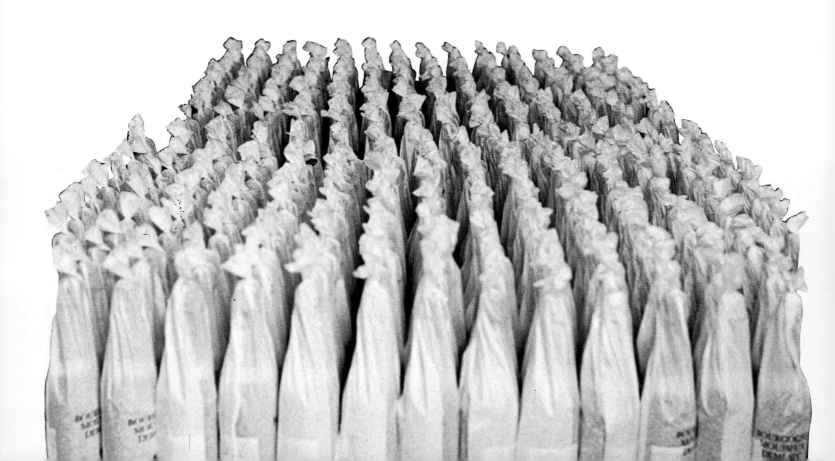

Henry Lucius Grégoire, from Davayé in the Mâconnais, often wins medals and prizes with his Bourgogne Mousseux. This delicious and refreshing wine has a charming hint of terroir.

The second fermentation of Kriter (produced by Patriarche) takes place in the bottle, but a process of filtering, not remuage, is used to clear the wine. Limpid colour, light taste, fresh and rather fruity. A very pleasant sparkling wine.

The word 'Crémant' comes from the Champagne district where it denotes a type of champagne with lighter than normal effervescence.

The Loire and Alsace, like Burgundy, have their Crémants.

The production of Crémant de Bourgogne is more expensive than that of Bourgogne Mousseux. Strict laws governing the pressing of the grapes reduces production of the must by 7 per cent.

Opposite page, below: A regiment of bottles, carefully wrapped in tissue paper, in the shop of Parigot & Richard, a small firm from Savigny-lès-Beaune.

Below: At André Delorme, in Rully, each bottle of Crémant is tested by smell before final corking.

Sparkling Wines

to be delicately removed. The bottles are placed on sloping shelves (*pupitres*) and rotated once a day by hand or by machine; this is called *remuage*. At the same time, each bottle is gradually tilted upright until it is vertical, and the sediment then accumulates naturally at the mouth of the bottle. After several weeks, when the bottles are completely vertical, the impurities are removed by an ingenious method called *dégorgement*.

In 1974, Burgundy produced more than six million bottles of wine made according to the *méthode champenoise*; this is one-fifth of all the sparkling wine made in France. The best-known specialist firms are: Simmonet-Fèbvre & Fils (the only one in Chablis); Moingeon-Gueneau Frères, Labouré-Gontard and Bouillot (all three in Nuits-Saint-Georges); Parigot & Richard and Moingeon & Remondet (in Savigny-lès-Beaune); André Delorme and Veuve Ambal (in Rully); la Cave Coopérative de Lugny, la Cave Coopérative de Viré and Henry Lucius Grégoire (in the Mâconnais).

Crémant de Bourgogne

Because Bourgogne Mousseux does not exactly conjure up an image of quality, a new *appellation* was created in 1975, Crémant de Bourgogne. The precise choice and blend of grapes is very important: the new wine must contain at least 30% each of Pinot Noir, Pinot Blanc and either Chardonnay or Pinot Gris. The remainder can be made up of Gamay (maximum 20% of the total), Aligoté, Melon or Sacy. Furthermore, the producers of Crémant must buy the actual grapes, not the wine, and must make the wine themselves. This poses problems for some firms which lack the means, the premises, the equipment or the expertise. Other regulations control transport of the grapes, yield per hectare, pressing techniques, maturation time, etc. Despite all these constraints, however, Crémant de Bourgogne will eventually replace the old Bourgogne Mousseux completely, and the changes will certainly improve both the quality and the reputation of the sparkling burgundies.

Other sparkling wines

In addition to Bourgogne Mousseux and Crémant de Bourgogne, both made by the rigorous *méthode champenoise*, there exist other sparkling wines that do not have the right to an *appellation contrôlée*. These are made in a closed vat, so that the second fermentation does not take place in the bottle but in a hermetically sealed tank. Other types of sparkling wine are made neither by the *méthode champenoise* nor in a closed vat, but simply by the addition of carbonic gas. These do not come wholly, or even partially, from the Burgundy vineyards. The best-known example is Kriter, a sparkling wine from Patriarche Père & Fils, which is quite pleasant and has enjoyed great success.

Réne Dauvistat has 22¼ acres of vineyards, exclusively of Premier Cru and Grand Cru level. His wines are matured in oak casks. Les Clos (5 acres) is a magnificent wine, with a fine, almost luxuriant bouquet and an expansive, agreeable taste.

At the Domaine de l'Eglantière, the wine is handled as little as possible, being allowed to develop on its own. The product is very pure and delicate; perhaps the best Chablis.

Simmonet-Febvre is a négociant who is very concerned with quality. He buys neither grapes nor wine, but must, so that he can exercise control over the making and élevage of his wine. His Chablis is a pleasant wine with a touch of vigour.

Like Simmonet-Febvre, Moreau buys the must and then makes the wine and personally supervises its élevage. Jean-Jacques Moreau detests oxidized wines: so his Chablis is very fresh, with an agreeable nose and taste.

The Albert Pic family has been making Chablis wines since 1799. Their Chablis has a wonderful pale green colour and clean, clear taste. Pic wines are marketed by the Regnard group.

Chablis

It is sometimes said that the character of a wine reflects its place of origin. I wholly concur with this sentiment as far as Chablis and its wines are concerned. Chablis wine seems to me as untypical a burgundy as the little town of Chablis is untypical of the Burgundy region. I have stayed several times in Chablis — a dreary, dismal little place, lacking in charm or warmth. Despite its favourable situation, halfway between Paris and Beaune and not far from the autoroute, it has only one fifteen-bedroom hotel, *L'Etoile*, which is the only place to get a good meal.

An incomparable wine

Chablis nevertheless produces a wine of extraordinary quality, with no equal either in Burgundy or the rest of the world. It is in no sense a tender, charming or kind wine; to the uninitiated, tasting it may almost come as a shock. In fact, compared with other white burgundies, perfume and taste may give an almost mineral-like, stony, cool impression. It is a very dry wine, that can taste almost salty (sometimes with a tang of salt licquorice). When young, Chablis is a limpid green; when older, it tends to be lemon-yellow. Despite its initial lack of charm, age gives it incomparable freshness, finesse, depth and suppleness. All these qualities make it an excellent accompaniment to seafood, particularly oysters.

Increasing production

Like all great white wines, Chablis is made exclusively from the Chardonnay grape, which was adopted from the Côte d'Or: in the Chablis district it is often called the Beaunois or Morillon. The surrounding landscape is a mixture of hills and small valleys, with Chablis itself situated in the Serein valley. With some local exceptions, the vineyards are tucked in between the fields and the woods. The law permits a maximum area of approximately 17,000 acres for this *appellation*, divided among 20 somewhat sleepy villages. The vineyards at present

under cultivation, however, only cover about 3,700 acres, roughly 20% of the total potential area. The wine growers have no complaint, however, since this land, by reason of its high calcium content and maximum exposure to the sun, is ideal for vines. Furthermore, greatly increased production could lower the market price. The area now under cultivation is, in any event, far bigger than it was 15-20 years ago, when it amounted to roughly 1,250-1,500 acres. At that time Chablis and the surrounding area were going through a period of severe depression. Land was cheap. Michel Poitout, manager of the Domaine de l'Eglantière, told me somewhat ruefully that while he had been away studying, one of his friends had bought some 30 acres of good vineyards for next to nothing, enabling the latter to build up a successful and increasingly profitable wine business. Even today, Poitout cannot raise enough money to buy any land of his own: since 1959, the revived fortunes of Chablis have led to rocketing price increases.

The frost peril

Chablis owes much of its newly won prosperity to the installation of a somewhat complex system of frost protection. As long as memory goes back, spring frosts have been a constant scourge in the valleys. Thus until about 1960, the Grand Cru les Clos, frequently ravaged by frost, was not very carefully tended by its disheartened owners. Because of this, the wine growers habitually planted their vines at the tops of the steep slopes, where it was extremely difficult to manoeuvre horses. Some growers were forced to do the work by hand — a long and costly operation. During the 19th century the *département* of the Yonne had a total of around 100,000 acres of vineyards; today this figure is not more than 5,190 acres, of which 3,700 acres are in Chablis. Wine-growing often used to constitute no more than a part of the peasants' livelihood and most of their production was retained for their own use. Gradually, wine-growing assumed greater importance, although

several vineyards were not very profitable. The first signs of a revival began to appear in 1952, coinciding with the time when Robert Vocoret introduced the tractor into the region. This innovation made it possible, for the first time, to utilize various types of land (for instance, with stony soil), unsuitable for working with horses. The revival proper, however, dates from several years later, when effective means were finally discovered for fighting frost, i.e. stoves and torches.

Stoves and torches

The small metal stoves now used for this purpose resemble rusty chimney flues. They generally burn fuel oil and give off a fair amount of heat, but are costly to buy and to run. For each acre, up to 100 stoves are needed. They have to be put in place individually, filled, lit, emptied and stored away at the end of the spring. At Maison Moreau, for example, with some 25 acres of Premiers and Grands Crus, it costs about 25,000 francs to keep the stoves burning for one night. It is easy to calculate the cost for 1974, for example, when it was necessary to light the stoves for three nights. Another problem with this method of heating is the risk of pollution. A number of wine-growers thing that, in the near future, the stoves will be banned in order to protect the environment. There are also small stoves which run on butane, but they, too, are costly to maintain.
In fact, a far simpler and commoner method of protection against frost is the torch. I have seen large heaps of them at the La Chablisienne cooperative. They are lit as soon as there is a threat of frost, and burn for seven hours at a stretch. They are produced by petrochemical companies like Mobil.

Water and wine

The third method used to combat frost, namely water, is the cheapest, cleanest and most efficient of all. The technique is as follows: narrow water pipes fitted with sprinklers are placed between the rows of

The 110-acre Domaine de Biéville, in Viviers, with its single owner, is drawing up the largest renovation programme in Chablis, and probably in the entire Burgundy region. It belongs to Maison Moreau and produces a Chablis with a slight hint of terroir.

Robert Vocoret and his two sons own 70 acres, of which 30 are Premiers Crus, including Les Forêts. A magnificent wine, delicate, fragrant and very clean tasting.

The Premier Cru Montmains (or Mont Mains) lies to the south-east of Chablis, on the slopes of the hills; the Domaine de l'Eglantière owns part of it. A rather elegant wine, not much perfumed; very clean, long aftertaste.

Below:
One of the pumping stations which helps to protect the vineyards of Chablis against frost.

Any reader keen to know more about Chablis and its problems (including soils) should buy William Fèvre's Les Vrais Chablis et les autres. This little book contains several maps and many lovely photographs of the Grand Crus. It can be obtained from the author, whose address is 14 rue Jules-Rathier, 89800 Chablis.

Crus of Chablis

Grands Crus:
Blanchots, Bougros, Les Clos, Grenouilles, Les Preuses, Valmur, Vaudésir.

Premiers Crus:
(Names in brackets indicate vineyards which may be reclassified under the name preceding them):
Monts de Milieu,
Montée de Tonnerre (Montée de Tonnerre, Chapelot, Pied-d'Aloup),
Fourchaume (Fourchaume, Vaupulent, Côte de Fontenay, Vaulorent,
l'Homme-Mort),
Vaillons, (Vaillons Châtains, Séché, Beugnons, Les Lys),
Montmains (Montmains, Forêts, Butteaux),
Mélinots (Mélinots, Roncières, Les Epinottes),
Côte de Léchet,
Beauroy (Beauroy, Troesmes),
Vaucoupin, Vosgros (Vosgros, Vaugiraut),
Les Fourneaux (Les Fourneaux, Morein, Côte des Prés-Girots).

The spelling of these names can often vary.

Chablis

vines. If there is a threat of frost, water is piped through the tubes and sprayed out, through the sprinklers, so that the vineyard is dowsed in a fine, artificial rain. The surrounding temperature is then maintained at a constant level and does not fall below 0°C. The water is obviously a much cheaper system than stoves. Fifty acres 'heated' by water is equivalent in cost to one acre heated by stoves. The system of water-sprinkling is very much in demand all over Chablis. The 25 wine growers who own the Premier Cru Fourchaume have jointly installed a pump which brings water from the River Serein to their vineyards. Several other pumps have already been installed and are now in use; among these is the largest in Chablis which services about 420 acres. The system has its drawbacks, however, as there still remains one element to be mastered: the wind. In the spring of 1976 strong wind drove the sprays of water in the wrong direction, so that there was considerable frost damage. Chablis has repeatedly suffered from hard frosts during recent years, but not as seriously or disastrously as before.

Petit-Chablis

The Chablis region has several areas of *appellation contrôlée* wine, the simplest of which, as its name indicates, is Petit-Chablis. The wine is mostly produced by growers on the outskirts of the region; the nearer the vineyards lie to the town of Chablis, the better the wine. The annual vintage of Petit-Chablis is on average well over 56,500 cases. (1975 was an exceptional year with about 107,000 cases.)
Petit-Chablis has no pretentions to being a great wine. In my opinion, its pleasant, vinous taste and lightly fruity bouquet make it an excellent *vin de carafe*. It must be drunk young, for if left too long it loses much of its charm and freshness, like a Beaujolais; and it is better drunk in the 12 months following the harvest. In 1975 a fairly large quantity of Petit-Chablis from the previous year's vintage was put on the market under the name Petit-Chablis Nouveau. This was an excellent new idea, since no other white burgundy is so suitable for this kind of presentation. It was devised by Maison Moreau, the largest in the region. However, the experiment was not very successful.

Montmains, produced by the estate of Albert Pic, is best laid down for about three years. The bouquet is often full, but without being exuberant. Fine, relatively full taste, though the aftertaste is sometimes less full.

Jean-Jacques Moreau, with 155 acres of vineyards, is the largest owner in Chablis. His Premiers Crus include some 12½ acres of Vaillons (or Vaillon). Fresh and supple wine with pleasant bouquet. Excellent taste, often quite subtle.

William Fèvre still works with small wooden casks in the vinification and maturing of his wine. A quarter of the barrels are renewed annually. Fine, full Vaudésirs, which can be left a few years to mature in the bottle without problem.

Jean-Claude Simmonet, of Simmonet-Fèbure, regards his Premier Cru, Mont (or Monts) de Milieu, as his great speciality. A full wine with a slightly saline, mineral taste.

La Montée de Tonnerre from the Domaine de l'Eglantière is a wine with a lasting taste, in which you can distinctly discern the chalk of the soil. Often too strongly perfumed when very young.

The Fourchaume of Regnard is often still amazingly clear in colour two years after the harvest. Vigorous bouquet, good earthy taste, which can be sometimes slightly metallic.

Chablis

Below:
Michael Poitout, manager of the Domaine de l'Eglantière.

Right:
Chablis, seen from the Grand Cru Les Clos, which was for a long time uncultivated because of the risk of spring frosts.

Opposite page:
A map of the Chablis area. Following analyses of the land structure, the Institut National des Appellations d'Origine proposed a major reallocation of land.

I tasted some very successful wines, as well as some mediocre ones, at Lamblin & Fils, a négociant in Milly. Among the better wines were a Petit-Chablis, a Bourgogne Blanc and a Fourchaumes. The latter revealed itself as a fine, distinctive, rather fleshy wine.

The Domaine de la Maladière belongs to William Fèvre. It is divided up among 11 Premier and Grand Cru vineyards. I have drunk his Vaulorent (which could equally well be called Fourchaume), with anguille en papillotes. A taste of sweet-sour apples.

La Chablisienne, a cooperative founded in 1923, produces, among other wines, a Premier Cru Fourchaume, which is often delicate and fragrant and which director Michel Tucki described as 'caressing the palate'.

Louis Michel enjoys an excellent reputation throughout Chablis. His Vaudésir has a strikingly agreeable taste, fleshy, with a flavour of peaches, but dominated by the characteristic freshness of Chablis.

Maison J. Moreau & Fils makes its wine from a tiny 3-acre vineyard in Vaudésir and Blanchots. It also buys must from other estates. Moreau's Vaudésir usually has a fine, strong and full taste.

The 5½-acre enclave of Moutonne is situated in Vaudésir. The differences between the two wines are considerable: Moutonne has more style and breeding. The name originates from a period when the vineyard belonged to some monks who, it is said, behaved like sheep when they had been drinking.

Chablis

Chablis tout court

Chablis comes above Petit-Chablis in the hierarchy of the *appellations.* The land that produces Chablis is more suited to vines and the degree of alcohol is fixed by law at 10°, whereas that of Petit-Chablis is 9.5°. The total vintage greatly exceeds that of Petit-Chablis, the average annual harvest being some 444,500 cases, of which about one-third is made by the La Chablisienne cooperative. Several *négociants* in Beaune (Bouchard Aîné, Bouchard Père & Fils, Chanson, etc.) buy regularly from the cooperative. These wines therefore can have a certain similarity, although much depends on the quality of the *cuvées* that one selects. In general, however, Chablis *tout court*, however, shows very marked differences; I have tasted several from the same vintage, some of which are extremely successful, while others are frankly bad. The Chablis from Domaine de l'Eglantière seem to me top-rate; it is a wine full of nuance and finesse, with a rare cleanness. This estate, in the village of Maligny, dates from 1968, and has 125 acres of vines. It belongs to a Parisian lawyer, Jean Durup, and is capably managed by the afore-mentioned Michel Poitout. Another excellent estate is the Domaine Laroche, with over 50 acres.

The Premier Crus

The average production of the Premiers Crus — those vineyards defined as such by law and producing wines with at least 10.5° of alcohol — is on average well over 52,000 cases a year. The Premiers Crus situated to

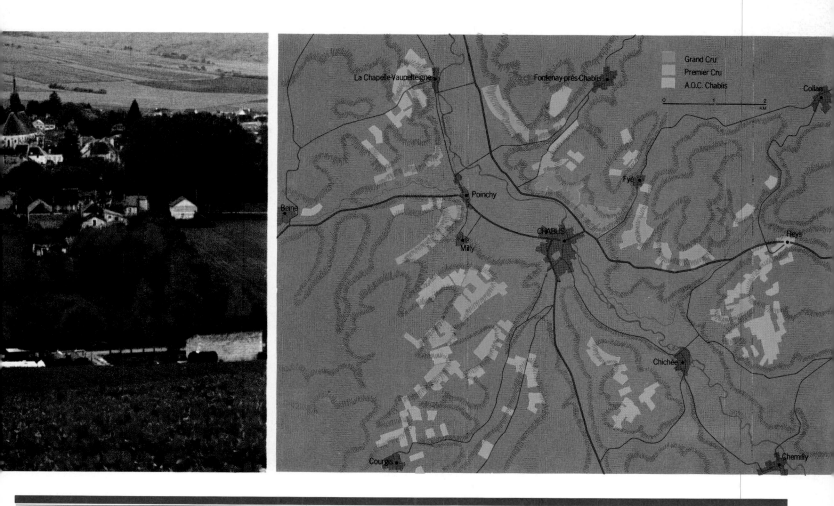

Chablis

the north of Chablis, on the right bank of the River Serein, are generally considered the best. Those of Fourchaume, Monts de Milieu and Montée de Tonnerre enjoy an excellent reputation, but I have also tasted some very good wines from Montmains, Beugnons and several other Premiers Crus. There are no less than 29 places with the right to the description Premiers Crus, and this diversity has led to legislation aimed at regrouping them under the 11 best known names. Thus the wines from Fourchaume, Vaupulent, Côte de Fontenay, Vaulorent and l'Homme-Mort could be reclassified under the single name of the most famous, Fourchaume. It is difficult to attribute a well-defined character to Chablis Premier Cru because of the wide variety of wines encompassed. The only really striking trait is a very much greater fullness than a Chablis *tout court*. It also needs longer to mature before developing all its potential. The degree of alcohol for Premiers Crus is legally fixed at 10.5° and the vintage varies from 88,000 to 187,000 cases.

The magnificent seven

The fullest and most generous Chablis, as well as the richest in alcohol (at least 11°), are those produced by the seven Grands Crus whose vineyards are in the north of the region, not far from the town of Chablis, on an extensive and, in places, quite rough hillside. These excellent vineyards cover an area of some 275 acres, with an average annual yield of 52,000 cases.

Each Grand Cru vineyard produces a wine with its own distinct personality, but one so elusive and so subtle that it is almost impossible to describe. The differences that occur within the same *cru* are due principally to the location of the vines, their age, and the methods of grafting and wine-making. Even experienced wine connoisseurs have great difficulty in telling one Grand Cru from another. Thus, in the course of a blind tasting, two owners of Grand Crus were only able to place them correctly after six attempts. Here is a brief general description of the 'Magnificent Seven', from north to south. The wines of Bougros are rather nervous and full of nuances. Those of Preuses are the roundest, with a stony, long-lasting taste. Vaudésir produces wines that are a little drier, livelier and finer than the others. Moutonne, owned by Domaine Long-Depaquit, is an enclave of land extending to Preuses and producing a wine, most of which is offered as Grand Cru by Maison Albert Bichot. The wine emanating from Les Grenouilles is so fragrant that the bouquet seems to explode out of the glass. Valmur also produces very fragrant, vigorous and fleshy wines. Les Clos generally yields wines which are firm, vigorous, sometimes a little flinty or almost spicy, with a long aftertaste; this vineyard also has an area producing a wine legally offered under its own name, Clos des Hospices, belonging to the Moreau family. Finally there is Blanchots, famed for perennially supple and fragrant wines; sometimes they are meatier and headier than the others, sometimes lighter.

Maison Moreau is the largest owner in the vineyard of Les Clos, which is often ravaged by frost. Its area is about 20 acres and includes the Clos des Hospices. This wine has a strong bouquet and a good, round, fairly long-lasting taste.

Until the French Revolution, Clos des Hospices belonged to the Chablis hospital; it was later bought by individual owners. The wine from this enclave is deeper, more fragrant, more subtle than that of Les Clos.

A narrow footpath separates the vineyard of Les Clos from that of Blanchots. The two wines are very different, the Blanchot from Vocoret is usually more supple and has a stronger bouquet than a Les Clos from the same year; it is also slightly lighter.

Les Preuses can be distinguished from all the other Grands Crus by its almost velvety fullness. La Chablisienne demonstrated this point very clearly. The wine also had a long-lasting mineral aftertaste.

The Sauvignon Blanc of Saint-Bris is nothing like a burgundy, bearing a closer resemblance to certain wines from the Loire. The 1975 from Maison Moreau has a very dry, light, lively taste.

In Irancy about 25 growers jointly cultivate about 360 acres of vineyard. Nowadays, the Pinot Noir is the most common variety of grape, although the César can still be found. Coulanges-la-Vineuse, another 'red' commune of Chablis, has some 200 acres which are cultivated by about a dozen growers.

In Bailly-sur-Yonne (immediately next to Saint-Bris-le-Vineux) an excellent Crémant de Bourgogne is produced by a group of growers. One of the brand names is Meurgis.

Chablis

Sauvignon de Saint-Bris and Bourgogne d'Irancy

In the area immediately surrounding Chablis, several less familiar and less impressive wines are produced. Because of their modest yield they are inevitably overshadowed by their celebrated neighbours. One of them, Sauvignon de Saint-Bris, is a very special wine. Not only is it the only wine in Burgundy without an *appellation d'origine contrôlée* (in 1974 it gained the lesser status of *vin délimité de qualité supérieure*), but it is also the only white burgundy produced from a grape not native to this area, the Sauvignon. The resultant wine, with little bouquet and not a great deal of taste, is more like a white wine from the Loire, such as a Sancerre, but thinner than a typical white burgundy. The village of Saint-Bris-le-Vineux is the centre of its production, and the vintage (at the most 47,750 cases) is divided between 30 growers who have formed a small cooperative. This village also produces a good Aligoté.

The other wine worth knowing in the Yonne comes from Irancy, a village situated in the centre of a natural amphitheatre containing some 155 acres of vineyards. Red and rosé wines, mainly based on the Pinot Noir, are grown there. Wine from Irancy has the right to carry the Bourgogne *appellation*. Compared with other burgundies, it gives a rather thin impression but if kept for several years it tends to become somewhat more rewarding. Bourgogne d'Irancy is not much exported because of the small quantity produced — on average up to 16,650 cases. The same is true of the wines of Coulange-la-Vineuse.

Côte d'Or

The Côte d'Or is more than a symbol: it is the very essence of Burgundy. Indeed, when the term 'burgundy' is used in the trade, it is often applied only to the wines of the Côte d'Or. The most celebrated red and white burgundies, in fact, come from this region, and here we find the names of the most prestigious of all *crus*: Chambertin, Clos de Vougeot, Romanée-Conti, Montrachet and many others. Here also, predominantly in Beaune and Nuits-Saint-Georges, you come across the names of firms which have established the reputation of Burgundy the world over. Some people say that the Côte d'Or owes its name to the precious wine it

produces, which seems reasonable, but actually it has another origin: each year, in autumn, when the leaves of the vines turn yellow, the sun transforms the vineyards into a carpet of gold.

Great diversity

The Côte d'Or (or simply the Côte, as it is known to the local inhabitants), comprises about 16,000 acres of vineyards; the zone starts south of Dijon and extends for 28 miles to the southeast. For most of its distance it runs parallel to *route nationale 74, La Voie Royale* or Royal Way, built by

Napoleon III. The best vineyards, those that are most open and receive the most sun, lie on the hillsides; others, situated on lower ground and frequently divided by the *route nationale*, are less well-favoured. The small vineyards of the Hautes-Côtes, in the hinterland of the Côte d'Or, are also well exposed. The composition of the subsoil plays an important role in the successful development of the vines, the best terrain being a mixture of calcium, clay and gravel. In each separate part of the vineyard, these elements are to be found in different proportions, or combined with other minerals, and these specific mixtures give

Côte d'Or

the wines their particular characters. The
soil of the plain generally contains more clay,
which is better for cereals than for vines;
indeed, wines from the plains are often
mediocre. In addition, water on the plain
stagnates and does not run away freely as it
does on the hillsides. These various factors
make for great diversity. Some of the Côte
d'Or vineyards — about 19,500 acres —
produce very simple wines, others wines of
exceptional quality.

Côte de Nuits and Côte de Beaune

Traditionally, the Côte d'Or is divided into
the Côte de Nuits and the Côte de Beaune.
The Côte de Nuits, the northern part, starts
south of Dijon and ends several miles south
of Nuits-Saint-Georges, beyond Corgoloin.
Predominantly red wines are produced here,
including most of the Grands Crus. In
general, the wines of the Côte de Nuits are
regarded as wines which keep for a long time,
while those of the Côte de Beaune mature
more rapidly. But there are many
exceptions, and, in fact, there are as many
light wines in the Côte de Nuits as there are
full-bodied ones in the Côte de Beaune, the
age of the vines and the methods of wine-
making being major influential factors on
quality. The Côte de Beaune starts at
Ladoix-Serrigny and ends south of
Santenay, and it is in this area that the Côte
d'Or produces, along with its excellent red
wines, white wines of Puligny-Montrachet,
Chassagne-Montrachet, Aloxe-Corton and
Meursault.

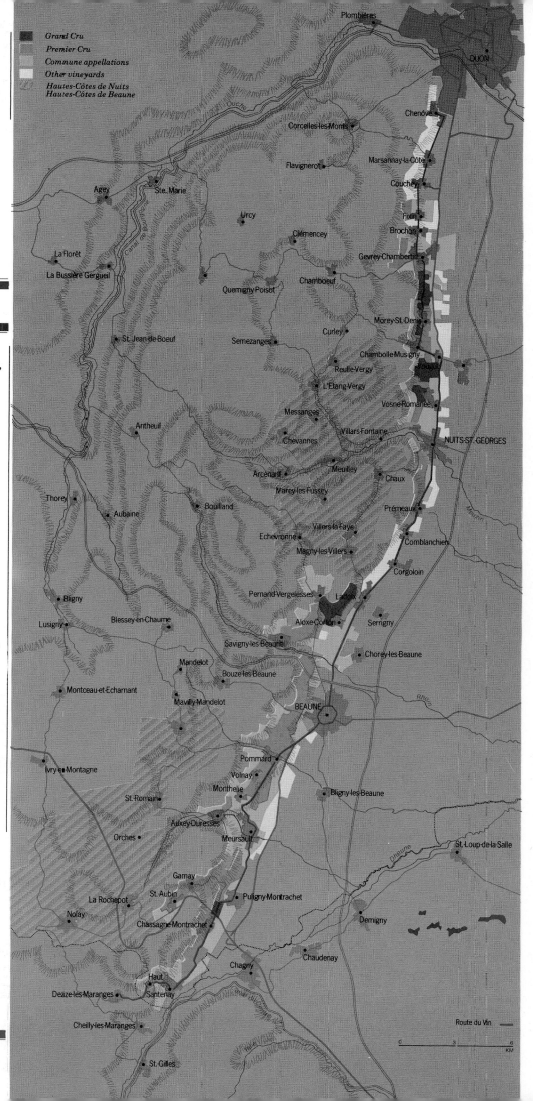

Grand Cru
Premier Cru
Commune appellations
Other vineyards
Hautes-Côtes de Nuits
Hautes-Côtes de Beaune

Route du Vin

Other good wines include:
Bourgogne Hautes-Côtes de Beaune from Alain Verdet in Arcenat (outstanding quality); Bourgogne Hautes-Côtes de Beaune from Jayer-Gilles in Magny-les-Villers; Bourgogne Hautes-Côtes de Nuits from the estate of Antonin Guyon in Savigny-lès-Beaune.

Mavilly-Mandelot is a small village to the west of Beaune. Château Mandelot produces a wine which, although a bit thin, is not without a certain charm, good red colour, Pinot Noir nose. Distributors: Bouchard Père & Fils.

The house of Geisweiler produces very pleasant red and white wines under the appellation d'origine of Hautes-Côtes de Nuits on its fine estate of Bévy. The vineyard of Bévy covers 173 acres. Another, more recent vineyard of 42 acres, near Nuits-Saint-Georges, produces another Hautes-Côtes de Nuits, the Cuvée Dames Hautes.

Jean Joliot and his sons live in Nantoux, where they own 16 acres of vineyards. Their red wine, perhaps a little severe and somewhat astringent, is nevertheless very good.

Below:
Cellars of the Domaine Thevenot-Le Brun & Fils in Marey-lès-Fussey. Maurice Thevenot was one of the first to replant in the Hautes-Côtes. He grows 27 acres of Pinot, 18 acres of Aligoté, Chardonnay and Pinot Gris, as well as 25 acres of blackcurrants.

Opposite page, above right:
In 1976, under the auspices of the Confrérie de l'Escargot, the marriage was celebrated between the Burgundy snail and the Aligoté of the Hautes-Côtes.

Opposite page, below:
A modern all-purpose tractor on the Domaine Hudelot. This tractor can be used on all types of terrain, is able to turn on its axis and is suitable for all kinds of work. The estate belongs to two brothers, Henri and Bernard, who has studied oenology and wine-growing. Their vineyard is in the Hautes-Côtes de Nuits, very near to Villars-Fontaine. The estate covers about 110 acres, but some of these are not productive.

Hautes-Côtes

A visitor to the Côte d'Or will not necessarily realize that the hills and valleys to the west conceal other vineyards. The Hautes-Côtes de Nuits and the Hautes-Côtes de Beaune constitute a single massive area divided up into 28 communes, all working in close collaboration. Although historians still cannot agree on the exact date when vines were introduced into the Arrière-Côte, we do know that wine-growing has been established there for several centuries. Pierre Forgeot believes that the first vines were planted there in the 16th or 17th centuries, but Michel Jovignot favours a later date at the end of the 17th century. In any event, wine-growing has been a feature of the Hautes-Côtes for about 200 years, reaching its peak at the end of the 19th century, with over 11,000 acres under cultivation. But 1878 proved a fatal year: the appearance of *Phylloxera* in Burgundy caused terrible devastation. This parasitic insect destroyed the vines one by one and since then the vineyards of the Hautes-Côtes have never made a full recovery.

A grave crisis

At the start of the 20th century, wine growers faced a series of problems. After a period of over-production from 1900 to 1905, which resulted in a fall in prices, the vines were attacked by two diseases, oïdium and mildew. Later, at the conclusion of World War I, certain *négociants* depressed prices still further by marketing red wines of inferior quality and of dubious origins, notably Algerian. This was the final blow for the wine growers of the Hautes-Côtes. In 1913 there had been 8,000 acres under cultivation; by 1955 there were only about 1,250 remaining acres entitled to use an *appellation contrôlée*. This tiny area diminished still further until around 1960 when the first signs of a recovery were evident.

The Château de Mercey in the Hautes-Côtes de Beaune region produces red and white burgundies of a consistently high quality. The château, which is owned by the Berger family, is near Cheilly-les-Maranges.

The cooperative of the Hautes-Côtes first began to mature its wine in wooden barrels with a part of the 1978 vintage. The result was so successful that, from 1981 onwards a large part of each vintage is to be left in barrels for six to nine months. The Hautes-Côtes de Beaune is slightly stronger than the Hautes-Côtes de Nuits.

Enlightened insanity

The revival of the Hautes-Côtes is due to the determined and brave efforts of several men, thanks to whom the area is beginning to prosper once more. Etienne Kayser, for example, fought for many years to get an *appellation contrôlée*: Maurice Thevenot had the courage to replant on a large scale; and since 1966, Bernard Hudelot has been so enthusiastic to buy land for wine-growing that his neighbours have often questioned his sanity. These and many others have dedicated themselves to the region and its wines. Happily, they have been rewarded with success: on 4 August 1961, the coveted *appellations* of Bourgogne Hautes-Côtes de Nuits and Bourgogne Hautes-Côtes de Beaune were granted. In 1968, a brand new cooperative brought in the harvest, and in 1974 La Maison des Hautes-Côtes was established.

The new cooperative

The new cooperative venture was of vital importance to the area, a great improvement on the barely functional, dilapidated older buildings. Wine growers new to the business were able to obtain reasonable prices for their grapes, without being compelled to invest heavily in buildings and materials. Their enthusiasm was not misplaced, and they were soon recording an increase in turnover. The cooperative, situated on the busy road between Beaune and Pommard, has made its mark with the public: everyone travelling that road regularly knows of its existence and many stop to sample its wine. *Négociants* are not the only customers, for many private individuals, particularly tourists, buy their wine 'on site'. The cooperative now has about 110 members who cultivate almost 745 acres on the Hautes-Côtes. It is equipped with such modern equipment as stainless-steel fermentation tanks which are self-emptying. Production is almost equally divided between the Hautes-Côtes de Nuits and those of Beaune. Some of the members also own land on the Côte d'Or

and the wine from those holdings is also made, bottled and sold by the cooperative. Since the 1981 harvest some of the red Hautes-Côtes wines have been matured in casks, which has greatly increased their quality. I also find the Rosé d'Orches (Bourgogne Grand Ordinaire) and the Aligoté very pleasant.

A pioneer

Some wine growers, particularly those who were in at the beginning, do not belong to the cooperative. Among them is Bernard Hudelot, who gave me an account of his

pioneering days. He and his brother Henri added to their vineyard a bit at a time, without capital, and consequently without the means to buy modern plant. They worked for years without taking a day's holiday, not even stopping on Sundays; but this strenuous effort finally paid off, so that today the Hudelots have a large estate, a modern tractor and a fine *cuverie* which they built themselves. If you consider that the land they bought not long ago for 3,705 francs per acre now fetches 20 to 25 times the price, it is easy to calculate the solid investment they made.

In addition to wine-growing, Lucien Jacob has political and professional interests. He is currently a deputy in the Côte d'Or. His 1975 red, which is very promising, has more colour than many Côte d'Or wines of the same vintage. However, recent harvests have produced lighter wines of less fine quality.

The Maison des Hautes-Côtes serves several thousand bottles of wine every year to its many visitors. Bernard Hudelot's wife created this label. The wines are delicious.

New methods of cultivation

Now that the vineyards of the Hautes-Côtes have almost all been restored, the younger owners have been quick to modernize their methods of cultivation. The vines are now trained up high to facilitate the work, to allow the passage of tractors and to avoid spring frosts; and the space between the rows of vines has been increased from 5 to 9 feet. In a conservative region like Burgundy, not everyone approves of new methods, and the *Institut National des Appellations d'Origine* has still not officially authorized them, but only granted temporary permission for their use. To qualify for an *appellation contrôlée* all wines are subjected to tests which allow the results of these new techniques to be verified. If the wine under inspection is of poor quality, it is not put on the market.

Pinot Gris

Most of the new strips of land under cultivation are to be found in the Hautes-Côtes de Nuits. Domaine de Bévy, of Maison Geisweiler, is notable for its 175 acres: after some fairly problematic initial attempts, it has succeeded in producing very pleasant, rather light, clear red wines. The slopes of Bévy enjoy an extraordinary microclimate, which has earned them the title of Côte d'Azur de la Côte d'Or. Bernard and Henry Hudelot also own some flourishing vineyards there, next to those of Maison Geisweiler. In the Hautes-Côtes, most of the grapes are Pinot Noir, Aligoté and Chardonnay, but Maurice Thevenot, an older, more reticent representative of those pioneering years, has managed to produce a white wine solely from Pinot Gris, a grape known in Burgundy under the alternative name of Beurot and in Alsace as Tokay d'Alsace. This wine has an unusually intense taste.

Some light wines

Compared with the Hautes-Côtes de Nuits, where all the vineyards are new, the Hautes-Côtes de Beaune is of long standing. Among the many wine growers I met there, Jean-Baptiste Joliot, of Nantoux, told me that in this zone wine-growing was actually more advanced than in the Hautes-Côtes de Nuits. This is borne out by the production figures: on average 177,750 cases for the Hautes-Côtes de Beaune, compared to 138,875 cases for the Hautes-Côtes de Nuits (*appellation contrôlée* wines only.) The vineyards to the southwest of Beaune mostly consist of old vines, which clearly improves the quality of the wine. The red wine of the Hautes-Côtes de Nuits is fairly light at the start and improves with age; patience is needed for it to reach its peak. If the Hautes-Côtes do not as yet produce fleshy or full-bodied wines, there are still a number of decent light wines to be had at reasonable prices. A blind tasting of the 1976 vintage, held in 1978, proved that the wines of the Hautes-Côtes, provided they are from a reputable grower and of a good vintage, could hold out pleasant surprises. The tasting included a bottle of Bourgogne Hautes-Côtes de Beaune from Jean Gros, which was vinous, with a good colour and a hint of vanilla in the taste (it had doubtless been kept in an oak cask) which was long-lasting. I also tasted a good Bourgogne Hautes-Côtes de Nuits from Maison Dufouleur Père & Fils. Of the nine wines tasted, these two Bourgogne Hautes-Côtes were given marks as good as two Premiers Crus Nuits-Saint-Georges from the highly reputed estate of Henri Gouges. During subsequent tasting sessions, the Hautes-Côtes wines were especially notable for their increasingly high standards.

In 1974, Bernard and Henri Hudelot lost their entire vintage through spring frost. This disaster put paid to several years of pioneering work. That is now all in the past, however; the Hudelots now have a worthwhile estate which produces good red and white burgundies. The best red Hautes-Côtes de Nuits is Des Genevrières.

Maurice Thevenot makes nearly all his wine from Chardonnay and Pinot Noir grapes. From Pinot Gris, however, he makes a rather rare white wine, requiring at least two years to mature, which has a strong bouquet and a delicate flavour.

Opposite page, above:
The Domaine Hudelot in Villars-Fontaine (Hautes-Côtes de Nuits).

Opposite page, below:
For just one day a year, on the first Sunday after the end of the harvest, hunting is permitted in the vineyards.

Right:
A beautiful bunch of Pinot Noir grapes.

Below:
Somewhere in the Hautes-Côtes the barrels are made ready for the new vintage.

The Maison des Hautes-Côtes in Marey-lès-Fussey, near Nuit-Saint-Georges, was set up by 25 wine growers from private funds and a subsidy from the Comité Interprofessionnel des vins de la Côte d'Or et de L'Yonne. The partly subterranean cellar of the building is used as a restaurant. Cheap, straightforward regional dishes are served, accompanied by local wines. In 1980 the Maison des Hautes-Côtes was further enlarged by the addition of a huge dining room to take 250 people, an event which underlines the immense success of the project.

The tourist route around the Hautes-Côtes is marked with dark brown signs.

An expanding region

Today the Hautes-Côtes comprise about 2,500 acres in production and very soon this will be more than 3,000 acres. It is hoped that this expansion will continue, and the area increased eventually to 5,000 acres, for wine is the only product that can bring prosperity back to the Hautes-Côtes.
All the means appear to be at hand to attain that objective. The new generation of wine growers receives specialized training in Beaune; a Comité d'Aménagement des Hautes-Côtes has been formed to encourage special activities in 60 villages; wine-tastings are organized; tourist maps and itineraries are freely distributed; and the Aligoté des Hautes-Côtes has been officially 'married' to the Burgundy snail. Visitors flock to *La Maison des Hautes-Côtes* to sample the restaurant's wines and regional specialities. Despite everything, however, most importers are still somewhat wary about letting burgundies from the Hautes-Côtes into their cellars: they argue that these wines are often too light and that their *appellation* is rather complicated. Nevertheless, it is probable — and naturally all the people of the Hautes-Côtes cherish the hope — that in the near future no cellar worthy of the name will be able to be without this wine.

The Clos de Langres, a vineyard of 7½ acres on the boundary of the Côte de Nuits and the Côte de Beaune, belongs to La Reine Pédauque. Clear colour, pleasant bouquet and supple in the mouth.

Paul Reitz, now a négociant, was formerly a wine grower in the Hautes-Côtes. He runs his business from a château in the centre of Corgoloin. Reitz's specialities are the Beaujolais Crus, but his Côte de Nuits-Villages is usually very acceptable. Other nice wines from this firm are the Corton, Volnay and Gevrey-Chambertin.

Right:
The famous 'Napoleon Awakening' in Fixin, by the sculptor Rude, who did the bas-reliefs on the Arc de Triomphe in Paris. The slab on which it is mounted comes from St Helena.

Below:
The Renaissance-style Château de Brochon. In about 1920 it belonged to the poet Stephen Liégard, who also owned a small vineyard.

Opposite page, above:
Ullaging in the cellars of the Domaine Clair-Daü, Marsannay.

Opposite page, below:
Mme Noëlle Vernet (née Clair) who manages the Clair-Daü estate, which is the largest privately owned wine-producing property on the Côte d'Or, with 91½ acres.

Côte de Nuits-Villages

The *appellation* Côte de Nuits-Villages (previously Vins Fins de la Côte de Nuits) is considered somewhat second-rate amongst the wines of the Côte de Nuits. This is because three of the communes (from north to south: Prissey, Comblanchien and Corgoloin) from which it comes do not have the right to use their names as *appellations*. Only the fourth, Fixin, is allowed to offer its wine under its own name. Being almost unknown, however, Fixin is often voluntarily declassified by the wine growers of the Côte de Nuits-Villages. Moreover, Côte de Nuits-Villages is frequently a blend of wines from more than these four communes.

The total area of production of the Côte de Nuits-Villages is about 800 acres, of which Fixin comprises 320 acres. Some years ago, the communes of Marsannay and Couchey applied to become part of this *appellation*, a suggestion vigorously opposed by owners in the five other communes. There is now little likelihood that this subject will be raised again.

Production of Côte de Nuits-Villages (on average 77,800 cases) varies quite a lot, depending mainly on the decision of the wine growers of Fixin. A small quantity of white wine is also produced, usually about 55 cases (the 240 cases of 1971 was a record).

Quarries of pink stone

For many years the village of Brochon produced wines for the Côte de Nuits-Villages *appellation*, but these vineyards, which cover almost 126 acres, have now been grouped under the Gevrey-Chambertin *appellation*. Its most impressive building is the Renaissance-style château which, around 1920, belonged to the poet Stephen Liégard, who also owned Craibillon (or Crébillon), a small 1¾-acre vineyard of good repute. Fixin and Brochon are in the north of the Côte de Nuits and Prissey, Comblanchien and Corgoloin in the south. Prissey (ancient Prisseum), to the south of Nuits-Saint-Georges, has only about 30 acres of vineyards.

Comblanchien owes its reputation mainly to its enormous quarries of beautiful pink-veined stone. When polished, this stone looks like marble, and has been used to decorate such famous buildings as the Opéra de Paris, Orly Airport and the Palais de Justice in Brussels. In Burgundy this stone is traditionally used both for public buildings and private homes.

The vineyards of Comblanchien cover an area of 135 acres. Corgoloin, the last commune in the Côte de Nuits, has 200 acres of vines and those of Clos de Langres form the boundary with the Côte de Beaune.

The Domaine Clair-Daü still offers its wine one year after the vintage. Very light claret colour, fruity bouquet, pleasantly refreshing taste. Should be drunk when young. Clair-Daü's red burgundy from Marsannay is also excellent.

The rosé from the Coopérative de Marsannay has a lively taste, full and fresh, and a light claret colour. Annual production is from 3,300 to 6,600 cases of red and rosé, one quarter of which is bottled by the Coopérative.

The Domaine Huguenot Père & Fils comprises 42 acres, about 22 of which are in Marsannay. Its wines are mostly sold in Belgium. The rosé, light claret, has a fairly vigorous bouquet and agreeable taste.

Marsannay

The vineyards of Côte d'Or, which originally began outside Dijon, have disappeared one by one, swallowed up by the town's urban development. At the end of the 19th century more than 220,000 cases of wine were being produced on 7,500 acres of land. Today, production is no more than 3,300 cases (of which only 850 cases can be described as *appellation contrôlée*). There are still about 40 wine growers in the Dijon area who make wine for their own consumption, but the majority produce barely 10 cases a year. Chenôve, for example, in the suburbs of Dijon, had a vineyard of about 125 acres in 1920, but this has virtually disappeared as the town has grown. The only vineyards still in use are the Clos du Roy and the Clos du Chapitre. There you can still see a very old and enormous wine press, the Pressoir des Ducs, dating from 1228 and still used in the 19th century. In a single operation, its immense stone could crush enough grapes to supply juice for 60 wine barrels.

A brilliant innovation

Now that the wine growers have disappeared from Dijon, Marsannay-la-Côte is the most northerly wine-growing commune in the Côte de Nuits, indeed in the entire Côte d'Or. For many years this village of 6,600 inhabitants has supplied the ordinary, everyday drinking wine of the people of Dijon. It is made from the Gamay grape and the wine growers have done so well out of it that they see no need to replace this common variety with the noble Pinot Noir. Another reason for using the Gamay is that during the 19th century and up to the beginning of the 20th, not a single Pinot Noir plant was to be found in Marsannay. However, increasingly intense competition from the French wine-growing region of the Midi has forced the Marsannay growers to lower their prices. The solution came on 23 September 1919, when Joseph Clair, a shrewd wine grower, introduced a rosé made from the Pinot Noir. The wine, which until then had hardly been known in Burgundy, was destined to single out Marsannay from all the other local communes.

One of the best French rosés

Joseph Clair's innovation was a tremendous success. The largest and best restaurant in Dijon bought the entire vintage and, with Clair again showing the way, a small cooperative was started in 1929, specializing in rosé but also producing red wine. During the 1960s, Marsannay, with the neighbouring commune of Couchey, was granted its own *appellation contrôlée*. Henceforth the red wine would be called Bourgogne Marsannay, and the rosé Bourgogne Rosé de Marsannay or Bourgogne Clairet de Marsannay. The rosé is the better, producing the roundness of a burgundy combined with an invigorating freshness. Frank Schoonmaker, the American writer on wine, described it as 'one of the lightest, fruitiest and best rosés in France'.

The production of Bourgogne Rosé de Marsannay is on average almost 22,200 cases, but an increase is expected. Domaine Clair-Daü, one of the largest estates in the Côte d'Or, including 65 acres in Marsannay, is an important producer of this wine.

On several occasions, as in 1972, André Bart, of Marsannay, produces a perfect Pinot-type wine in his Hervelets Premier Cru, although not very fleshy and without much finesse.

The fragrant Clos Napoléon has received many awards. Its breeding does not appear until after it has aged for two or three years. Fairly vigorous, this wine is lighter than that of Clos du Chapitre or Clos de la Perrière.

Clos de la Perrière is a Premier Cru which produces a deep-coloured wine with a generous, open, strong taste. A good-quality wine. This Fixin needs to be kept for at least three to four years. The owner of this vineyard is Philippe Joliet who lives in the Manoir de la Perrière, overlooking the vineyards.

Clos du Chapitre is more 'imperial' then Clos Napoléon. In 1972, the old vines produced a wine which Pierre Gelin considered the best since 1949. It has more colour, bouquet and body than other wines from Fixin and keeps for a long time.

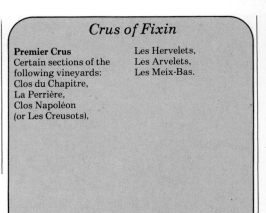

Crus of Fixin

Premier Crus
Certain sections of the following vineyards:
Clos du Chapitre,
La Perrière,
Clos Napoléon
(or Les Creusots),

Les Hervelets,
Les Arvelets,
Les Meix-Bas.

The spelling of these names can often vary.

Fixin

The best wine of the Côte de Nuits, after the Marsannay rosé, comes from Fixin. The Pinot Noir grape gives this wine the same deep colour, generosity and warmth as those from more famous communes.

Vines were introduced into this region by the Romans, but the history of the village of Fixin is even older. A tomb found close to the village probably dates back to 2000 BC, the period when the Egyptian civilization of the Pharaohs was at its peak; and a Roman spring of chalybeate water has, since 1827, fed a local public wash-house. Its smooth stone columns are worthy of adorning a temple of hygiene, even if the water itself looks decidedly murky.

The commune of Fixin contains the hamlet of Fixey and has about 900 inhabitants. This figure will almost certainly grow in years to come, if the mayor is successful in making it a suburb of Dijon, a project that is not universally popular, especially with the wine growers.

Memorial to Napoleon

Fixin was formerly the summer residence of the Dukes of Burgundy and at one time the place where certain citizens of Dijon settled when retiring to the country. With the arrival of motor traffic, however, Fixin is nowadays swamped by visitors from home and abroad. In Whitsun 1975 the village was besieged by tourists from 40 different *départments* of France and from six foreign countries. The object of their pilgrimage was not the vineyards, but the immense reverent memorial to Napoléon Bonaparte in Noisot Park.

This 15-acre park was originally created by Claude Noisot, a former grenadier commander of the Imperial Guard, who decided to build in it a full-sized replica of the house on St Helena where Napoleon ended his days. The park contains one work of art, a bronze statue by the sculptor François Rude entitled 'Napoleon Awakening'. François Noisot bequeathed his park to the commune of Fixin.

Natural protection

Compared with other wine-growing communes in the Côte d'Or, Fixin enjoys a very special microclimate, with the result that the village has thus far been spared the ravages of nature. Only one shower of hail within living memory has caused any damage. The village and vineyards of Fixin lie in the valleys of the Saône and the Ouche, south of Lake Kir. Since hail showers generally follow watercourses, they usually bypass Fixin, (except on 12 July 1979 when between 30% and 50% of the crop was destroyed by hail). Furthermore, the vineyards are located on the slopes of a hill crowned by trees which provide effective protection from the wind. Finally, the soil, consisting mainly of clay, encourages rainfall to drain away, so somewhat diminishing the risk of decay. One Fixin wine grower remarked to me: 'Nature is our best insurance'.

The commune possesses 315 acres of vineyards with an average annual vintage of 18,300 cases of red wine. The variation may seem surprising, considering the mildness of Fixin's climate, but is explained by the fact that Fixin sells part of its vintage under the *appellation* of Côte de Beaune-Villages and not under its own name. In the last resort, the quantity of available wine depends on market trends.

Similar to Gevrey-Chambertin

Fixin closely resembles Gevrey-Chambertin in colour, generous taste, fairly high alcohol content, solid structure and keeping potential. As a rule, however, it lacks the breeding and distinction of Gevrey-Chambertin, and could perhaps be likened to a less gifted younger brother. This criticism does not apply, however, to the superior wines of the commune, which may legitimately be compared with the *crus* of Gevrey-Chambertin. Back in 1855, Doctor Lavalle wrote that the price of a Clos de la Perrière was often as high as that of a

Chambertin. Today many connoisseurs find it very hard to distinguish, at a blind tasting, between, say, a Clos du Chapitre from Fixin and a Gevrey-Chambertin of the same vintage.

The best Premier Crus

In my opinion, Clos du Chapitre produces the best Fixin: an impressive wine with a good colour, remarkable bouquet, meaty and mellow in taste, with a hint of raspberries. This Premier Cru vineyard, entirely rented out to Domaine Gelin & Molin, extends from behind the village church for about 12 acres. Another Premier Cru enjoying an excellent reputation is the 12-acre Clos de la Perrière, dominated by the old Perrière manor, once the property of the Cistercians and now owned by Philippe Joliet who lives there with his family. Visitors are always welcome to taste the wine and admire the fine cellars. The wine has a strong, firm constitution: a classical Burgundy, delicious with game. Of the other Premiers Crus — Meix-Bas, Arvelets, Hervelets and Clos Napoléon — the last deserves special mention. In the 19th century Claude Noisot, founder of the park, managed to buy this little vineyard intact, and wishing to immortalize the emperor's name in the area he called it Clos Napoléon. Today this 5-acre vineyard belongs to Pierre Gelin and Andre Molin, who produce a good wine for laying down, although it is a little lighter and thinner than that of Clos du Chapitre.

Above:
View of Fixin from the Clos Napoléon.

Below:
Old gateway to the manor of La Perrière in Fixin. Here you can drink Clos de la Perrière and see a 13th-century winepress.

Chez Jeannette *is the best restaurant in the village, followed by* La Petite Taverne *where they serve a* coq au vin *made with the lees of the wine from the Domaine Gelin.*

Bernard Drouhin, of the Domaine Drouhin-Laroze, cultivates 45 acres, using both modern and traditional wine-making methods. A very clean, balanced Gevrey-Chambertin, with a very successful bouquet and plenty of fruit in the mouth.

The firm of Joseph Faiveley, in Nuits-Saint-Georges, owns 25 acres in Gevrey; Grands Crus, Premiers Crus and commune. The latter is no more than a good-quality wine. However, the excellent La Combe aux Moines is an especially well-balanced Premier Cru (of which Faiveley owns 2¼ acres); a much more distinguished wine.

Henri Rebourseau lives in a magnificent house which in one direction looks out onto a large park, and in the other onto a 13½-acre vineyard of appellation contrôlée Gevrey-Chambertin. This property, which also includes some 6 acres of another vineyard, produces an excellent, robust wine. The quality of any vintage — even recent ones — is highly reliable.

Although Louis Latour's 1972 Gevrey-Chambertin lacked suppleness four years after its vintage, his 1971 was very satisfactory: good colour, lively bouquet, almost peppery, full-bodied taste, long aftertaste. Several other vintages were also very satisfactory.

The 25-acre Cazetiers vineyard is the most extensive of the Premiers Crus in Gevrey-Chambertin. From it the Domaine Clair-Daü produces a wine with a lot of bouquet and good backbone, for keeping a long time. The Clos de Fonteny, another property owned by Clair-Daü, also deserves a mention. It is lighter in taste.

The Clos des Varoilles (a great Premier Cru from 15½ acres) and Romanée (an equally good Premier Cru from 4 acres) belong to the Domaine des Varoilles. A wine of the Gevrey-Chambertin appellation, Clos de Meix des Ouches (3½ acres), belonging to the Maison Naigeon-Chauveau, deserves special mention.

Gevrey-Chambertin

I once knew a wine importer who always started a visit to Burgundy with a good lunch in Gevrey-Chambertin. At the end of the meal he once more felt 'at home'. I can understand this: Marsannay and Fixin are the first places on your route, but Gevrey-Chambertin is the real Burgundy. This commune has eight Grand Crus — including the famous Chambertin — as well as many other wines of exceptional quality. My friend was particular, too, about his choice of restaurant, for he invariably lunched at the *Rôtisserie du Chambertin*, particularly renowned for its excellent regional specialities and local wines. Pierre and Céline Menneveau offer their guests a wonderful variety of wines, including their own Gevrey-Chambertin as well as such elegant dishes as *ravioli aux truffes, gigot de poulette aux morilles* and *bavarois aux poires*. Visitors go through a small wine museum to reach the restaurant proper.

Chapter of disasters

The ancient village of Gevrey was, in 630, known as Gibriacus. Some experts believe that the name, derived from *grabos*, means 'goat', but others think it means 'bearded man'. The vineyards of Gevrey became famous shortly after this and for several centuries the village was the scene of many disputes between bishops, abbots and dukes.

In 1257, there was so much local suffering that the abbot of Cluny authorized a small fortified château to be turned into a powerful stronghold for the protection of the villages. These precautions did not, however, prevent Gevrey from being pillaged and destroyed yet again in 1336. These misfortunes continued throughout the centuries, particularly during the religious wars of the 16th century. The archives reveal that in 1579 only 80 of the former 400 families still remained. The château has survived to the present day, despite being badly damaged in 1976 when a serious fire destroyed much of the main body of the building; fortunately the tower and the living quarters of the present owner, Mme Masson, were untouched. Today the village has 3000 inhabitants, the majority of whom are either directly or indirectly involved in wine-growing. Several other small businesses have also started up in Gevrey, mainly producing jam, electrical equipment and machines for the metallurgical industry and asphalt. To the north, along the *route nationale*, there is a bottling plant owned by the makers of the aniseed aperitif, Ricard. In addition, one of the largest marshalling yards of the S.N.C.F. (the French railway system) handles a daily traffic of 3,500-4,000 trucks. Yet in spite of all this industrial development, Gevrey-Chambertin is still principally famed for its excellent wine, and

above all, its Grand Cru, Chambertin, whose name has been synonymous with that of the village since 1847.

Bertin's field

So great is the reputation of Chambertin that, in spite of the natural conservatism of the people of Burgundy, brightly coloured hoardings at either end of the vineyard, which extends for one-third of a mile, advertise the exact whereabouts of this supreme *appellation*. They are, needless to say, much photographed. The famous vineyard, covering just over 30 acres and yielding between 3,850 and 5,500 cases of wine annually, owes its existence to an enterprising peasant named Bertin, who owned some land next to the vineyard of Clos de Bèze, which was cultivated by monks from the abbey of the same name. Bertin reckoned that his land should also produce good wine — and he was quite right; very soon the wine from 'le champ de Bertin' was as celebrated as that from Clos de Bèze. When Bertin died, the monks bought his vineyards and thus became the proprietors of Chambertin. Its reputation grew steadily, reaching its peak in the Napoleonic era.

JUDGMENT OF PARIS 30th ANNIVERSARY CELEBRATION - MAY 24, 2006
Younger Vintages Observations

BERRY BROS. & RUDD

COPIA

		9 USA Official Panelists (points)	9 UK Official Panelists (points)	USA & UK Official Panelists (points)	All Panelists - Honorary and Official(points)
White Burgundy	First	Puligny-Montrachet Premier Cru Les Pucelles 2002, Domaine Leflaive (47)	Puligny-Montrachet Domaine Leflaive (44)	Puligny-Montrachet Premier Cru Les Pucelles '02, Domaine Leflaive (91)	Puligny-Montrachet Domaine Leflaive (332)
	Second	Beaune Premier Cru Clos des Mouches 2002, Domaine Drouhin (37)	Chassagne-Montrachet Louis Jadot (39)	Beaune Domaine Drouhin (72)	Beaune Domaine Drouhin (297)
	Third	Meursault Premier Cru Charmes 2002, Domaine Roulot (33)	Beaune Domaine Drouhin (35)	Chassagne-Montrachet Louis Jadot (67)	Bâtard-Montrachet Louis Latour (288)
	Fourth	Chassagne-Montrachet Premier Cru Les Caillerets, 2002, Louis Jadot (28)	Mersault 1er Cru Domaine Roulot (27)	Mersault 1er Cru Domaine Roulot (60)	Corton-Charlemagne Bonneau du Martray (270)
	Fifth	Bâtard Montrachet Grand Cru 2002, Louis Latour (26)	Bâtard-Montrachet Louis Latour (26)	Bâtard-Montrachet Louis Latour (52)	Chassagne-Montrachet Louis Jadot (263)
	Sixth	Corton-Charlemagne Grand Cru 2003, Domaine Bonneau du Martray (18)	Corton-Charlemagne Bonneau du Martray (18)	Corton-Charlemagne Bonneau du Martray (36)	Mersault 1er Cru Domaine Roulot (230)
Chardonnay	First	Talley Rosemary's Vineyard 2002 (48)	Ramey Hyde Vineyard 2002 (41)	Talley Rosemary's Vineyard 2002 (84)	Talley Rosemary's Vineyard 2002 (321)
	Second	Patz & Hall Hyde Vineyard 2004 (33)	Patz & Hall Hyde Vineyard 2004 (37)	Ramey Hyde Vineyard 2002 (72)	Ramey Hyde Vineyard 2002 (315)
	Third	Ramey Hyde Vineyard 2002 (31)	Talley Rosemary's Vineyard 2002 (36)	Patz & Hall Hyde Vineyard 2004 (70)	Patz & Hall Hyde Vineyard 2004 (300)
	Fourth	Peter Michael Point Rouge 2003 (27)	Chateau Montelena 2003 (31)	Chateau Montelena 2003 (57)	Chateau Montelena 2003 (277)
	Fifth	Chateau Montelena 2003 (26)	Peter Michael Point Rouge 2003 (28)	Peter Michael Point Rouge 2003 (55)	Peter Michael Point Rouge 2003 (240)
	Sixth	Mount Eden 2002 (24)	Mount Eden 2002 (16)	Mount Eden 2002 (40)	Mount Eden 2002 (227)
Red Bordeaux	First	Château Margaux 2000 (38)	Château Margaux 2000 (42)	Château Margaux 2000 (80)	Château Margaux 2000 (346)
	Second	Château Rauzan Segla 2000 (37)	Château Montrose 2000 (36)	Château Rauzan Segla 2000 (63)	Château Rauzan Segla 2000 (281)
	Third	Château Haut-Brion 2000 (34)	Château Latour 2000 (34)	Château Montrose 2000 (61)	TIE: Château Haut-Brion 2000 (278) and Château Latour 2000 (278)
	Fourth	Château Leoville-Las-Cases 2001 (30)	Château Leoville-Las-Cases 2001(28)	Château Latour 2000 (59)	
	Fifth	TIE: Château Montrose 2000 (25) / Château Latour 2000 (25)	Château Rauzan Segla 2000 (26)	Château Leoville-Las-Cases 2001(58)	Château Montrose 2000 (258)
	Sixth		Château Haut-Brion 2000 (23)	Château Haut-Brion 2000 (57)	Château Leoville-Las-Cases 2001(239)
Cabernet Sauvignon	First	TIE: Shafer Hillside Select 2001 (38) / Ridge Monte Bello 2000 (38)	Stag's Leap Wine Cellars Cask 23 2001 (42)	Ridge Monte Bello 2000 (77)	Shafer Hillside Select 2001 (318)
	Second		Ridge Monte Bello 2000 (39)	Stag's Leap Wine Cellars Cask 23 2001 (76)	Ridge Monte Bello 2000 (294)
	Third	Staglin Family Vineyard 2001(37)	TIE: Joseph Phelps Insignia 2002 (30) / Clos du Val Reserve 2000 (30)	Staglin Family Vineyard 2001 (64)	Staglin Family Vineyard 2001 (286)
	Fourth	Stag's Leap Wine Cellars Cask 23 2001 (34)	Staglin Family Vineyard 2001 (34)	TIE: Shafer Hillside Select 2001 (59) / Joseph Phelps Insignia 2002 (59)	Stag's Leap Wine Cellars Cask 23 2001 (284)
	Fifth	Joseph Phelps Insignia 2002 (29)	Shafer Family Vineyard 2001 (27)		Joseph Phelps Insignia 2002 (274)
	Sixth	Clos du Val Reserve 2000 (13)	Shafer Hillside Select 2001 (21)	Clos du Val Reserve 2000 (43)	Clos du Val Reserve 2000 (224)

Borda Count System used for tallying results

These scores will be confirmed at 12:00 pm on Thursday, May 25 and posted on www.copia.org

GEVREY-CHAMBERTIN 1ᴱᴿ CRU CLOS St-JACQUES APPELLATION GEVREY-CHAMBERTIN CONTRÔLÉE DOMAINE ARMAND ROUSSEAU PÈRE & FILS GEVREY-CHAMBERTIN (CÔTE-D'OR)	GEVREY-CHAMBERTIN CLOS St-JACQUES Appellation Contrôlée Domaine CLAIR-DAÜ Propriétaire à Marsannay-la-Côte (Côte-d'Or)	Gevrey-Chambertin 1ᴱᴿ CRU - LAVAUX-St-JACQUES Domaine F. Tortochot & Fils	GEVREY-CHAMBERTIN LES COMBOTTES APPELLATION CONTROLEE Louis Jadot NEGOCIANT A BEAUNE (CÔTE-D'OR)	AUX COMBOTTES 1970 DOMAINE DUJAC	Joseph Drouhin GRIOTTE-CHAMBERTIN APPELLATION CONTROLÉE JOSEPH DROUHIN AUX CELLIERS DES ROIS DE FRANCE ET DES DUCS DE BOURGOGNE

The Domaine Armand Rousseau owns just over 6 acres of the Clos Saint-Jacques. An extraordinary wine, full-bodied and balanced, with a strong bouquet, a hint of terroir and long-lasting aftertaste in good years. Less successful years produce a lighter wine, but one which is still very good.

The Clos St Jacques is a Premier Cru which produces wines of Grand Cru quality. This can be seen in the outstandingly high and consistent quality of the Clos St-Jacques from the Domaine Clair-Daü (which owns a third of the vineyard). Deep colour, intense bouquet, lasting and variegated aftertaste.

Wine-growing has been carried on for three generations at the Domaine Tortochot. Gabriel Tortochot makes a remarkable Lavaux-Saint-Jacques from his 1½-acre strip: supple, delicious and very characteristic of this appellation.

The Premier Cru of Les Combottes is situated between Latricières-Chambertin and Clos de la Roche in Morey. In good years, the wine made by Louis Jadot is rather full-bodied, often supple, generous and robust, with a long aftertaste.

Even in less good years, the Domaine Dujac, which owns 2½ acres in Les Combottes, managed to produce a good, perfectly balanced wine with as much body and fruitiness in the taste as in the bouquet. It has been followed by other good wines.

Joseph Drouhin, owner of 1¼ acres in Griotte-Chambertin, produces an absolutely delicious wine, deep and velvety, with a perfume that gradually gets richer over the years. It is an elegant, yet firm and generous wine of great quality, even in lesser years such as 1980.

Napoleon and Chambertin

Chambertin was Napoleon's favourite wine. His taste for it was probably formed when, as a young artillery officer, he stayed in the Côte d'Or on several occasions. By 1798 he was so fond of this wine that except for an occasional glass of champagne he never drank anything else. Bourrienne relates: 'Before his (Napoleon's) departure for Egypt, he laid in good stocks of wine from Burgundy, delivered by a man from Dijon called James. Several cases of this burgundy twice crossed the desert of the Suez isthmus on the backs of camels, and what we brought back to Fréjus tasted just the same as when we left. Moreover, James accompanied us to Egypt.' Subsequently, Soupé & Pierrugues, on the rue Saint-Honoré in Paris, made regular deliveries of their Chambertin to Napoleon and a representative of that firm went on all the emperor's campaigns. Napoleon usually chose a five- to six-year-old Chambertin and drank half a bottle with each meal. All his drinks had to be served cold and diluted with water; and unfortunately, even Chambertin was no exception to this rule. Such barbarous habits were in keeping with the emperor's bad table manners; he is said to have stuffed down even the finest food with his fingers. Naturally, Chambertin played its part in the Russian campaign, and on Napoleon's return from Moscow in 1812, some astute wine merchants put on the market a Chambertin described as 'back from Russia'. In fact, the quantity sold far exceeded the amount Napoleon had taken to Russia in the first instance. Another story claims that Napoleon failed to drink Chambertin before the battle of Waterloo and that this was one of the reasons for his defeat. One certain fact, however, is that the emperor's death on St Helena was hastened by the absence of fresh vegetables and the drinking of Bordeaux instead of Chambertin.

In praise of Chambertin

Chambertin's praises have long been celebrated in word and song. In 1813, the making of Chambertin was featured in a comic opera, *Le Nouveau Seigneur du Village*, which played to full houses in Paris. Camille Rodier wrote of Chambertin: 'This wine possesses in the highest degree all the qualities that characterize a perfect wine — body, colour, bouquet and finesse'. Others, more fancifully, have compared Chambertin to the symphonies of Beethoven, particularly the Fifth. Alexandre Dumas claimed that the future never looked so rosy as through a glass of Chambertin. Gaston Roupnel, who lived in Gevrey and is buried there, wrote that Chambertin is 'as firm and full-bodied as the greatest Corton; it possesses the delicacy of a Musigny, the velvety nature of a Romanée, the fragrance of a Clos Vougeot . . . and it stands alone as the greatest burgundy'. All in all — none but the highest accolade for the wine that is famous the world over (average production 5,700 cases).

*Opposite page:
Signs and posters west of the village.*

*Above:
The Domaine Louis Rémy has its own entrance to Latricières-Chambertin, where it owns about 1½ acres.*

*Below:
A cellarman at the Domaine Armand Rousseau.*

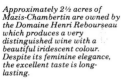

Approximately 2½ acres of
Mazis-Chambertin are owned by
the Domaine Henri Rebourseau
which produces a very
distinguished wine with a
beautiful iridescent colour.
Despite its feminine elegance,
the excellent taste is long-
lasting.

I have tasted and enjoyed the
Mazy-Chambertin from the
Domaine F. Tortochot & Fils:
deep colour, delicate bouquet,
long-lasting taste with
undeniable finesse. The
vineyard consists of 1¾ acres.

The Domaine Camus owns 42
acres in Gevrey-Chambertin: 4
Chambertin, 3¾ Latricières,
17¼ Charmes (the largest owner
there), almost 1 Mazis, while the
rest is less well-known vineyard.
The wines are deeply coloured
and strong; need to be kept.

The Domaine Taupenot-Merme
in Morey-Saint-Denis owns 3¾
acres of Gevrey-Chambertin. It
is a wine with a great deal of
personality, both vigorous and
mellow, round and fruity. This
estate also produces a good
Gevrey-Chambertin.

Although the firm of Joseph
Drouhin does not own any
Charmes-Chambertin, I tasted
on its premises a very agreeable
wine, with a deep colour, a mild
but seductive bouquet and a full-
bodied taste just beginning to be
supple without any heaviness.

Charles Rousseau, owner of the
Domaine Armand Rousseau,
sells a great deal of his wine to
famous restaurants in France
and Belgium, including the Villa
Lorraine in Brussels. His wines
are made in stainless-steel tanks
and the Charmes-Chambertin,
from his 3¾-acre vineyard, is
warm and supple.

Not one but several

It might be well asked whether Chambertin
deserves its present-day reputation, since
the wine tends to vary considerably even
though the composition of the soil is
identical throughout the vineyard. The size
of the holding, the age of the vine and the
experience and ability of the individual
grower all play central rôles. Thus the 20 or so
owners of Chambertin, plus a handful of
négociants-éleveurs, each produce a
Chambertin of markedly different character.
To appreciate the diversity of these wines,
you should taste at one sitting a Chambertin
de Trapet (quite light), a Rémy (very heavy),
a Jaboulet-Vercherre (rather mediocre) and a
Rebourseau (an aristocrat). The truth is,
there is not one Chambertin but several.
Nevertheless, certain features remain
constant: to me Chambertin spells colour,
power and baroque splendour. It is an
extraordinary burgundy which unites in a
single taste and bouquet an amazing

Like Taupenot and Rousseau, Henri Rebourseau owns 2¾ acres of Charmes-Chambertin. The vines are 15 years old, and produce a pleasant, full, supple wine with nuances. The colour is beautifully deep, sometimes almost bluish — a sign of youth.

There is a striking difference between the taste of Gabriel Tortochot's Charmes-Chambertin and his Mazis. The Charmes (almost 1½ acres) is more supple, fuller, with a creamier aroma.

The Domaine Trapet Père & Fils owns about 2¾ acres of Chapelle-Chambertin and 3¾ acres of Latricières. The Latricières is the better of the two: well-bred, strong bouquet, very agreeable, long-lasting taste.

The house of Faiveley in Nuits-Saint-Georges produces a wide range of fine wines from its own vineyards. One of these is the graceful and elegant Latricières-Chambertin (from 3 acres), a very subtle wine with a long-lasting aftertaste.

Gevrey-Chambertin

measure of warmth, grace and robustness, qualities that appear only after long years of ageing — for Chambertin requires a great deal of patience. When young, it can shock with its savage harshness, but after seven or eight years it begins to develop suppleness. You could compare it to a peacock slowly and majestically opening its train to reveal the true vivid, glowing colours.

Chambertin Clos de Bèze

Chambertin and Chambertin Clos de Bèze are neighbours and both can be called Chambertin, but Chambertin itself may not be used in conjunction with Clos de Bèze. It is a subtle but justified distinction, as the wine of Clos de Bèze often has a trifle more finesse, breeding and delicacy. As we have seen, Clos de Bèze was planted, before Chambertin, by the monks of the abbey of Bèze, who acquired it from Duke Amalgaire in 630. About seven centuries later, it was sold, like Chambertin, to the Chapter of the cathedral at Langres. The bishops were evidently more interested in profitability than direct responsibility, for they promptly rented out the vineyards. In the 18th century they were taken over by Claude Jobert, who cultivated them successfully and unequivocally named them Jobert-Chambertin. Today Clos de Bèze has an area of about 38 acres and is divided up between a dozen owners; it produces on average 5,100 cases a year. To an even greater extent than Chambertin, it deserves to be called 'the king of wines, and the wine of kings'. This expression need not be taken too literally for it really applies, as one grower in Gevrey-Chambertin put it, 'to all the kings of life and pleasure', all *bons vivants*, at least those who are fairly well off, since the wine of kings certainly commands a king's ransom.

Opposite page:
Charles Rousseau, owner of the Domaine Armand Rousseau, showing off some of his best bottles.

Left:
Sign to the château of Gevrey-Chambertin which was badly damaged by fire in 1976.

Right:
All those who have travelled the road to Chambertin will recognize this little house belonging to the Domaine Pierre Damoy. Chambertin lies on gentle slopes running from east to west, so benefiting from the maximum amount of sunshine.

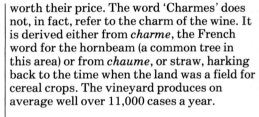

Pierre Gelin and his son-in-law, André Molin, each own a strip of Clos de Bèze, totalling 1¼ acres. Their 1972, which is still very heavy and dark, will develop and reach its peak in years to come. Other vintages also display similar strength.

Louis Latour owns 2½ acres of Chambertin Cuvée Héritiers Latour. Good years produce a wine with a fine, generous taste which needs years of keeping to develop fully.

Comparison of several vintages of Chambertin from the Domaine Armand Rousseau made me realize how much these wines need to age. Even after 12 years, despite its charm and finesse, the 1964 had still not opened up. Even wines from lighter years are still excellent.

Louis Rémy, in Morey, owns just under an acre in Chambertin. He makes a full-bodied wine with a nutty scent. He also owns 1½ acres of Latricières from which he produces a wine with plenty of character, although not in the same class as a Chambertin.

The Domaine Trapet Père & Fils owns 8½ acres of Chambertin. The wine tends sometimes to be rather light, but the quality is still satisfactory. The quality of the wine improves in the great vintage years when there has been plenty of sun.

Henri Rebourseau owns 2½ acres of Chambertin. The wine from this vineyard usually has a fine, pure taste which can linger for as long as half an hour. Unfortunately, Rebourseau sells very little bottled wine; most of the production is sold to Nicolas in barrels.

Latricières-Chambertin

French law until 1982 confirmed the high value of Chambertin and Chambertin Clos de Bèze by limiting their yield to 30 hectolitres per hectare, below the general level for Grands Crus. Today the permitted yield is 35 hectolitres per hectare, the same as the other Grands Crus of the Côte d'Or. (See page 14). Latricières-Chambertin is generally placed in the second rank of Grand Crus, as it is located in the southern section of Chambertin. About 200 yards wide, it lies on the same gentle slope, but there is a slight difference in the composition of the soil, which is rendered a little harder by a thin bed of silica. This vineyard began to be cultivated around 1508, very much later than the other two Chambertins, and so high was the quality of the wine that it was spontaneously christened Latricières, meaning 'small miracle'. The diminutive adjective is justified by its figures, for the 17 acres produce some 2,600 cases of wine annually. Although it does not possess the taste, body or nobility of Chambertin, it does have a certain elegance, a shorter ageing time and a more realistic price.

Charmes-Chambertin

The heir apparent to Chambertin is Charmes-Chambertin. This is the best known of the second class Grand Crus because its total area is as large as that of the other five — roughly 78 acres. It comprises Charmes-Chambertin (about 31 acres) and Mazoyères-Chambertin (about 47 acres). The wine from Mazoyères can be sold as Charmes-Chambertin, which suits all the wine growers, as the name Mazoyères is not well known or easy on the tongue.
A good Charmes, from old vines, has a deep red, almost purple colour, and a velvety taste. The trouble is that not all Charmes-Chambertins possess these attractive qualities. I have tasted some that shame their label —sour, rough and decidedly not worth their price. The word 'Charmes' does not, in fact, refer to the charm of the wine. It is derived either from *charme*, the French word for the hornbeam (a common tree in this area) or from *chaume*, or straw, harking back to the time when the land was a field for cereal crops. The vineyard produces on average well over 11,000 cases a year.

Mazis-Chambertin

Mazis-Chambertin and Charmes-Chambertin are both good wines, but there the similarity ends. If the latter wine has the attributes of a cultivated gentleman, Mazis (Mazys, Mazy) is more like a pretty young girl in silk and lace. It is finer, lighter, more feminine, ready to drink earlier and therefore very balanced. Situated to the south of Clos de Bèze, Mazis-Chambertin comprises about 31 acres, which produces some 2,700 cases annually. The name 'Mazis' is derived from *maison*, house, as there were several small dwellings on the land between Gevrey and Morey six centuries ago.

Griotte-Chambertin

Griotte-Chambertin is a modest vineyard which, with an area of 13½ acres, reaches almost the size of its neighbour, Chappelle-Chambertin (see below). These two Grand Crus are only separated from Chambertin Clos de Bèze by a road, but for some reason Griotte-Chambertin's production of 720 cases a year is barely half that of Chappelle-Chambertin. Consequently, this generous wine is rarely seen outside France. The word *griotte* means a morello cherry, and possibly recalls a former time when cherry trees were planted there; alternatively, it could mean 'stony ground'.

Chapelle-Chambertin

The monks of Bèze christened this area Chapelle-Chambertin when they built a chapel here in 1155. The vineyard could equally well have been called *ermitage*, since a hermit spent part of his life here in the 16th

CHAMBERTIN CLOS DE BÈZE
APPELLATION CONTRÔLÉE

Domaine Armand Rousseau Père et Fils
GEVREY-CHAMBERTIN (CÔTE-D'OR)
MISE AU DOMAINE   Product of France

CHAMBERTIN CLOS DE BÈZE
Appellation Contrôlée
Ancien Domaine Comte de St-Quentin

Domaine CLAIR-DAÜ
Propriétaire à Marsannay-la-Côte (Côte-d'Or)

CHAMBERTIN CLOS DE BÈZE

DOMAINE DROUHIN-LAROZE

Joseph Drouhin

CHAMBERTIN-CLOS DE BÈZE
APPELLATION CONTROLÉE

JOSEPH DROUHIN

In 1961, Charles Rousseau bought 2¼ acres of Clos de Bèze, with no guarantee of its profitability. This exceptional wine combines characteristic vigour with delicate nuances.

The Domaine Clair-Daü owns just under 5 acres of Chambertin Clos de Bèze, which produces a high-quality wine with lasting aftertaste. Occasionally a hint of liquorice in the bouquet.

Drouhin-Laroze's Chambertin Clos de Bèze comes from about 5 acres. The bouquet of the heady, extraordinarily full-bodied 1969 had still not fully flowered in 1976. A wine for patient wine lovers, to be kept a long time.

The only thing the two companies, Drouhin and Domaine Drouhin-Laroze, have in common is that they are both owners in Clos de Bèze. Joseph Drouhin has only half an acre, from which he produces a sumptuous wine, with a deep colour and seductive bouquet.

Crus of Gevrey-Chambertin

Grands Crus:
Chambertin,
Chambertin Clos de Bèze,
Charmes-Chambertin (or
Mazoyères-Chambertin),
Chapelle-Chambertin,
Griotte-Chambertin,
Latricières-Chambertin,
Mazis-Chambertin,
Ruchottes-Chambertin.

Premiers Crus:
Les Varoilles,
Clos Saint-Jacques (or
Village Saint-Jacques),
Aux Combottes,

Bel-Air, Cazetiers,
Combe-aux-Moines,
Estournelles, Lavaut,
Poissenot, Champeaux,
Les Goulots, Issarts,
Les Corbeaux,
Les Gemeaux Cherbaudes,
La Perrière,
Clos Prieur (part),
Le Fonteny, Champonnets,
Au Closeau, Craipillot,
Champitonnois (or Petite
Chapelle),
Ergots, Clos du Chapitre.

The spelling of these names can often vary.

Gevrey-Chambertin   Côte de Nuits

century. The site of the chapel, totally destroyed during the French Revolution, has been completely taken over by vineyards. Of all the Grand Cru wines, Chapelle-Chambertin is certainly the lightest, with body replaced by finesse. Its area is about 13½ acres, roughly identical to that of Griotte-Chambertin, but its production is much higher: well over 2,170 cases a year (as opposed to 720).

Ruchottes-Chambertin

From the viewpoint of quality, Ruchottes-Chambertin occupies the bottom rung of the Grand Crus ladder. Very little is exported, as only an average of 920 cases a year are produced from its 7½ acres.

Premier Crus

Even with the inclusion of all these Grand Crus, the treasures of Gevrey-Chambertin are far from exhausted, since this commune also encompasses some 210 acres of Premiers Crus. These, and particularly the best of them, are situated to the north-east of the village on fairly steep slopes where the soil is mainly composed of clay and chalk. A highly regarded Premier Cru is the 17-acre Clos Saint-Jacques, producing a very well-bred wine, tasting much like Chambertin and selling at the price of a Grand Cru. Lavaux has a very different character: it is a wine of exceptionally fine and supple taste, almost atypical of Gevrey-Chambertin, but unfortunately it sometimes lacks depth and nuances. Varoilles, a 15½-acre vineyard belonging entirely to the Domaine des Varoilles, is placed on the same level as Saint-Jacques. Other Premier Crus which I enjoyed very much were the Estournelles St Jacques, Cazetiers, La Combe aux Moines and Combottes.

Over-production

Generally speaking, a wine with the plain *appellation* Gevrey-Chambertin should be a simplified version of the Grands and Premiers Crus, with a good, dark colour, a bouquet full of nuances and a velvety taste. In fact, this is far from the truth, and it is quite difficult to find a decent Gevrey-Chambertin 'tout court'. The village has effectively succumbed to the temptation of over-production. Although Gevrey has many acres of vineyards less than Beaune, it produces more wine than any other commune on the Côte d'Or: well over 189,000 cases on average. It has also expanded its vineyards on the less hilly side of the *route nationale*, where the soil yields wine of lesser quality. The wines produced by nearby Brochon (previously Côte de Nuits-Villages) are now sold as Gevrey-Chambertin.

*Opposite page:
Three splendid bottles from the Domaine Armand Rousseau, which owns about 31 acres. its Grands Crus are always stored in new casks.*

*Above left:
A wine grower uses a trailer to take his grapes to the small local cooperative, made up of 139 growers who share about 150 acres.*

*Left:
The Gault-Millau food guide has awarded its 'Clé d'Or' to the Rôtisserie du Chambertin, the finest restaurant in the Côte d'Or.*

The best part of Ruchottes-Chambertin is probably Clos des Ruchottes, which was added to the estate of Charles Rousseau in 1977.

Morey-Saint-Denis

A little farther to the south of the internationally renowned Gevrey-Chambertin is one of the most modest communes of the Côte de Nuits: Morey-Saint-Denis. Make no mistake, however; Morey-Saint-Denis is just as much a part of Burgundy as the other wine-growing communes that surround it, and the quality of its wine is equally exceptional. Throughout its long history, Morey has always played a minor rôle. During the late Middle Ages it was a modest hamlet belonging first to the barony of Vergy, and then to the abbey of Cîteaux, which owned several vineyards, including Clos de Vougeot. Its origins are very ancient, for it was inhabited at the time of the Phoenicians, and many coins from the Gallo-Roman era have been found in the vineyards. Historians think the name 'Morey' comes from the word *Moriacum* — an estate worked by a Moor. The memory of the tragic happenings of 1636 is still alive today. In that year, during the Thirty Years' War, the village of Morey was completely destroyed by fire. This disaster, followed by other calamities, caused such general fear and suffering that the inhabitants tended to adopt a bitter, pessimistic attitude to life. Centuries of neglect and oppression accustomed them to making do with very little, for which reason they were nicknamed the 'wolves of Morey'. It was not until around 1950 that the village began to be properly rebuilt. Even today, a local handbook underlines the point that 'the inhabitants of Morey do not suffer from hunger any longer'. The population has increased considerably since the start of the present century, from 460 inhabitants in 1914, to 560 in 1939 and 790 in 1982.

Eating and drinking

Morey-Saint-Denis is nowadays very peaceful. The old part of the village lies to the west of the *route nationale 74*, while new buildings are springing up on the east side of the road. You can lunch either at the friendly inn *Le Castel de Très Girard* or, more cheaply but well, at the local *routier*. The village also boasts a bar, a baker-cum-confectionery and a general food store.

The church of Morey-Saint-Denis, built on the site of a 15th-century fortified chapel, is quite large but architecturally undistinguished. Wine-growing remains the principal activity in this village where there are only two industrial concerns — a road-building firm and a workshop for repairing agricultural equipment. The village formerly possessed its own foundry, in an area called 'Les Fourneaux', which is now planted with vines.

Modest reputation

Although Morey-Saint-Denis has for hundreds of years produced an excellent wine, its reputation was, until recently, relatively modest. The Grands Crus, such as Clos de la Roche, Clos de Tart or Clos Saint-Denis, are admittedly famous, but other wines of lesser quality remain almost unknown.

The most obvious reason for this comparative neglect is the very small amount of wine produced, particularly in comparison, for example, with Gevrey-Chambertin. Thus in 1973, an abundant vintage, Morey-Saint-Denis produced only 44,000 cases of wine, while Gevrey-Chambertin and Chambolle-Musigny produced at least five times that quantity. Because *négociants* would be unable to cope with a sudden increased demand for this wine, they are reluctant to sell Morey-Saint-Denis, even though they concede it merits a reputation at least equal to that of Gevrey-Chambertin or other wines of the Côte de Nuits. Furthermore, the addition of another *appellation* to those already in existence does not conform to their current policy of concentrating sales efforts.

Unknown for too long

Even before legislation relating to *appellations contrôlées* was introduced, this typical attitude of the *négociants* meant that Morey-Saint-Denis was always sold as Gevrey-Chambertin or Chambolle-Musigny. During the 1920s, Camille Rodier, in his interesting book, *Le Vin de Bourgogne*, declared: 'It is regrettable that this wine should always be sold under the name of its two neighbouring communes, Gevrey-Chambertin and Chambolle-Musigny, thus helping to enhance the reputation of these two *crus*. It would be better for Morey to be sold under its own name, thus gaining the reputation it so justly deserves.' Eventually, when Morey-Saint-Denis was awarded its own *appellation contrôlée*, local growers spared neither effort nor expense in trying to promote the virtues of their wine. But these were difficult years, and their modest incomes prevented them embarking on a costly publicity programme. Nor were they helped by clients who kept secret their discovery of a great burgundy at a reasonable price. The longer the wine remained unknown, the cheaper it was. Finally, Morey did not then have the good fortune, like Chambertin, to be associated with a celebrity who, by habitually drinking it, brought the wine popularity and world fame.

Change for the better

The situation has now changed, thanks mainly to various specialist writers who, in books and articles, often quote Morey as an excellent burgundy which still represents good value. A small group of enthusiasts gradually became established, and as this circle grew, so did the demand, leading to a rise in price. Morey-Saint-Denis is no longer content merely to be a 'lucky find'; indeed it exploits its newly found fame. On 25 February 1975, for example, the famous chef, Paul Bocuse, was decorated with the

Opposite page:
Morey-Saint-Denis surrounded by its vineyards. It is said that the first vines were planted here in the 3rd century.

On 16 May 1979, in the Vatican, Georges Bryczek gave a number of bottles of wine to Pope John-Paul II, a Pole by birth, like Bryczek. The bottles contained Cuvée du Pape Jean-Paul II, a wine produced by a small vineyard where the first vines were planted in 1920, the year of the Pope's birth. This wine (2,000 bottles a year) is excellent and very strong; it should be kept for at least 10 years. Bryczek owns another 10 acres of vineyards (also in Gevrey-Chambertin) and is helped in the business by his son Édouard.

Right:
The most picturesque cellar in Morey is that of Georges Bryczek, who created all the works of art displayed there.

Below:
Georges Bryczek, whose wines are often judged to be the best in the commune. The age of the vines, some of which may be more than 80 years old, is a contributory factor to his success.

Morey-Saint-Denis

Légion d'Honneur by President Valéry Giscard d'Estaing. The ceremony was followed by a lunch, the menu for which was as follows:

Soupe de truffes;
Escalope de saumon de Loire à l'oseille with a Montrachet 1970, Domaine de la Romanée-Conti;
Canard Claude Jolly, with a Châteaux Margaux 1926;
Petites salades du Moulin;
Fromages, with a Morey-Saint-Denis 1969, Domaine Dujac;
Desserts, with a Champagne Roederer 1926.

As you can see, Morey-Saint-Denis, served as an accompaniment to the cheese, was given the place of honour and considered good enough to follow a Châteaux Margaux. Today, Morey-Saint-Denis enjoys a high reputation, but the growers hope for even greater things. Jean-Marie Ponsot, the commune's mayor and president of the wine growers' association, told me: 'We particularly want to extend our reputation to Paris. The memory of our patron saint, Saint Denis, is cherished by Parisians: he was the first bishop of Paris and honoured it with his martyrdom'.

Some white wines

Apart from its Grands Crus, Morey-Saint-Denis produces yearly about 27,000 cases of red wine and, on average, about 255 cases of white. The latter comes predominantly from the estate of Jean-Marie Ponsot, owner of a 3½-acre strip of Premier Cru Monts Luisants, which is planted with Chardonnay grapes. These *monts*, which are really hills, owe their name to the glowing shafts of light that bathe the yellowing vine leaves in autumn. The bouquet of Morey-Saint-Denis develops in three stages: during fermentation, there is a scent of the undergrowth, which later takes on the fragrance of sweet-briar. Eventually, after several years' ageing, there is an aroma of nuts. Its beautiful golden colour is comparable to that of a Meursault; and it also has brilliance. The taste, which is fairly full-bodied, is very clean. Though somewhat lacking in nuances, it has a powerful personality that bursts through after long years of ageing without losing any of its freshness. The 1970, which I drank six years after its vintage, was just such a wine. Jean-Marie Ponsot likes to serve it with seafood (it goes very well with lemon), a terrine or a good sauerkraut. Unfortunately, this vineyard lies fairly high up and is therefore subject to the whims of nature, which often diminishes an already far from abundant vintage. In 1977, for example, not a single drop of wine was produced as the result of a violent hailstorm.

A balanced wine

It would be true to say that Morey-Saint-Denis broadly produces two sorts of wine, each with a very particular style.
The first, and less plentiful, is a light wine, without a great deal of character. I had the impression, during my visit to Morey, that its reputation is on the decline. It is mainly produced by two cooperatives: one in Morey-Saint-Denis itself, the Coopérative des Vins Fins, and the other in Gevrey-Chambertin, the Coopérative de l'Union des Propriétaires de Vins Fins. These two cooperatives account for nearly 10% of the total vintage. The second, more abundant, wine seems to me the perfect compromise between the vigorous, generous Gevrey-Chambertin and the elegant Chambolle-Musigny. If one compared the wines of the Côte de Nuits to a choir, the wines of Morey would be ranked not with the sopranos or baritones, but with the tenors. Strength and finesse are perfectly balanced. The good wines of Morey, such as those of Domaine Dujac, are renowned for their fruitiness. Although not comparable to the youthful freshness and fruitiness of Beaujolais, they are light and velvety, sometimes with an aroma of plums. Experts claim to detect in them a whole gamut of scents — violets, strawberries, mushrooms, truffles, plus the very smell of the earth itself. It is the complexity of the bouquet, above all, which makes Morey-Saint-Denis such an exceptional wine. Yet in addition to all these qualities, it has to be said that Morey-Saint-Denis is seldom hard or firm. I agree with the saying: 'Morey-Saint-Denis wears a cloak of rubies with a velvet train'.

Clos des Lambrays

The Premiers Crus of Morey-Saint-Denis are not well known, and so many problems have arisen simply over advertising the name of the commune that there is little general inclination to promote them. However, I have tasted some excellent Premiers Crus. Clos-Sorbés, for example, comes from 8 acres owned by Georges Bryczek, a former sculptor from Poland. He owns the most original and picturesque cellar in the whole of the Côte d'Or, and almost every year his Morey *tout court* is classed in blind tastings among the best of the commune. Another good Premier Cru is that of Pierre Amiot,

Opposite page, bottom left:
The courtyard of the Domaine Dujac; note the handsome gallery leading to the entrance of the house.

Opposite page, bottom centre:
The manager of Clos de Tart, Henri Perraut, who has been in charge of vintages there since 1969.

Opposite page, bottom right:
Jacques Seysses, owner of the Domaine Dujac, personally takes part in the wine-making process.

Right:
The entrance to Clos de Tart.

Below:
Preparing the barrels before the harvest at Clos de Tart.

owner of a small 3-acre vineyard in Charmes. In 1981 the Premier Cru Clos des Lambrays was promoted to Grand Cru. This was the first time such a promotion had occurred since the passing of the legislation relating to *appellations d'origine côntrolées*. The vineyard lies next to the Clos de Tart and covers just over 21 acres. Apart from one small section, this land has been owned since September 1979 by three people: the brothers Fabien and Louis Sayer, wine growers in Mercurey, and the horse-breeder Roland de Chambure. They have introduced some much needed reorganization to the vineyard and full production will be resumed in 1985.

Bonnes-Mares

The vineyards of Bonnes-Mares, the smallest of the Grands Crus of Morey, cover part of this commune and part of Chambolle-Musigny. A stone cross marks the boundary between the small 4½-acre strip in Morey and the larger 32-acre holding in Chambolle. Bonnes-Mares in Morey belongs to Domaine Clair-Daü, which also owns about 1½ acres in Chambolle. It makes very tannic, fat and full-bodied wine which needs laying down for many years, particularly the good vintages.

Clos de Tart

The Grand Cru Clos de Tart adjoins Bonnes-Mares and its cellars are right in the centre of Morey. The vineyard owes its name to the monks of the abbey in the village of Tart-le-Haut, who acquired it in 1145. An alternative name for this vineyard is 'la Forge'. Ever since it was purchased by the monks, it has had only one owner at a time — a rare occurrence in Burgundy. In 1932 Clos de Tart was bought by Maison Mommessin of Mâcon, and Henri Perraut has been the manager since 1969. The wine is handled with the greatest possible care; bottling, for example, is done by using natural gravity rather than pumps. As a result, the wine

1976 was a very good year throughout the Côte d'Or, except for Clos de la Roche, which was partially devastated by hail.

The Côte Rôtie vineyard, mentioned as one of the Premiers Crus of Morey-Saint-Denis, has not actually existed for some years.

At Clos de Tart, an ancient wine-press dating from 1579 is capable of extracting the juice from three tonnes of grapes in 48 hours: today a modern press can do the same job in three hours. A gravity-based system, rather than with a pump, is used for bottling at Clos de Tart.

The Premier Cru Aux Charmes is next to the Grand Cru Mazoyères-Chambertin in Gevrey (sold as Charmes-Chambertin). Pierre Amiot's wines are often subtle and delicate.

Known in the past as a heavy, dull wine, Clos des Lambrays appears to be improving under new ownership. It has now become a fresher, more lively wine, robust but not too heavy. The first of the new-style Clos des Lambrays was first made in 1979. The wine is left to mature for two years in barrels, in contrast to the past, when it was left for much longer.

The part of Bonnes-Mares in Morey-Saint-Denis (together with a strip in Chambolle) belongs entirely to the Domaine Clair-Daü. Very dark colour, very tannic, powerful bouquet and quite full-bodied. Needs to age for a long time.

Clos de Tart is very carefully tended: in 1975, a very damp year, three people spent hours on end picking out all the rotten grapes before the vintage. Deep colour, sumptuous bouquet, vigorous taste, elegant character (although some vintages, including that of 1976, have been rather disappointing).

The Domaine Dujac of Jacques Seysses owns 2¾ acres of Clos Saint-Denis. I usually find their wine very pleasant. Shimmering colour, pleasant bouquet, balanced, restrained and fruity. The 1976 was a success.

Clos de la Roche, of which Jean-Marie Ponsot owns 7½ acres, is a wine that requires ageing for at least five years. Powerful, but eventually acquires a velvety charm.

Morey-Saint-Denis

Côte de Nuits

Bouchard Père & Fils usually buys a quarter of Clos de la Roche's grapes every year. In good years the wine is characterized by a strong aroma of violets and a long-lasting aftertaste. Needs patience.

Clos de la Roche, where Louis Rémy owns about 1½ acres, can be recognized by its iron gate. Heavily coloured wine, pleasant bouquet, vigorous taste, delicious.

The Domaine Dujac owns 2½ acres of Clos de la Roche. I was impressed by the 1972 with its magnificent bouquet, its backbone and its softness. I was equally impressed by the power and elegance of the more recent vintages.

Although he lives in Gevrey-Chambertin, Charles Rousseau is aware that his Clos de la Roche (produced from 3¾ acres) surpasses his Charmes-Chambertin: indeed, it often comes near to perfection and its seductive taste often reveals the fragrance of plums.

Morey-Saint-Denis

possesses a finesse worthy of a Chambolle-Musigny, making it the most elegant of all Moreys. With its sustained colour, strong perfume, vigour, fruitiness, long aftertaste and slight taste of the soil, it may not possess the high breeding of its neighbours, but it has always given me great pleasure. This 18½-acre vineyard produces about 2,100 cases a year.

Clos Saint-Denis

It seems strange that the inhabitants of Morey should, in 1927, have chosen the name of Saint-Denis to add to that of their commune, when its reputation has always been overshadowed by that of Clos de la Roche (see below). Perhaps they did not consider the name Morey-la-Roche to be sufficiently distinguished for a wine village? The Saint-Denis has the fruity suppleness of Morey; its bouquet is often very agreeable, although it is notable not for its fullness but for its nuances. This very likeable wine is lighter and more supple than that of la Roche. At the start of the present century, the vineyard only covered about 5 acres, but the purchase of land belonging to neighbouring vineyards has now increased the area to about 16 acres. The average annual vintage is around 1,900 cases.

Clos de la Roche

Clos de la Roche, which is sunnier than Clos Saint-Denis, produces a more full-bodied wine. It adjoins the vineyard of Gevrey-Chambertin and is separated from Latricières-Chambertin by Les Combottes. This is the reason why, according to Jacques Seysses, able manager of the Domaine Dujac, a Clos de la Roche tasted blind is very hard to distinguish from one of the great Chambertins. Charles Rousseau of Gevrey-Chambertin claims that his Clos de la Roche is superior to his Charmes-Chambertin. The quality of Clos de la Roche is recognized, but in addition to strength it

has elegance — with the hidden muscle power of an acrobat rather than the obvious brute force of a boxer. It has a rather fruity bouquet, variously evocative of bilberries, nuts and violets, and a long aftertaste. Clos de la Roche has a very ancient history. In the Gallic period, it was the site of Druid rituals. Like Clos Saint-Denis, its size has greatly increased, growing from 11 acres to nearly 38 acres. Average production is about 4,800 cases. A quarter of its grape harvest is normally bought by Maison Bouchard Père & Fils, who are responsible for the wine-making, *élevage* and eventual sales.

The Clos des Lambrays vineyard was sold in September 1979 — just before the harvest — for 10 million francs. The vineyard, which had belonged to Camille Rodier, was in very bad condition. Under its new ownership, production has been about 10 hectolitres per hectare (only 7 hl in 1981) for the first three years. A small part of the Clos des Lambrays belongs to another owner who only produces a few dozen litres of wine each year. The new owners had to lift about one-third of the old vines and replace them by new ones. The cellars also needed a lot of renovation. Until 1984 vinification will probably be carried out on the Sayer estate in Mercurey, then afterwards in Morey-Saint-Denis. The maturing of the wine in the barrels and the bottling are already concentrated in the latter location. The wine is then shipped in wooden casks, much of it to the United States.

Opposite page:
The Domaine Dujac at harvest time. Jacques Seysses and his American wife live in this delightful house.

Above:
Like those of the Hautes-Côtes, the vineyards in the Côte de Nuits are sometimes bordered by walnut trees. Fernand Point, master of French cuisine (La Pyramide in Vienne) said: 'The taste of walnut oil goes very well with red wine'.

Chambolle-Musigny

At one time, anyone in Burgundy who was deformed or very ugly was described as being like 'the Good Lord of Chambolle', an allusion to the wooden crucifix which adorns the door of the local church and depicts Christ with a distorted body and hideous face. Happily, the creator of this primitive work was not responsible for building the houses in Chambolle, or the village would be in a sorry state today, all the more since it is frequently flooded by the river Grône. This little river, which flows through the village, is transformed by sudden storms into a raging torrent, inundating roads and cellars, as it did in 1944 and 1965. Indeed, the village

derives its name from such unforeseen rises in the river level. Chambolle comes from *campus ebulliens* or *champ en ebullition*, meaning 'the boiling field'. By 1110 the Latin name had already evolved into Cambola; and Musigny was added to the name Chambolle in 1882.

The lay brothers of Vougeot

Chambolle was for many years a nondescript hamlet. In the 13th century, however, the lay brothers of Cluny, who had already begun similar cultivation in Vougeot, settled in Chambolle and started to plant vines and make wine as a leisure activity. By about 1350, the village had become quite important and a coach used to stop there. Like many of the villages of the Côte d'Or at this period, Chambolle had a leper hospital. The memory of this is perpetuated in the sculpted head of a leper on the front of the house belonging to the wine grower Jean Brunet, and in a field called *La Maladière*. In about 1450 Chambolle became a village of some standing when it built its own chapel which was enlarged at the end of the 16th century.

A link with California

Nowadays Chambolle-Musigny is a peaceful, hospitable spot, as is underlined by an inscription that appears in several places: 'Le bon vin et l'amour font passer d'heureux jours' (Good wine and love make for happiness). Each year a prize is awarded to the house with the best display of flowers. Although there are no noteworthy monuments, two curiosities of interest to visitors are the very old linden tree, next to the church, its hollow trunk large enough for a children's hiding-place, and a small cave once inhabited by a vagabond, and said to be the entrance to an underground passage leading to Morey-Saint-Denis. This is unverified because nobody has ever dared to explore it.
Chambolle is probably one of the very few villages in France without either a *tabac* or a

regular restaurant. Nevertheless, the 470 inhabitants are in no way isolated: they are experienced wine growers, participating in all the activities of the Burgundy wine industry and their commune has close ties with Schwabenheim in Germany and Sonoma in California. The bonds that unite Chambolle and this distant American town, also famous for its wines, testifies to a mutual feeling of fraternity and respect.

Limestone soil

During the 19th century, the wine-growing area of Chambolle underwent several fluctuations. In 1828, the commune comprised 470 acres; in 1855, 385 acres; in 1870, 635 acres and in 1890, 740 acres. The present area is about 535 acres. The greater part of the land in Chambolle does not belong to the people of the village, most of whom work in the vineyards only for a share of the harvest. Every year, the mayor registers about 100 *déclarations de récolte*, indicating that the vineyards of Chambolle, like those in other parts of Burgundy, are very fragmented. Although the soil of the Côte de Nuits consists mainly of clay, that of Chambolle is principally limestone. Furthermore, this relatively thin layer of soil covers a very hard, stony subsoil which obstructs the growth of the vine roots. This very particular soil composition lowers the yield per hectare (the annual total — commune appellation and premiers crus — is 51,100 cases) and gives the wine a distinct personality.

A seductive wine

Chambolle-Musigny is clearly distinguishable from all the other red wines from the Côte de Nuits. The only burgundy to which it can really be compared is a Volnay from the Côte de Beaune. Chambolle-Musigny is remarkable above all for its feminine delicacy, manifest both to nose and palate, in contrast to the other wines of the Côte de Nuits which are notable for their virility. The breeding and elegance of Chambolle-Musigny sometimes evokes comparison with a Margaux; indeed, its astonishing finesse has all the grace and fragility of hand-made porcelain. Camille Rodier writes: 'The wines of Chambolle-Musigny have a fine, exquisite bouquet and many experts consider them the most delicate in the whole Côte de Nuits'. Do not imagine, however, that Chambolle-Musigny is in any way trivial; beneath that feminine elegance it is sound and firm. I find this wine extremely seductive; indeed, with its sumptuous bouquet and its subtle taste, it should give satisfaction to the most fastidious wine lover.

Musigny

By far the best wine to be found hereabouts is Musigny. Gaston Roupnel describes it as follows: 'Musigny is a wine of silk and lace, supremely delicate, with no hint of violence yet much hidden strength. Savour it carefully. Smell the scents of a damp garden, the perfume of a rose, a violet bathed in morning dew.' These poetic comparisons seem entirely appropriate to me as every Musigny I have ever tasted has left an indelible memory. Its bouquet evokes flowers as well as strawberries and raspberries; and every sip reveals amazing nuances of taste. It evokes the paintings of the old Dutch masters and their gently tinted winter landscapes; the longer you gaze at them, the more distinct are the tiny figures, the sharper the colours. Musigny, with its incomparable taste and bouquet,

fully deserves the most glowing tributes. It is interesting to record that at a dinner held during the festivities celebrating 2,500 years of the Persian Empire, a Musigny 'Vieilles Vignes' from Domaine Comte de Vogüé was among the great French wines served.

Slopes of limestone soil

Unlike many of the wines of Bordeaux, the noble burgundies do not come from great estates endowed with impressive châteaux and huge vineyards. Musigny, for example, seems no different from the fields that surround it; in fact, the vines of this Grand Cru cling to a slope of rather sparse limestone soil next to the Clos de Vougeot. There is nothing outwardly to distinguish them from any other vines or to hint at the fact that they produce a truly great wine. However, when rain storms carry the topsoil down to the foot of the slope, the growers promptly collect it all and replace it with the greatest care. I have been told, though I have not actually seen it, that before the men leave the vineyard, they scrupulously shake their boots clean so as not to waste any of the precious earth.

The total area of Musigny, formerly divided into 'grand' Musigny and 'petit' Musigny, is about 26 acres, producing 2,650 to 4,400 cases a year. The Domaine Comte Georges de Vogüé owns the largest parcel of some 18 acres, Maison Faiveley has almost 3 acres, Domaine Jacques Prieur (Meursault) about 2 acres, Joseph Drouhin 1¾ acres and Domaine Roumier three-quarters of an acre. The Domaine Clair-Daü and the Maison Leroy also each hold a strip.

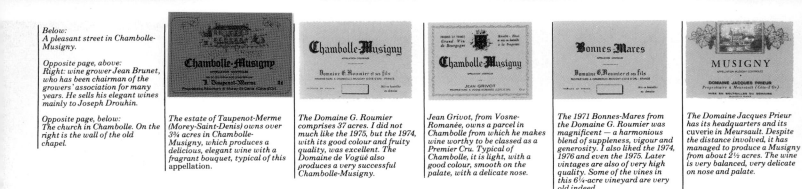

The estate of Taupenot-Merme (Morey-Saint-Denis) owns over 3¾ acres in Chambolle-Musigny, which produces a delicious, elegant wine with a fragrant bouquet, typical of this appellation.

The Domaine G. Roumier comprises 37 acres. I did not much like the 1975, but the 1974, with its good colour and fruity quality, was excellent. The Domaine de Vogüé also produces a very successful Chambolle-Musigny.

Jean Grivot, from Vosne-Romanée, owns a parcel in Chambolle from which he makes wine worthy to be classed as a Premier Cru. Typical of Chambolle, it is light, with a good colour, smooth on the palate, with a delicate nose.

The 1971 Bonnes-Mares from the Domaine G. Roumier was magnificent — a harmonious blend of suppleness, vigour and generosity. I also liked the 1974, 1976 and even the 1975. Later vintages are also of very high quality. Some of the vines in this 6¼-acre vineyard are very old indeed.

The Domaine Jacques Prieur has its headquarters and its cuverie in Meursault. Despite the distance involved, it has managed to produce a Musigny from about 2½ acres. The wine is very balanced, very delicate on nose and palate.

Musigny Blanc

Musigny also produces a small quantity (90-165 cases) of white wine. The former Comtesse de Vogüé, who loved white wine, had three-quarters of an acre planted with Chardonnay for her own consumption. Musigny Blanc, with less than 2,000 bottles a year (and not a single bottle in 1975), is therefore rare and commands top prices. Because of the high demand, this output has to be allocated among regular importers, particularly in America and Belgium. Musigny Blanc does not age long in oak casks, but is bottled three or four months after the vintage. I have tasted the 1974, gold with green tints, a faintish perfume and a very pure, fresh taste. In my opinion, white Musigny is not as distinguished as red Musigny, but with attentive making and handling can be excellent. In any event, because of its sheer rarity, drinking it is an exceptional privilege.

Bonnes-Mares

Whereas Musigny lies to the south of Chambolle-Musigny, the other Grand Cru, Bonnes-Mares, is situated in the extreme north. A small section (4½ acres) of this 38-acre vineyard extends into Morey-Saint-Denis, and belongs entirely to the Domaine Clair-Daü (see page 61). The origin of the name is unknown, but some people think it is linked to the Mares, goddesses who protected harvests. Others believe it refers to the nuns of Tart-le-Haut, like the Clos de Tart in Morey-Saint-Denis. A third theory is that the term is derived from an ancient expression meaning 'working and tilling'. The annual vintage of Bonnes-Mares averages 4,275 cases of red wine.

The Musigny that I tasted on Joseph Faiveley's premises was comparable to a beautiful, intelligent woman. I was so taken with it that I had little inclination to try another. The vineyard covers almost 3 acres.

Joseph Drouhin wants to keep the old vines on his 1¾-acre plot of Musigny as long as possible. The wine has a good bouquet with a fragrance of flowers and fruit, especially raspberries. Delicious taste, fruity, full-bodied and elegant.

Jean Servelle owns 2½ acres of Charmes. I liked his wine very much: light, pleasant, round and with a cheerful colour. Servelle also produces an Amoureuses (1 acre), and a Chambolle-Musigny tout court (8¾ acres).

Jean-Marie Roumier, from the Domaine G. Roumier, has a favourite Amoureuses. I can understand this, as I liked its elegant distinction, and its pleasing bouquet which harmonized perfectly with its long aftertaste.

Chambolle-Musigny

A difference in style

Like Musigny, Bonnes-Mares has a feminine quality, but there the resemblance ends. Bonnes-Mares is somewhat rounder, more full-bodied, more passionate but less refined, though not without elegance or distinction. The qualities of the two wines can be compared, perhaps, to those of two celebrated film actresses, Catherine Deneuve and Elisabeth Taylor — both very beautiful, both very talented and internationally famous, yet each with her own style, personality and temperament. Of all the wines of Chambolle-Musigny, Bonnes-Mares is the one that requires the longest ageing. The Drouhin-Laroze 1972, for example, can certainly wait 30-40 years to be drunk. Like Musigny, Bonnes-Mares belongs mostly to the Domaine Comte Georges de Vogüé, although Domaine Roumier also owns about 6 acres.

The Premiers Crus

In addition to its Grands Crus, Musigny and Bonnes-Mares, Chambolle proudly boasts several Premiers Crus. The best of these, Les

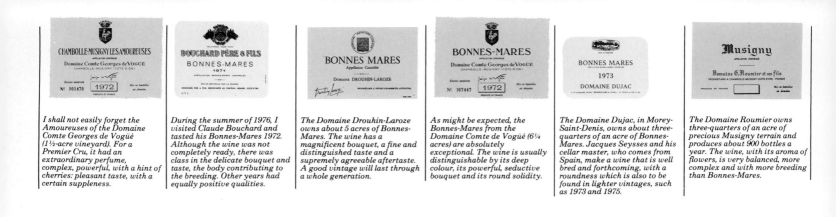

I shall not easily forget the Amoureuses of the Domaine Comte Georges de Vogüé (1½-acre vineyard). For a Premier Cru, it had an extraordinary perfume, complex, powerful, with a hint of cherries: pleasant taste, with a certain suppleness.

During the summer of 1976, I visited Claude Bouchard and tasted his Bonnes-Mares 1972. Although the wine was not completely ready, there was class in the delicate bouquet and taste, the body contributing to the breeding. Other years had equally positive qualities.

The Domaine Drouhin-Laroze owns about 5 acres of Bonnes-Mares. The wine has a magnificent bouquet, a fine and distinguished taste and a supremely agreeable aftertaste. A good vintage will last through a whole generation.

As might be expected, the Bonnes-Mares from the Domaine Comte de Vogüé (6¼ acres) are absolutely exceptional. The wine is usually distinguishable by its deep colour, its powerful, seductive bouquet and its round solidity.

The Domaine Dujac, in Morey-Saint-Denis, owns about three-quarters of an acre of Bonnes-Mares. Jacques Seysses and his cellar master, who comes from Spain, make a wine that is well bred and forthcoming, with a roundness which is also to be found in lighter vintages, such as 1973 and 1975.

The Domaine Roumier owns three-quarters of an acre of precious Musigny terrain and produces about 900 bottles a year. The wine, with its aroma of flowers, is very balanced, more complex and with more breeding than Bonnes-Mares.

Amoureuses, situated near Musigny, comprises nearly 13 acres. The price of this wine often equals or sometimes even exceeds that of Bonnes-Mares. A good one has a warm colour and an extraordinary perfume that is often reminiscent of cherries. It has the finesse of a Musigny, although not the same depth or delicacy. The alcohol content is often 13.5°. In Chambolle-Musigny they like telling you the anecdote about the lady visitor who was asked by a wine grower whether she liked Les Amoureuses. 'Certainly,' she replied, 'especially when my husband is drinking it!'

The other Premiers Crus, rarely sold under their own names, are generally offered under the *appellation* 'Chambolle-Musigny Premier Cru'. Les Charmes, however, with its attractively full and supple taste, is an exception to this rule. The area of the vineyard is 14½ acres, and since it is situated north of Les Amoureuses and south of the vineyard of Beaux-Bruns, the locals were unable to resist inventing a punning comment to the effect that 'les beaux bruns charment les amoureuses'.

At its best, the Musigny from the Domaine Comte Georges de Vogüé is almost black in colour; its bouquet and taste are very intense, yet have a remarkable finesse at the same time. This highly civilized wine is one of the greatest in the world.

The Comte de Vogüé owns three-quarters of an acre of Chardonnay and produces from it a rare wine, Musigny Blanc. I liked the 1973, with its pleasant freshness, its exquisite taste and its suppleness. The bouquet was still not quite at its peak. Other vintages confirmed these impressions.

Opposite page:
The white grapes of the Musigny made by the Domaine Comte de Vogüé are crushed in this modern (Vaslin) winepress.

Below:
This young cellarman obviously believes in getting right into the fermentation vat to get a closer look. This photograph was taken no longer ago than 1976 by the grower Jean Brunet.

The Comte de Vogüé's daughter, whose family is connected by marriage to the owner of Moët & Chandon, has married a member of the Ladoucette family, a name well known to lovers of Pouilly-Fumé, wine from the Loire.

The most extraordinary Musigny ever made was the 1865. I was fortunate enough to drink a bottle at Chanson Père & Fils. Apparently the wine fermented for three years.

Behind Chambolle-Musigny there is a small chapel overlooking a ravine.

The Grône has flooded several times in the past, notably in 1744, 1803, 1816 and 1826.

Domaine Comte de Vogüé

The most important estate in Chambolle-Musigny is undoubtedly the Domaine Comte Georges de Vogüé, comprising a total area of approximately 31 acres. Owning land in Bonnes-Mares, Les Amoureuses and Chambolle-Musigny, it controls more than 70% of Musigny production. This estate has for a very long time specialized exclusively in making Chambolle-Musigny and obviously brings to it a wealth of skill and experience.

The history of this estate dates back to the Middle Ages, to a time when the Musigny family provided generations of chamberlains, counsellors and governors to the Duchy of Burgundy. The illustrious family has since died out and is remembered only by the vineyard name. The first mention of a Vogüé is in records from 1776, and today this family is the biggest owner in Musigny. Alain Roumier has followed in his father's and grandfather's footsteps to become manager of the estate; and his son has attended the agricultural and wine-making college in Beaune.

Alain Roumier uses oak fermentation vats and stores one-third of his vintage, in new barrels, for about 18 months. Handled with extreme care, the wine is clarified only three or four times, preferably with egg white. Alain Roumier likes to use traditional methods up to the point when the wine is bottled; then, regretfully, as he admits, he has to carry out filtration to satisfy his American customers who insist on having their wine perfectly clear. Not all the vintage is bottled on the estate; after a rigorous selection of the best *cuvées*, the remainder, sometimes as much as one-third of the vintage, is sold to commercial firms.

Charles Noëllat, the second owner of Clos de Vougeot, has 6½ acres. His wine, which is less in demand today, used to enjoy an excellent reputation. Its bouquet is light and its taste pleasant but lacking depth.

During a comparative tasting of four Clos Vougeot 1971, that of Louis Jadot was unanimously judged the best: solid colour, subtle bouquet, clean body and a taste with a suggestion of oak. Other years displayed a similar high quality.

Part of the Clos de Vougeot is owned by the Domaine Jacques Prieur (8 acres in the past, now just over 3 acres). A classic wine for laying down, with colour, bouquet and strength. The aftertaste can be a little bitter sometimes. The label has been slightly changed recently.

Jean Grivot from Vosne-Romanée has received several awards for his Clos de Vougeot (from about 5 acres). This is a fine wine in all respects — colour, bouquet and taste.

The Clos Vougeot from Maison Faiveley, specialists in red burgundy, is a wonderfully generous wine, robust without being heavy. Taste and aftertaste are most distinctive; the bouquet is quite discreet. From 2½ acres.

The Domaine René Engel, owner of 3½ acres on the upper slopes of Clos de Vougeot, produces a deliciously full wine. Delicate, slightly reserved bouquet, pleasant colour, very supple.

Vougeot

People are often surprised to discover that outside the world-famous Clos de Vougeot there is a small village actually called Vougeot. Even if its 200 inhabitants play down its importance, there it is; and you can stroll down the main street, lined with houses and intersected by side turnings, for about half a mile. Happily, *route nationale 74* which formerly ran through the centre of Vougeot, is now diverted round it, but the village is still besieged by innumerable tourists and wine lovers, particularly in summer. Some firms exploit the situation by inviting the tourists in and offering them

wine at inflated prices. The best known, *La Grande Cave*, does have large, beautiful cellars that are worth a visit; but as you leave, you are pestered by salesmen for orders. It is run by the Maison Chauvenet, a firm which sells directly to the public in France. Across the street is the tasting and sales room of Domaine Bertagna, which owns 30 acres in several villages and produces agreeable Vougeot Premiers Crus. Also located in this village is the dynamic firm of Jean-Claude Boisset.

Arrival of the monks

The village and the name of Vougeot date from the start of the 10th century. During this period a toll was set up on the Vouge, a small river which forms the boundary between Vougeot and Chambolle-Musigny. There was then almost no wine-growing in the area, and the land that nowadays makes up Clos de Vougeot was forested or lay fallow. One vineyard, located on a slope at the edge of a plantation of chestnut trees, produced wine for the use of the owner only. This was the situation until the monks of

Drouhin-Laroze has more than 2½ acres of Clos de Vougeot, with vines at the top as well as the bottom of the vineyard. The wine is very successful, having a powerful bouquet, a delicate yet robust taste and a lingering aftertaste.

Joseph Drouhin owns 2¼ acres of Clos de Vougeot. Like many of this company's wines, its Clos Vougeot gives an impression of elegance: very fruity bouquet, robust but not heavy taste, long-lasting aftertaste.

Bouchard Père & Fils owns no land in Clos de Vougeot, but the wine it sells under this appellation is very pleasant. The wine is often very fruity in nose and taste, having plenty of vigour and little acidity.

The only white wine of Vougeot is that of L'Héritier-Guyot. The wine seems somewhat heady, almost sensual, with a hint of oak in the taste. Little freshness or breeding.

Cîteaux arrived at the beginning of the 12th century; they had recently broken away from the abbey at Cluny in order to observe a more rigorous discipline. These monks decided to build a monastery and a church at Vougeot, close to the hills and the toll bridge. They obtained the materials from a local stone quarry.

A walled vineyard

In order to gain the blessing and favour of the church, many of the faithful gave or lent land to the Cistercians, who immediately turned it into vineyards. Gradually, the monks added to their holding, and towards the middle of the 12th century their vineyards had grown so appreciably that they were obliged to build a *cuverie* and a cellar on the site. Even at that time, the wine produced by the monks was of exceptional quality. During the 13th and 14th centuries, they finally achieved their original aim — a vineyard of 125 acres belonging to a single owner. This estate, which the Cistercians enclosed with a high wall, was from then on known as Clos de Vougeot. From that date until the present day, the size of the vineyard has remained identical — 125 acres.

Monk-cum-architect

At the end of the 14th century, lack of space for accommodation and wine-making compelled the monks to put up new buildings. On 13 October 1367, Philip the Bold gave permission for a château to be built near Vougeot; five years later this château, situated at Gilly-lès-Vougeot, was

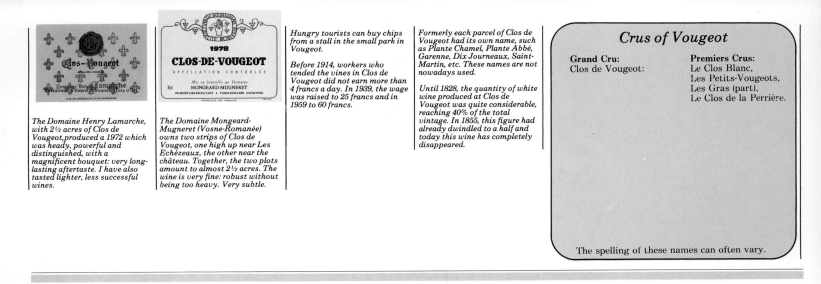

The Domaine Henry Lamarche, with 2½ acres of Clos de Vougeot, produced a 1972 which was heady, powerful and distinguished, with a magnificent bouquet: very long-lasting aftertaste. I have also tasted lighter, less successful wines.

The Domaine Mongeard-Mugneret (Vosne-Romanée) owns two strips of Clos de Vougeot, one high up near Les Echézeaux, the other near the château. Together, the two plots amount to almost 2½ acres. The wine is very fine: robust without being too heavy. Very subtle.

Hungry tourists can buy chips from a stall in the small park in Vougeot.

Before 1914, workers who tended the vines in Clos de Vougeot did not earn more than 4 francs a day. In 1939, the wage was raised to 25 francs and in 1959 to 60 francs.

Formerly each parcel of Clos de Vougeot had its own name, such as Plante Chamel, Plante Abbé, Garenne, Dix Journeaux, Saint-Martin, etc. These names are not nowadays used.

Until 1828, the quantity of white wine produced at Clos de Vougeot was quite considerable, reaching 40% of the total vintage. In 1855, this figure had already dwindled to a half and today this wine has completely disappeared.

Crus of Vougeot

Grand Cru:
Clos de Vougeot:

Premiers Crus:
Le Clos Blanc,
Les Petits-Vougeots,
Les Gras (part),
Le Clos de la Perrière.

The spelling of these names can often vary.

finished. The Château Vougeot that exists today, however, is not as old, dating from the 16th century. Camille Rodier in his book *Le Clos de Vougeot* tells how the château, which was to have been the grandest and most beautiful in the region, developed into the building that now stands.

Once the project had been approved, Dom Loisier, the 48th prior of Cîteaux, gave responsibility for drawing up the plans to a young monk who was an architect. The latter lost no time in presenting these plans to his superiors. He was very proud of his work, boasting that this château, stylistically perfect, would be unique in France, the crowning glory of the abbey. The prior examined the plans, thought long and hard, pressed the hands of the young architect and promised to submit them to the chapter. A month later, the result of the conference was announced. The chapter had decided to have the plans revised by another monk. In place of the original ambitious project, a massive, ugly building was substituted. 'My son,' said the prior, 'here are the new plans. Yours have been changed, but you will sign these and personally see they are carried out: thus your name will remain forever linked with this building, as a punishment for your sinful pride and vanity.' And so it was. In 1555, however, just as the work began, the young monk, exhausted by toil and grief, died. For this reason the château of Clos de Vougeot has become a symbol of the proverb: 'Pride goes before a fall'.

The last cellar master

The French Revolution put an end to the wealth of the abbey of Cîteaux. On 13 February 1790, the state confiscated all its property and sold it at auction. It was bought by M. Focard, a wood merchant in Paris. The new owner, however, was not able to meet his new obligations and Dom Goblet, the monks' last cellar master, was asked to stay on; it was he who, for several years, continued cultivating Clos de Vougeot for

the state. He did his work so well that when he retired, he was given two silver spoons and forks and enough wine to last him the rest of his life. In 1800 Dom Goblet put Napoleon Bonaparte in his place. Returning from the battle of Marengo, the consul passed through Dijon and sent a messenger to Clos de Vougeot to obtain some bottles of wine. Dom Goblet replied to the messenger: 'I have some 40-year-old Clos de Vougeot. If your master wants it, tell him to come personally and ask me for it'. The records of Clos de Vougeot do not mention a visit from Napoleon, so we must assume that while he was in Dijon, he had to make do with his beloved Chambertin.

The breakup

After M. Focard, Clos de Vougeot had several successive owners, until in 1828 it was acquired by Julien-Jules Ouvrard, son of Gabriel-Julien Ouvrard, an important gunsmith and director of the 'Négociants réunis', then an influential bank. Julien-Jules Ouvrard remained the owner until his death in 1861. For several years the property was the object of many disputes and despite the serious efforts of an English group to buy it, the Clos was finally bought in 1889 by a speculator and five *négociants*. The breaking up of Clos de Vougeot was a *fait accompli*. Two years later, 15 owners divided up the land, amongst them Léonce Bocquet, who bought the château, then partly in ruins. He had it completely renovated and, after his death in 1920, the land was once again split up, this time among 19 owners. Since then, the fragmentation has continued and today more than 80 owners have plots in the 125-acre Clos de Vougeot.

Les Chevaliers du Tastevin

The last owner of the château of Clos de Vougeot was Etienne Camuzet, who, after the foundation of La Confrérie des Chevaliers du Tastevin, put it at their

disposal, and finally sold it to them. The fraternity officially took possession of it on 29 November 1944 through a public company called Les Amis du Château du Clos de Vougeot. Etienne Camuzet was the first president. This society now owns the château, and has sensibly and astutely made it the focal point of a campaign designed to promote the wines of Burgundy. Several times a year, meetings of the Chevaliers are held here, complete with picturesque ceremonies and candle-lit dinners. The château is also visited by thousands of visitors who come to admire its ancient cellar, which has been transformed into a great banqueting hall, and its immense *cuverie*, with its fermentation vats and four impressive old winepresses, originally built by the monks of Cîteaux and requiring the muscle-power of a dozen men to work them. Arlott and Fielden mention in their book, *Burgundy Vines and Wines*, that during World War II some German prisoners were only just prevented from demolishing them for firewood.

Papal choice

Clos de Vougeot is famous in history because of the wines that the abbey of Cîteaux supplied to the nobility of Europe and to the princes of the church. Thus, when the papacy was established in Avignon, the monks always reserved their best *cuvée* for the pope and the equally appreciative cardinals. In 1336, Petrarch suggested that the reason the cardinals persistently refused to return to Rome was that: 'In Italy there is no Clos de Vougeot, and they did not believe they could lead a happy life without this wine, which they considered as their second *élément* (i.e. the wine used in the celebration of the Eucharist), and like the nectar of the gods'. After the Revolution, an officer of the French army, Colonel Bisson, gained notoriety for a gesture that was a tribute to his perceptiveness as a lover of good wine. While travelling north with his regiment, he

Top left:
The courtyard of the château of Clos de Vougeot.

Top centre:
The sign of Champy Père & Fils beside the route nationale.

Top right:
These gates, surmounted by the sign, once formed the entrance to the vineyard. There used to be large trees in front, but they disappeared during work to widen the route nationale.

Above:
Clos de Vougeot with the front of the château at upper right.

crossed Burgundy, and on passing Clos de Vougeot, gave the order to his soldiers to present arms. By doing so he was paying homage to one of the loveliest parts of France and one of her finest wines.

Three types of wine

Tradition has it that through the ages there have been three types of Clos de Vougeot: the *cuvée* for popes, the good wine for kings and priors, and the run-of-the-mill quality for monks. Whether or not this is true, it is an established fact that the vineyards situated on a hillside can be divided into three sections running more or less parallel to the *route nationale*. The top part, with its reddish-brown soil and scattered pebbles, is composed of limestone and clay; this section, steep enough for rain-water to drain away, gives the best grapes of the Clos. At the foot of the slope, alongside the road, the earth is dark brown, with more clay; it is damper and also more fertile because the roots of the vines are more easily nourished. Down here, drainage is poor because there are few pebbles and the ground is relatively flat; so there is increased risk of spring frosts and attacks of mildew in rainy years.
This soil, so often wet, produces a thinner wine, lacking in strength; only in dry years, as a rule, does this lower, poorer part of the Clos de Vougeot yield good wines. Finally, the section midway up the slope gives a wine which combines the qualities of the wines both from above and below.

Burgundy in miniature

As has already been stressed, however, the siting of a vineyard is not the only factor to determine the quality of a wine. In Clos de Vougeot, as elsewhere, the final result depends, too, on the age of the vines, the way they are pruned and the wine-making methods that are employed. A competent, dedicated grower who owns one of the lower

parcels of Clos de Vougeot, may turn out a better wine than a less efficient grower with a holding in the upper part of the vineyard. You become aware of these differences in terrain, methods and wine-growing expertise by tasting several Clos de Vougeot of the same vintage: some are clear, others full-bodied, some clean and others bitter, some excellent, others mediocre.
Basically, Clos de Vougeot is Burgundy in miniature. This vineyard demonstrates incontrovertibly that the choice of a burgundy should always be based on the name of the owner, the estate or the *négociant*: he alone, in fact, gives the most certain guarantee of quality on which you can depend.

The owners' association

Because of the varying quality of Clos de Vougeot, the Syndicat de Défense du Clos de Vougeot resumed its activities in 1976, on the initiative of its president, Pierre Rebourseau. As its name indicates, this association has a definite objective: to protect the quality of the wine. The first suggestion put to the members was that the yield per hectare be reduced, and this was accepted, together with other proposed measures. Pierre Rebourseau, for example, wanted to restore the beautiful wall around Clos de Vougeot and hoped that the funds needed would be supplied by the owners. Many of them, however, particularly those whose vines were not situated near the wall, refused to contribute: Pierre Rebourseau therefore approached Les Chevaliers du Tastevin.
Not all 80 owners of the Clos de Vougeot make or bottle the wine themselves, for almost half of them possess no more than 1¼ acres. Those with under an acre harvest too few grapes to produce a good wine for their own account. They are normally obliged to sell their crop, or, if they have no professional conscience, they mix it with

Vougeot

grapes originating from another area. This does not imply, however, that the largest owners necessarily make the best wine. The Domaine du Château de la Tour, which comprises buildings erected in 1890 on the north side of the Clos, owns the largest area (15 acres) but its wine is in no way exceptional.

A perfect balance

Because of its innumerable variations, it is impossible to give a precise description of Clos de Vougeot. Michael Broadbent, in his book, *Wine Tasting*, asserts, quite rightly, that the wine lover will be doing well to find a round, full-bodied, tasty wine for long keeping. In my opinion, the good Clos de Vougeot wines possess qualities that are perfectly balanced. By and large, it could be defined as somewhat introverted, not extending a welcome with open arms but demanding better acquaintance for full appreciation. For those with the patience to explore its feel and taste, the wine gradually reveals itself as neither too heavy nor too hard, possessing body and breeding, not excessively robust, sometimes as supple as velvet. A typical Clos de Vougeot has a delicate bouquet in which you can sometimes distinguish the fragrance of various flowers, and sometimes the aroma of mint or truffles. The aftertaste may linger for several minutes.

Clos Blanc de Vougeot

While the production of the Grand Cru Clos de Vougeot is about 15,900 cases, that of village and Premier Cru is much lower. The annual production of red Vougeot is on average 4,900 cases, while that of the

At the Domaine Tortochot I tasted the 1972 Clos Vougeot as well as the 1973. The former had a powerful bouquet, a strong colour and a very long-lasting aftertaste. The 1973 was also very balanced, although lighter, but still very harmonious. More recent vintages have displayed similar characteristics.

In good vintage years the estate of Coquard & Fleurot of Morey-Saint-Denis produces a wine which is very pleasant but needs time to open up.

Henri Rebourseau works 6¼ acres in Clos de Vougeot. He produces a diffident wine with a delicate bouquet and a mellow, velvety, long-lasting taste. Solid colour and perfect balance: very characteristic.

Opposite page, above left: Maison Moillard from Nuits-Saint-Georges is proud to show that it owns vines in the Clos de Vougeot.

Opposite page, above right: Old hods for carrying grapes, dating from 1826.

Opposite page, below: The magnificent cuverie in the château of Clos de Vougeot. It has been turned into a museum and is visited by thousands of tourists every year.

Below: A view of the Château de la Tour, taken from Vougeot. Although this is the largest owner in Clos de Vougeot, its quality is often disappointing.

Also worthwhile: Clos de Vougeot from André Zittener Père & Fils (Gevrey-Chambertin and Switzerland) who produce a clean, elegant wine from 3¾ acres.

It is difficult to define the boundaries of the bigger holdings in Clos de Vougeot, even though each comprises a precise area. The approximate sizes are: Château de la Tour 14¾ acres, Jacques Prieur 3 acres, Charles Noëllat 6½ acres, Henri Rebourseau 6¼ acres, Champy Père & Cie 5½ acres, Jean Grivot 5 acres, Domaine Zittener 3¾ acres, Drouhin-Laroze 3¾ acres René Engel 3½ acres, Domaine des Varoilles (sharecropping) 3¼ acres, La Reine Pédauque 2½ acres, Henry Lamarche 2½ acres, Joseph Faiveley 2½ acres, Joseph Drouhin 2¼ acres, Moillard 1½ acres, Jaboulet-Vercherre 1¼ acres, Thorin 1¼ acres, Ropiteau-Mignon ½ acre, Coquard-Fleurot ½ acre, Tortochot ½ acre, Leroy ½ acre, Mongeard-Mugneret 2½ acres.

Vougeot

white is about 550 cases. The Vougeot pattern is therefore rather untypical of a Côte de Nuits commune: plenty of red Grand Cru, followed by Premier Cru and village *appellations* with more white than red. The Premiers Crus are somewhat rare and those I have tasted, like Le Clos de la Perrière, Les Cras and Les Petits-Vougeots, were agreeable but not very inspiring. The white wine of Le Clos Blanc de Vougeot separated by a road from Clos de Vougeot, is, on the other hand, excellent, possessing fragrance, breeding, body and a faint taste of oak. Even though it lacks a little freshness, it is very pleasant with well-seasoned veal, pork or chicken. Le Clos Blanc de Vougeot belongs entirely to the Maison l'Héritier-Guyot of Dijon, a firm equally well known for its *cassis*. The Guyot method of pruning vines, a procedure known to all wine growers, was perfected by a partner of M. l'Héritier.

Crus of Vosne-Romanée

Grands Crus:
Romanée-Conti.
Richebourg,
La Tâche,
Romanée-Saint-Vivant,
Romanée,
Grands-Echézeaux,
Echézeaux.

Premiers Crus:
Aux Malconsorts,
Les Beaux-Monts,
Les Suchots,
Les Gaudichots,
Aux Brûlées,
Les Chaumes,
Les Reignots,
Le Clos des Réas,
Les Petits-Monts.

The spelling of these names can often vary.

Below:
Henry Lamarche, of the estate of the same name, in his office. He works with his son, and their estate comprises 25 acres divided between Grands-Echézeaux, Clos de Vougeot and Pommard.

La Grande Rue, a celebrated vineyard in Vosne-Romanée, is a monopole which was already known in 1786. According to François Lamarche, if La Grande Rue is not classed as a Grand Cru, it is because it was not appreciated for many years, and has often been the object of rivalry. The prices of La Grande Rue are generally higher than those of Clos de Vougeot.

The Domaine René Engel owns about 17¼ acres, mainly in Vosne-Romanée itself. It also owns land in Les Brûlées, Echézeaux and Grand Echézeaux. Very good wines are produced from all the holdings, but even the simple Vosne-Romanée is a worthwhile wine: fine bouquet, lively and elegant taste.

Father René and son Gérard Mugneret jointly cultivate 17¼ acres, of which they own half. Their wine is fined with egg white and is not filtered. The bottles have a wax seal. I have pleasant memories of both Les Suchots (perfect balance between fruit and wood) and Vosne-Romanée. René and Gérard each have their own label.

The estate of Jean Gros is the sole owner of the Premier Cru Clos des Réas, which lies to the south of the village and covers about 5¼ acres. It produces a fine, supple, deep-coloured wine. The estate owns 37 acres in all, with land on the Hautes-Côtes de Nuits.

Vosne-Romanée

Although Gevrey-Chambertin, Morey-Saint-Denis, Chambolle-Musigny and Vougeot all produce some great wines, Vosne-Romanée has some claim to be described as the true treasure house of the Côte de Nuits. Here, indeed, are the richest, most brilliant, most precious wines in the whole of Burgundy. Vosne-Romanée has seven Grands Crus: Romanée-Conti, Richebourg, La Tâche, Romanée-Saint-Vivant, Romanée, Grands-Echézeaux and Echézeaux. Each of them enjoys an almost legendary world-wide reputation, justifying the opinion of Gaston Roupnel that 'Vosne-Romanée is the central pearl of the Burgundian necklace'. Vosne-Romanée's 650 inhabitants are deeply involved with wine-growing, and the town's streets and paths seem to have been laid out with the intention of not encroaching on the vineyards. Visitors are not afforded special treatment. Although they can eat very well at the best local restaurant, *La Toute Petite Auberge*, Vosne has no hotel, and the only accommodation is a tent on the campsite alongside *route nationale 74*, or one's car.

The battle of Nuits

Vosne-Romanée goes back many centuries: in 639, it was called Vaona, and the Dukes of Burgundy maintained a hunting lodge there. Most of the houses, however, were built in the 19th century, for the village was destroyed in 1870 during the Franco-Prussian War and only one 16th-century house and the 18th-century château were left standing. In Vosne-Romanée, the *Maison du vin*, located near the *route nationale*, is not owned by the commune, but was built by François Gros, a wine grower who runs it on a commercial basis. Most of the houses in Vosne bear a plaque or notice with the name of an estate or *négociant-récoltant*, as almost all the local vineyards belong to the villagers.

1978

ECHEZEAUX

APPELLATION CONTROLÉE

Mis en bouteille au Domaine

MONGEARD-MUGNERET

PROPRIÉTAIRE-RÉCOLTANT A VOSNE-ROMANÉE (CÔTE-D'OR)

PRODUCE OF FRANCE

Together with his son Vincent, Jean Mongeard cultivates the estate of the Domaine Mongeard-Mugneret, which extends for just under 44½ acres. With his 12 acres, he is also the largest owner of Echézeaux (fine, subtle wines of great quality) and, with 4½ acres, the second largest owner of Grands Echézeaux (after the Domaine de la Romanée-Conti; also an excellent wine). Mongeard also produces a fine Vosne-Romanée (from 8¾ acres).

Right:
The famous stone cross standing at the foot of Romanée-Conti. The very stony soil of this vineyard is analyzed as follows; 0.003 chlorides, 0.007 organic matter, 0.725 silica, 0.174 alumina, 0.088 lime, 0.002 iron, and 0.001 others.

Below:
Grape-pickers in Vosne-Romanée. In addition to its famous Grands Crus, this commune produces roughly 47,000 to 78,000 cases of Premiers Crus and appellation villages. At Flagey-Echézeux, which does not have an appellation village wine, only the Grands Crus have the right to an appellation d'origine.

Romanée-Conti is one of the few vineyards which is celebrated in a song, written and sung by Anne Sylvestre.

The Société Gros Frères at Soeurs, established in the Château Gros, has an excellent reputation for its wines. In 1982, however, I was informed that they were not prepared to be visited by the author. I am told this estate cultivates 18 acres.

Vosne-Romanée

The Romanée-Conti estate

Romanée-Conti is the wine *par excellence* of Vosne-Romanée: no other vineyard boasts such a prestigious name. This estate, owned by two families, consists of two monopoly holdings: Romanée-Conti has 4¾ acres and La Tâche 15 acres. These two wines are both Grands Crus, as are four other wines from strips belonging to the estate: Richebourg (8¾ acres), Grands-Echézeaux (8¾ acres), Echézeaux (11¼ acres) and Montrachet (1¾ acres), (see the section on Puligny-Montrachet, page 132). The Domaine de la Romanée-Conti also cultivates a large part of the Grand Cru Romanée-Saint-Vivant (13 acres), the remainder of which belongs to the Domaine Marey-Monge. The joint owners of Romanée-Conti are the Villaine family (who also own vines in Bouzeron, near Chagny) and the Leroy family (who own the Maison Leroy in Auxey-Duresses). One representative of each family is responsible for the day-to-day running of the estate — M. Aubert de Villaine and Mme Lalou Bize-Leroy. Both are fully involved with the estate's activities and, of course, with the sale of its wines. M. Aubert de Villaine handles exports to the USA and Britain; Maison Leroy sells to all other markets. Domaine de la Romanée-Conti has long been in great demand despite its very high prices. In 1975, however, the American importer, Frederic Wildman, deterred by exorbitant prices, cancelled his contract as exclusive buyer. With no exports to the USA, the estate was compelled to lower its prices by 30% or even 40%, but despite this price drop, the wines of Romanée-Conti still remain the preserve of the rich.

Wines from the Domaine de la Romanée-Conti are always sold in mixed cases. The 1976, for instance, was sold with three bottles of La Tâche, two Romanée-Saint-Vivant, Richebourg and Grands-Echézeaux, and one Romanée-Conti.

Harvests in the snow

It is often questionable whether certain wines are worth their price and if customers are really capable of appreciating their true qualities. With regard to Romanée-Conti, however, it is important to stress that the high prices do not stem merely from exclusive distribution or scarcity, but from the loving care that goes into obtaining the best possible quality. The age of the vines has a lot to do with this: 30- and 40-year-old plants are not uncommon on this estate. Quality rather than quantity, needless to say, is the principal aim of the owners and the *régisseur* André Noblet. The harvest is gathered as late as possible, when the grapes are really ripe, even if the weather is bad. As Mme Bize says: 'The grape is the master'. October is often very sunny in Burgundy and the harvests on this estate begin a month later than elsewhere. At this time of year it is possible to employ a large number of pickers, and the entire harvest can be

gathered in less than ten days. In rainy years, the damaged grapes are picked first so that the good fruit can ripen better. In 1965, La Tâche had three harvests: two for the spoiled grapes and the third, starting in November in the snow, for the grapes that were finally ripe.

Above:
Pickers from the Domaine de la Romanée-Conti, enjoying their meal.

Below left:
The overflowing baskets of grapes are quickly taken back to the cuverie.

Below right:
Pickers in a green sea of vines.

Highest standards

After a final sorting of the grapes, prior to fermentation, an only partial removal of the stalks allows sufficient tannin into the wine. Vinification is still carried out in wooden vats, but doubtless these will soon be replaced by stainless-steel vats, under test for years. Following a fermentation and maceration period of about three weeks, during which the temperature is steadily raised (a team even spends nights beside the vats) the wine is put into new oak barrels, where it remains for some 18 months, absorbing more of the tannin contained in

the wood. A careful watch is kept over the vats during vinification and in the course of the *élevage* in barrels, since it is essential for the wines to be worthy of their label. So great is the concern for standards that in 1950 and 1951, for example, only wine from La Tâche was marketed, in 1960 only the produce of La Tâche and Romanée-Conti, and in 1968 only wine from Montrachet. Although prices are high, the constant attention to detail required for turning out a perfect wine eats into the potential profitability of this estate, which employs about 15 families. Should it prove absolutely essential to reduce expenses, a saving may

The Château de Vosne-Romanée has a vineyard of 14¾ acres, from which it produces a wine with a solid colour, rich in alcohol and tannin, with a good, natural taste. Since 1948, Lionel Bruck (Hasenklever) has been in charge of the vinification, bottling and sales.

The Premier Cru Les Brûlées is situated just to the north of Le Richebourg. Its owner, Henri Jayer, often produces a wonderfully balanced wine combining body and suppleness. Jayer also owns vines in Le Richebourg and Les Beaumonts.

Jean Grivot owns about 8¾ acres in Vosne-Romanée. His Les Beaumonts is a remarkable wine: along with a delicious bouquet, it possesses the satiny splendour that typifies a Vosne-Romanée. A very good 1976.

The Domaine du Clos Frantin and a part of Les Malconsorts belong to the Maison Bichot. This Premier Cru is of excellent quality: delicate bouquet, strong, elegant taste, and a touch of hardness in the aftertaste.

La Grande Rue is an excellent Premier Cru, if not one of the best. Often more successful than Les Malconsorts, it has a lovely bouquet, is elegant with a hint of terroir, and has a lingering aftertaste. Sometimes, however, extremely disappointing.

The Domaine de la Romanée-Conti owns 11½ acres of Les Echézeaux. Even during mediocre years such as 1958, the wines are of perfect quality: rather light, fragrance of violets, fruity taste, prolonged aftertaste.

be possible on such items as packing-cases or bottles, but no economy is ever permitted which might prejudice the quality of the wine.

The vineyard of Romanée-Conti

The Domaine de la Romanée-Conti owes its international reputation to the vineyard of Romanée-Conti, a Grand Cru with no equal in Burgundy, apart from Montrachet Blanc. Cultivated since 1232, this vineyard has only changed hands nine times in over 700 years. It originally belonged to the abbey of Cîteaux, then to the abbey of Saint-Vivant, and after that remained the property of the Croonenbourg family for more than two centuries. Madame de Pompadour tried to get her hands on it several times but it was the Prince de Conti who finally acquired it in 1760. He kept it for more than 30 years, until 1793, when the revolutionaries drove him abroad and confiscated his lands. The vineyard was sold to Nicolas Defère, head of the public gardens in Paris. Later, briefly, it was the property of the banker Ouvrard, and finally it was bought by the Duvault-Blochet family, from which M. Aubert de Villaine is descended. The Villaine and Leroy families, forming a *Société civile*, have been the joint owners of the vineyard since 1942.

Renewing the vineyards

In the early 1940s, Romanée-Conti was the only vineyard in Burgundy which still had vines pre-dating the *Phylloxera* invasion. However, the 50- or 60-year-old plants were yielding such a small vintage (200-300 bottles per year) that they were no longer profitable. Furthermore, the soil was 'tired' because of the special treatment applied to protect the vines from *Phylloxera*. Consequently, it was decided in 1945 to replant the vineyard completely — a radical measure which curtailed all vintages between 1946 and 1951. Today, this 4½-acre Grand Cru produces 3,000 bottles annually; in 1973, its most abundant year, the figure was 9,627 bottles.

Absolute perfection

Romanée-Conti is one of the rare Grands Crus that is easy to find without a map. It can be located by the large stone cross which, many years ago, was placed at the foot of the gentle slopes of the vineyard. The vines are impeccably maintained in perfect rows on the beautiful reddish-brown soil. The wine itself, with its magnificent, shimmering colour, brilliant as a ruby, its penetrating bouquet dominated by the fragrance of sweet-briar, and its unique softness, is unforgettable. For André Simon it evokes 'oriental splendour' with its sumptuousness and velvety finesse; and, in addition, there are innumerable subtle nuances in the lingering aftertaste. All these qualities are balanced to a rare degree of perfection, particularly if good sense and patience are exercised. Even when young, Romanée-Conti is quite palatable, but it is like a fruit that is not yet completely ripe. As with its other red wines, the Domaine de la Romanée-Conti never sells a Romanée-Conti until it has been in bottle for at least six months; after that it should be left in the cellar for at least 12 years before it is really fit for drinking.

The Domaine Ropiteau owns nearly an acre of Les Echézeaux. The vines are more than 15 years old, and give a pure, full-bodied wine with an aroma of violets. Of his magnificent 1972, André Ropiteau confided: 'This is a wine that makes me truly happy.'

The owner of La Grande Rue, Henry Lamarche, also has about three-quarters of an acre of Les Echézeaux. He makes a very distinguished wine with an agreeably long aftertaste.

It was with some trepidation that I tasted a Grands-Echézeaux 1963 in the company of Lalou Bize-Leroy. Despite the late harvest that year, this wine had a rich bouquet, and a slightly earthy, spicy taste: a true symphony of taste and fragrance. A striking wine with a lingering aftertaste, typical of years like 1976 with a lot of sun.

Since the harvest of 1976, the wine from La Romanée has been matured, bottled and sold by Bouchard Père & Fils. It is a deep-coloured wine with a very fragrant bouquet and a strong taste with more than a hint of oak and tannin; there is also a slight fruitiness about it. This is a fine, firm burgundy which improves with keeping. Bouchard also sells Les Reignots (1½ acres) from the same estate.

La Tâche

La Tâche, with its 15 acres, is three or four times larger than Romanée-Conti. This was not the case, however, until after World War I. The vineyard then covered about 3½ acres. An application to the Court of Appeals in Dijon added some 11½ acres of the neighbouring vineyard Les Gaudichots to La Tâche on 6 December 1932. La Tâche (French for 'task') has a personality very different to that of Romanée-Conti and has often been the subject of controversy. In the USA, the high price of La Tâche is not considered consistent with its quality; the 1959, 1961, 1963, 1966 and 1967 vintages, for example, were severely criticized. My own opinion is more favourable, although admittedly I have only tasted the more recent vintages. The 1972, for instance, is an impressive wine, with all the characteristics of a great La Tâche. But the taste of the 1976 is quite simply overwhelming.

If Romanée-Conti has a velvet and satin quality, La Tâche is more earthy, with the scent of freshly picked herbs, subtle spices, mushrooms and (especially the 1965) strawberries. The aftertaste, less prolonged than that of Romanée-Conti, is nevertheless pleasantly persistent. Annual production, monopolized by the Domaine de la Romanée-Conti, is about 1,720 acres.

Richebourg

The 20-acre Grand Cru Richebourg is larger than La Tâche because 7½ acres which once belonged to the Premier Cru Les Verroilles vineyard were added during the 1930s. Richebourg also possesses a rich and individual personality, quite different from the Grands Crus already mentioned. If La Tâche is lighter than Romanée-Conti, Richebourg is more full-bodied. It left me with an impression of abundance and almost unbounded generosity, an almost indecently luxurious taste and a prolonged aftertaste. The bouquet is extraordinary, charged with fragrance, almost sensual. Even Maurice Healy, basically a lover of Bordeaux, describes it with enthusiasm: 'One sniff and the glory was revealed. Oh, what a bouquet! All the flowers of the garden, purged of their excess of sweetness, seemed to join in the tribute.' Richebourg has more body than fruitiness, yet lacks neither grace nor breeding. The vineyard, divided among eight owners, has an average annual production of 2,500 cases.

Romanée-Saint-Vivant

Romanée-Saint-Vivant is a 23¼-acre vineyard next to Richebourg. Like Romanée-Conti, this vineyard once belonged to the abbey of Saint-Vivant, and still bears its name. The wine (about 2,600 cases a year) is notable for its power, long-lasting quality and magnificent bouquet, which is sometimes slightly spicy. More elegant and reserved than a Richebourg, though with less breeding than a Romanée-Conti, it is a very great wine, which in my view encompasses all the richness of Burgundy.

ROMANÉE St-VIVANT
Appellation Contrôlée

Distribué exclusivement par
MOILLARD

La Romanée-Saint-Vivant (1¾ acres) is one of Moillard's best wines. It is often supple, sumptuous, and astonishingly mellow for its vintage, with a pleasant though still rather undeveloped bouquet.

Romanée St-Vivant
Les Quatre Journaux
Louis Latour Négociant à Beaune (Côte d'Or)
Mise en bouteilles dans les caves du propriétaire

Louis Latour owns 2½ acres called Les Quatre Journaux in La Romanée-Saint-Vivant. Although I drank bottles from the same vintage which were very dissimilar, on the whole, I found this a great wine. Powerful yet velvety in bouquet and taste.

ROMANÉE-St-VIVANT
MAREY-MONGE
APPELLATION ROMANÉE-ST-VIVANT CONTROLÉE

The 13 acres of La Romanée-Saint-Vivant owned by the Domaine Marey-Monge is leased to the Domaine de la Romanée-Conti. This wine is delicious, delicately fragrant, elegant and powerful, with a persistent taste, very subtle.

ROMANÉE SAINT-VIVANT
APPELLATION CONTROLÉE

Michel Voarick of Aloxe-Corton owns a part of La Romanée-Saint-Vivant en métayage. Even in lighter years, Voarick managed to produce a good wine with a very velvety bouquet and very full taste.

Opposite page:
Historic photograph of René Engel and his late son Pierre, who died suddenly in 1981. The Domaine René Engel (about 17¼ acres) has since been managed by Pierre's son Philippe. René Engel (born 1894) is the author of several books and a regular contributor to the review of the Chevaliers du Tastevin. His book, Propos sur l'art de boire, is very well known. Even at the ripe old age of 86, he still managed to write another book, Vosne-Romanée, on his own village.

Below:
A pile of packing cases and, inset, Lalou Bize-Leroy and Aubert de Villaine, the two directors of La Romanée-Conti. Lalou and Marcel Bize go climbing nearly every weekend. Lalou has done many first ascents and had to refuse an invitation to join an Everest expedition because of lack of time.

More than a half of this vineyard has been leased to the Romanée-Conti estate by the Marey-Monge family since 1966. Parts of the remainder belong to Charles Noëllat (about 5 acres), Louis Latour (2½ acres) and Moillard (1¾ acres).

La Romanée

Less ancient than the vineyards of Romanée-Conti and Romanée-Saint-Vivant, La Romanée dates from the end of the 18th century. With its 2 acres, it is the smallest vineyard in France with an *appellation contrôlée*, smaller even than the Château Grillet in the Rhône valley, and with a lower yield (220 cases).

The vineyard is owned by the Liger-Belair family. Since 1976, wine from La Romanée has been matured, bottled and distributed exclusively by Bouchard Père & Fils. Before that, La Romanée was handled by Bichot for many years. My own impression is that the wine has improved in quality since 1976, and its quality today compares very well with other Grands Crus. It is a deep-coloured wine, which clings to the glass and has a strong taste and aroma of oak, fruit and tannin. It should be kept for six to ten years.

Grands Echézeaux

The commune of Flagey-Echézeaux is situated east of *route nationale 74*, at Vosne-Romanée, on what is locally called 'the bad side'. Here the vines border the road to the left and right. The wines produced on the lower slopes ('bad side') are not even allowed to use a village *appellation*; those from the upper slopes ('good side') attain a sufficiently high standard to be sold either as Vosne-Romanée, Échézeaux or Grands-Echézeaux. Of the latter two wines, Grands-Echézeaux is the better. The vineyard adjoins Clos de Vougeot, and has an area of 22½ acres. The quality of Grands-Echézeaux tends to be erratic, but in good years equals that of the wines of La Tâche. It is fragrant, with breeding and a light hint of *terroir* and spices; though not forceful, it is a very

Charles Viénot from Prémeaux makes a very good Richebourg. In 1976 the 1972 was still young with an as-yet undeveloped bouquet and a fairly rich taste. Rather full-bodied. Later vintages display a similar robustness.

The Domaine de la Romanée-Conti's Richebourg 1971 promises to become pure nectar by the year 2000. Powerfully fragrant, well structured, very richly flavoured, and with a long aftertaste. I have also enjoyed, among other years, the 1973 and 1976.

The estate of Charles Noëllat covers about 44½ acres. I have not found all the wines from this estate equally pleasant. But among those which I most enjoyed is the Richebourg (from about 2½ acres) which has a deep colour and a full, long-lasting taste; a very elegant wine.

The 1972 La Tâche silenced all critics with its beautiful deep colour and magnificent bouquet. Very characteristic earthy taste with hints of herbs, freshly mown grass and mushrooms. A pity that all vintages are not of the same quality.

Romanée-Conti is an extraordinary wine. It often has beautiful ruby tints and a silky bouquet reminiscent of flowers, particularly sweet-briar. The taste is equally wonderful, with delicacy and roundness in perfect balance.

*Below:
Vosne-Romanée at harvest time.*

*Opposite page, left:
Michel Gouges, one of the two brothers who run the Domaine Henri Gouges in Nuits-Saint-Georges. Marcel is in charge of vinification and Michel of the sales.*

*Opposite page, right:
Nuits-Saint-Georges is an important wine-growing town, twinned with Tamines in Belgium and Bingen in Germany. It boasts many leading wine firms and a cooperative.*

pleasant wine. A restaurateur told me that one day he had the misfortune of dropping a bottle of Grands-Echézeaux 1934 and was still able to smell the bouquet for about an hour afterwards. When we were in René Engel's cellar, where he kept his Grands-Echézeaux, he remarked cheerfully: 'There are only songs here.' Annual production is about 2,800 cases.

Echézeaux

The wine of Echézeaux (a name probably derived from *chaumières* — thatched cottages) is clearly distinguishable from Grands-Echézeaux. Light in bouquet and body, it has a fairly lingering aftertaste. It must be chosen with greater care than the other Grands Crus of Vosne, since some merchants sell Echézeaux of sub-standard quality. Its area is rather large for a Burgundy *appellation* — 76 acres. About 10,600 cases are produced annually.

La Grande Rue

La Grande Rue is a long, narrow vineyard, bordered on one side by La Tâche, and on the other by Romanée-Conti, Romanée-Saint-Vivant and La Romanée. Despite its glittering neighbours, La Grande Rue is only classed as a Premier Cru; yet it merits more than this, for it towers above certain Echézeaux. The bouquet is flowery and even when young this wine has a lot of charm and lingers long in the mouth. Like all the great wines of Vosne, it takes some time to reach its peak. But once mature, what a wonder! Henry Lamarche was given La Grande Rue (3¾ acres) as a wedding present before the war and he and his son, François, still own it. La Grande Rue produces at least 8,000 bottles which quite rightly fetch higher prices than the other Premier Crus of Vosne-Romanée.

Variable village wines

The other Premier Crus of Vosne-Romanée often produce some quite remarkable wines, such as Beaux-Monts, Les Suchots (the two wines are sometimes rather alike) and Les Malconsorts, all of which enjoy a good reputation. With approximately 120 acres of Premiers Crus, Vosne-Romanée also has roughly 230 acres of *appellations village*. Despite the confident assertion of Courtépée in 1774: 'There are no mediocre wines in Vosne', they should be chosen with great care as the variations in quality are sometimes considerable.

A good Vosne-Romanée can be recognized by its bouquet, which should be penetrating, subtle and slightly spicy, and by its aristocratic, velvety taste — a blend of flamboyance and delicacy. Finally, of course, there is its incontestable elegance.

Henri Remorquet owns about 2½ acres of Les Allots (appellation Nuits-Saint-Georges). This wine, both supple and full-bodied, takes on a very balanced bouquet after being laid down for about 12 years.

Maison Faiveley owns about 17½ acres in Nuits-Saints-Georges. This wine is fruity, full-bodied without being heavy, with a closed and compact bouquet. Its distinctive aftertaste is not excessively tannic.

It was during the scorching hot summer of 1976 that I tasted a 1974 Nuits-Saint-Georges from the cask, in the cellars of Labouré-Roi. For a simple Nuits-Saint-Georges, the wine had a great deal of breeding, quite a lot of body, a little astringency and a beautiful shimmering colour. Six years later I tasted the 1978, which was also perfect.

One of the most modest wines of the Hospices de Nuits comes from the vineyard of Les Fleurières (appellation contrôlée Nuits-Saint-Georges). The wine has a solid colour and an as-yet undeveloped bouquet; it is full-bodied, fleshy and with a long aftertaste.

Louis Latour's 1971 Nuits-Saint-Georges is very typical: beautiful colour, powerful bouquet, virile taste, prolonged aftertaste, rich in alcohol. The 1972, equally robust, was very successful. Subsequent vintages display the same robust qualities.

Jean Grivot regularly wins medals for his Nuits-Saint-Georges Les Boudots. I liked the 1974 very much; full of vigour, very tannic and with a good colour. Jean Grivot owns about 2½ acres of this vineyard.

Nuits-Saint-Georges

Côte de Nuits

Nuits-Saint-Georges, described ironically in certain quarters as 'the kidney of Burgundy', is the last important commune in the Côte de Nuits. A lot of wine flows through this town, as many *négociants-éleveurs* have their headquarters here. The best known are Moillard, Geisweiler & Fils, Joseph Faiveley. Labouré-Roi, Dufouleur Père & Fils and

Lionel J. Bruck. Two firms specializing in sparkling burgundy are established here: Bouillot and Moingeon Frères, who have taken over Labouré-Gontard. There are also several makers of liqueurs, especially *cassis* and *prunelle* (Maison Vedrenne). Finally, Pampryl produces an enormous amount of fruit juice. One thing is certain, nobody is likely to die of thirst in Nuits-Saint-Georges.

Walnut trees

Looking at the traffic jams on the *route nationale*, which runs through the village, it is hard to imagine what the scene used to be in the old days. Until the 18th century the area was covered with walnut trees, and this is commemorated in the name of the town, which comes from the Latin: *Nutium* or *Nuys*.

Nuits-Saint-Georges, more than other communes in the Côte d'Or, has delved into its history. An archaeological dig has brought to light the remains of an important Gallo-Roman villa in the Bolards vineyard. The site covers more than 25 acres and the villa comprises houses and artisans' workshops, evidence of which is to be found in the variety of materials found there. Coins, statuettes and pieces of pottery have also been discovered. In the summer, the finest of these objects are displayed in the church tower.

Clos de Thorey, with its 11½ acres, covers about two-thirds of the Premier Cru Aux Thorey. Owned by Moillard, the Clos produces a fleshy, supple, distinguished wine with a lingering aftertaste.

The young wine grower Alain Michelot owns 15 acres in Nuits-Saint-Georges. He makes an excellent Chaignots; powerfully fragrant, fruity, round, balanced, with a magnificent aftertaste.

Faiveley is a tenant of Clos de la Maréchale (23½ acres). The wine has a beautiful deep colour, a fairly reserved bouquet and great suppleness. An ample, delicious wine.

Maurice and Robert Chevillon cultivate some 32 acres, of which 3 are in Les Cailles. This vineyard has very old vines and produces a wine which is very frank and full-bodied, and which becomes more and more velvety over the years.

Marcel and Michel Gouges possess 4½ acres of the Premier Cru Les Pruliers. I had the opportunity to taste the 1973, with its light bouquet, on three occasions and each time I was struck by its taste of bitter plums. Subtle bouquet. Other vintages were sometimes more robust and more fragrant.

Although Maurice Chevillon works in close collaboration with his son, he sells Les Pruliers (3½ acres) with a label showing only his name. The wine, though with little power or colour, is nevertheless very lively.

German influence

In the 19th century, Nuits-Saint-Georges had already succumbed, albeit peacefully, to German influence. As in Champagne, a number of enterprising young Germans had settled in the region, hoping to find jobs in the wine-growing industry. This explains not only the origin of names such as Geisweiler and Hasenklever, but also the large consumption of beer which a reporter complained about in 1886. The same writer remarked that 'the air of Nuits is very healthy, a little sharp on the teeth, and there are few epidemics there.'

Trip to the moon

The international reputation of Nuits-Saint-Georges has even spread to the Moon. The astronauts on the Apollo 15 mission named one of the largest Moon craters Saint-Georges, in memory of Captain Andart, hero of Jules Verne's *From the Earth to the Moon*, who celebrated his success by opening a bottle of Nuits-Saint-Georges.
The famous Confrérie des Chevaliers du Tastevin was founded in Nuits-Saint-Georges in 1934, at a ceremony held at the Caveau Nuiton. It was some time before the restaurants of Nuits gained a wide reputation or attracted customers in large numbers — astonishing for a town situated in the heart of Burgundy and overflowing with good wines. In the last few years, however, Jean Croitet, owner of the *Restaurant de la Côte d'Or*, has successfully raised the standard of his cuisine. Two other restaurants, located just outside the village, which serve more simple food, are *La Gentilhommière*, where you can enjoy excellent food, and *Au Sanglier*, where the food is certainly quite acceptable.

Hospices de Nuits

Like Beaune (see page 100) Nuits-Saint-Georges has its *hospices*, owning a vineyard with a total area of 25 acres (the best vines being those of Les Saint-Georges, Les Porets and Les Boudots). Here, however, the wine auction does not take place in November, but in the spring, on the Sunday before Palm Sunday. These wines, having had four months to mature, are thus easier for the buyers to judge. On the Saturday afternoon and Sunday morning, before the auction, there is a tasting of all the wines of Burgundy to which thousands of wine lovers are invited. The idea of a public sale of the wines of the Hospices de Nuits-Saint-Georges had been put forward as early as 1934, but the war and other events forced the administrators to postpone their plans, and the first auction did not actually take place until 1962.

Premier Crus

The *appellation* Nuits-Saint-Georges is made up of some 640 acres producing an annual harvest of 97,000 cases. The white wine is minimal by comparison and does not exceed 700 or so cases a year. Expansion here, as throughout the Côte d'Or, began in the 1970s as more vineyards came under cultivation, particularly at the tops of the slopes near Vosne-Romanée. Nuits-Saint-Georges, contrary to what might be expected of the largest commune in the Côte d'Or, does not possess a Grand Cru. The vineyard named les Saint-Georges in 1892 is a Premier Cru, as is the famous Les Vaucrains. Henri Remoriquet, president of the wine growers' association since 1972, maintains that the growers have always refused the distinction of a Grand Cru so as to avoid creating differences (non-existent, as they believe) between their best wines. The same attitude is also encountered in the Côte de Beaune.

Opposite page:
Grape pickers returning for lunch.

Below:
The Hôtel-Restaurant de la Côte d'Or, which serves excellent food, is on the road which leads through Nuits-Saints Georges. In the past, the restaurant looked out onto a stream, but this has now been covered to form a parking lot. Even in Nuits-Saints-Georges, time does not stand still.

Crus of Premeaux

Premiers Crus:
Clos de la Maréchale,
Clos Arlots,
Clos des Argillières,
Clos des Grandes Vignes,
Clos des Corvées,
Clos des Forêts,
Les Didiers,
Aux Perdrix,
Les Corvées-Paget,
Les Clos-Saint-Marc.

The spelling of these names can often vary.

Crus of Nuits-Saint-Georges

Premiers Crus:
Les Saint-Georges,
Les Vaucrains,
Les Cailles, Les Porrets,
Les Pruliers,
Les Haut-Pruliers (part),
Aux Murgers,
La Richemone,
Les Chaboeufs,
La Perrière,
La Roncière, Les Procès,
Rue-de-Chaux,
Aux Goudots, Aux Cras,
Aux Chaignots,
Aux Vignes-Rondes,
Aux Thorey (part),
Aux Bousselots,
Les Poulettes,
Aux Crots (part, including Château Gris),
Les Vallerots (part),
Aux Champs-Perdrix (part),
Perrière-Noblet (part),
Aux Damodes (part),
Les Argillats (part),
En La Chaîne-Carteau (part),
Aux Argillats (part).

The spelling of these names can often vary

The wines of Premeaux

Although the area of the Nuits-Saint-Georges *appellation* is not the largest in the Côte d'Or, it is the longest, measuring almost 4 miles from north to south and including the vineyard at Premeaux. This is a village south of Nuits-Saint-Georges which borders the *route nationale*. The vineyards planted along this narrow strip of land between the *route nationale* and the top of the slopes, enjoy a very long-standing reputation, for they date from before 1250: Premeaux produces only Premiers Crus, such as Clos des Corvées and Clos des Forêts, very close to Nuits-Saint-Georges, west of the *route nationale*.
Clos de la Maréchale, with its 24 acres, is at the southernmost tip of the commune and the last wine entitled to the Nuits-Saint-Georges *appellation*. After this, the quality of the land rapidly deteriorates. Clos de la Maréchale, leased in its entirety to the

Maison Faiveley, in fact produces three different *cuvées*, the best from the north of the vineyard, the poorest from the south. These *cuvées* are eventually mixed, yet the result, far from being disagreeable, has given me much pleasure.

Virile and robust

A good Nuits-Saint-Georges is a classic burgundy — full of colour, fragrance and body. Rarely simple, it has neither the baroque splendour of a Gevrey-Chambertin, the fruity balance of a Morey-Saint-Denis,

the delicate grace of a Chambolle-Musigny, nor the aristocratic elegance of a Vosne-Romanée. In comparison with all these wines, Nuits-Saint-Georges seems more robust, with more tannin, and there is a slight fragrance of bitter fruit or burnt oak in its indefinable aroma. Of all the wines from the Côte de Nuits, those of Nuits-Saint-Georges are often the slowest to develop. Comparative tastings of wines of the same vintage from different communes, yet

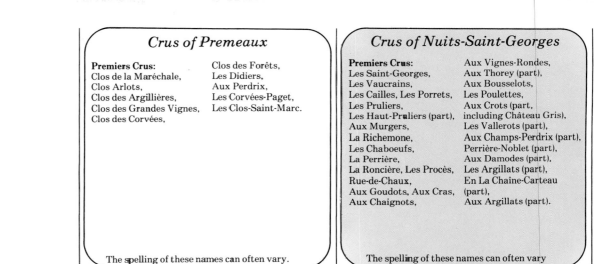

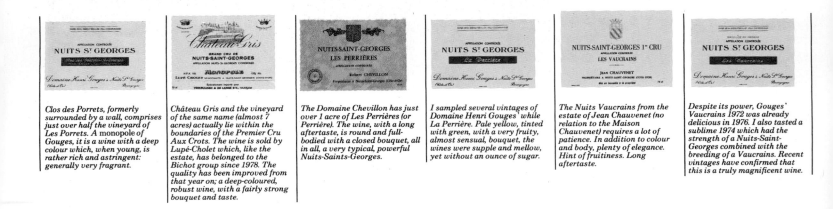

Clos des Porrets, formerly surrounded by a wall, comprises just over half the vineyard of Les Porrets. A monopole of Gouges, it is a wine with a deep colour which, when young, is rather rich and astringent: generally very fragrant.

Château Gris and the vineyard of the same name (almost 7 acres) actually lie within the boundaries of the Premier Cru Aux Crots. The wine is sold by Lupé-Cholet which, like the estate, has belonged to the Bichot group since 1978. The quality has been improved from that year on; a deep-coloured, robust wine, with a fairly strong bouquet and taste.

The Domaine Chevillon has just over 1 acre of Les Perrières (or Perrière). The wine, with a long aftertaste, is round and full-bodied with a closed bouquet, all in all, a very typical, powerful Nuits-Saints-Georges.

I sampled several vintages of Domaine Henri Gouges' while La Perrière. Pale yellow, tinted with green, with a very fruity, almost sensual, bouquet, the wines were supple and mellow, yet without an ounce of sugar.

The Nuits Vaucrains from the estate of Jean Chauvenet (no relation to the Maison Chauvenet) requires a lot of patience. In addition to colour and body, plenty of elegance. Hint of fruitiness. Long aftertaste.

Despite its power, Gouges' Vaucrains 1972 was already delicious in 1976. I also tasted a sublime 1974 which had the strength of a Nuits-Saint-Georges combined with the breeding of a Vaucrains. Recent vintages have confirmed that this is a truly magnificent wine.

produced by the same *éleveurs*, show Nuits-Saint-Georges to be better structured than the others, yet also more guarded and secretive, although without any harshness or roughness. In fact, they are very typical burgundies, and their relatively high degree of alcohol has prompted the saying: 'Un verre de Nuits prépare la vôtre'.

There is a modern tendency to drink burgundies too young, an error to be strenuously avoided with a good vintage Nuits-Saint-Georges; these need at least a dozen years in bottle before they are ready for drinking.

Les Saint-Georges

Generally speaking, Nuits-Saint-Georges can be divided into two groups, according to their style. On the one hand, there are the lighter wines produced from vineyards to the north of the commune, on the boundary of Vosne-Romanée; on the other, there are the more robust wines from the south of the commune. The latter are often the more typical, and they include Les Saint-Georges, a Premier Cru adjoining Premeaux.

In the 19th century, Doctor Lavalle wrote: 'Nuits-Saint-Georges is at least comparable to a Corton from Aloxe or a Lambrays from Morey-Saint-Denis.' In 1920, Camille Rodier awarded Les Saint-Georges prime of place for longevity, colour, bouquet and finesse. I would agree, unhesitatingly, that Les Saint-Georges is today the fullest, most powerful wine of the commune, though I maintain it has less breeding than Les Vaucrains. Les Saint-Georges is a very old vineyard, first planted around the year 1000. Nowadays this Premier Cru covers about 18 acres, divided up among many owners.

The Domaine Henri Gouges owns one-seventh of the Premier Cru Saint-Georges, (about 2½ acres). Deep colour, but not opaque: powerful, full, but less subtle than a Vaucrains, with an extraordinarily long aftertaste.

Opposite page:
After a number of difficult years, the Château Gris is now doing much better. The house has been completely renovated and the vineyard reorganized.

Right:
Jean Croitet, owner of the Hôtel-Restaurant de la Côte d'Or.

Below:
Beautiful vaulted cellar of the Domaine Henri Gouges.

The somewhat austere frontages of houses in Nuits-Saint-Georges often conceal pretty enclosed courtyards and flower gardens.

Les Vaucrains

In my opinion, Les Vaucrains is at least the equal of Les Saint-Georges, although it has a lesser area of some 16 acres. If several great Nuits-Saint-Georges wines were served at the same meal, Les Vaucrains would precede Les Saint-Georges, for although it has the customary strength of a Nuits-Saint-Georges, it also possesses a finesse that the others lack, rather like a heavily built musician who looks as if he ought to play percussion but actually performs beautifully on the violin. Les Vaucrains — the name comes from a small valley with stony ground — has been divided up between several owners, including the Domaine Chevillon with 3¾ acres, the Domaine Henri Gouges with 2½ acres and Alain Michelot with 1¾ acres.

Plums and pears

Near Les Saint-Georges and Les Vaucrains are several excellent quality Premiers Crus, such as Les Cailles (9½ acres), producing a wine which is sometimes very velvety, with a rather particular taste, and Les Perrières (10 acres), whose wine is robust and spirited, with a prolonged aftertaste.
Les Pruliers produces a wine which I greatly respect. Its name is a variation of *pruniers*, or plum trees, and with a little imagination you can, in fact, detect the taste of green plums or plum stones. When very young, the wine has an almost metallic taste.
Les Porrets, or Porets (9 acres), deriving its name from *poirets* or *poiriers* (pear trees), gives wine which some say resembles the taste of very ripe pears. To the north of Nuits-Saint-Georges, near Vosne-Romanée, there are another three Premiers Crus: Les Chaignots (13¾ acres), Les Boudots (15¾ acres) and Richemone (5½ acres).

A rare white wine

The largest amount of white wine from Nuits-Saint-Georges comes from two vineyards, Clos Arlots (in Premeaux), and La Perrière — the latter particularly worth visiting. When Henri Gouges bought the Clos de Porrets in 1934, some rows of Pinot Noir vines produced, by a quirk of nature, bunches of white grapes. Out of curiosity, Henri Gouges took several grafts of these vines and planted them in 1-acre parcels of La Perrière. The wine that resulted from this astonishing Pinot Noir Blanc was delicious, more reminiscent of a white Condrieu from the Côtes du Rhône than a white burgundy. Its straw-yellow colour, faintly tinted with green, its intensely fruity perfume, its vinosity and its roundness make it a quite exceptional wine. Unfortunately, the Domaine Gouges produces only about 65 to 220 cases of this rare wine and, consequently, it is very expensive. A quarter of the vintage is nearly always reserved for the great Parisian restaurant, *Taillevent*.

Daniel Senard is one of the rare growers to produce a white Aloxe-Corton. His 55-acre vineyard turns out about 1,500 bottles a year. This very fruity wine requires long ageing to develop fully. The grape is Pinot Gris.

Many years ago the Domaine Chandon de Briailles replanted a plot of Les Bressandes with white grapes — one section with Chardonnay, the other with Pinot. The result was a wonderful, rather astringent, white Corton, which was very successful at Lasserre in Paris.

Louis Latour's Aloxe-Corton is like a red-cheeked boy, with a beautiful colour and a round, fleshy taste. This wine improves with ageing: bouquet and taste become richer.

Clos des Meix (4 acres) owned by Daniel Senard, is the most southerly of the Grands Crus of Aloxe-Corton. The very harmonious 1972 will not be ready to drink before 1985. However, I have also tasted lighter, less successful wines from the same vineyard.

This vineyard, next to Clos des Meix, and owned by Louis Latour, comprises about 6 acres. It has a delicate personality for a Corton: light bouquet, firm taste. It ages well.

Corton-Pougets' 3¾ acres provide Louis Jadot with a sumptuous wine, which after being kept some years, has a richly fruity nose, powerful taste and very long-lasting aftertaste. It can be laid down for at least 10 years.

Aloxe-Corton

Côte de Beaune

Below:
Bad weather can be the cause of rotting grapes, as this picture testifies. In the 1980s, however, anti-rot treatments have come into fashion, on a large scale and very effectively. Not only in Burgundy but also in Champagne and other regions these treatments have saved huge quantities of grapes in rainy years.

Experts disagree about the origin of the name Corton: some think it derives from 'Curtis' of Otho, a Roman emperor and elderly favourite of Nero. Others think the word comes from 'Cortis' or 'Curtis', a country estate.

The vineyard of Les Bressandes owes its name to three old ladies from Bresse who once owned it.

The traveller heading for Beaune, after leaving Nuits-Saint-Georges and Premeaux, crosses some of the least interesting parts of the Côte. Instead of hospitable wine-growing villages, surrounded by lush vineyards, you come across communes such as Comblanchien and Corgoloin, straggling haphazardly along the road. La Reine Pédauque's vineyard, Clos des Langres, is the last in the Côte de Nuits, its southern wall forming the boundary with the Côte de Beaune. Before reaching the next area of

beautiful vineyards, you pass through Ladoix-Serrigny, made up of two twinned communes which produce Corton, Aloxe-Corton Premier Cru and a more modest wine, Côte de Beaune-Villages. After Ladoix, you come to Aloxe-Corton, a tiny village with a giant reputation.

Charlemagne's gift

Situated several hundred yards from *route nationale 74*, Aloxe-Corton is very ancient

Corton du Clos du Roi is probably Moillard's best wine. Produced on a 2½-acre vineyard, this magnificent wine is full-bodied and ample, and has lovely nuances. Often very tannic.

Michel Voarick cultivates 42 acres but owns only about 15 acres himself. He makes his wine in oak vats, removing the stalks from the grapes. I very much liked his Clos du Roi (1¼ acres) which had a forthcoming bouquet and full, robust taste.

The label of Clos du Roi (2½ acres) of Pierre Dubreuil-Fontaine carries the fitting inscription 'J'aime à vieillir'. In fact, this wine needs keeping for at least five to ten years. Firm, subtle and excellent taste.

Right:
The remains of this small château overlook Daniel Senard's property. The tower is 19th-century but the wall is much older.

Below:
This copper vat in Louis Latour's cellars is movable and, thanks to a double casing which can be filled with hot air, it enables some of the grapes to be heated in chilly autumns, so that fermentation can begin.

Centre:
Several bottles from Daniel Senard.

Bottom:
Test tubes in Jean Latour's office. He is responsible for the vinification at Domaine Louis Latour, and supervises the development of the wine with the utmost care and attention.

and was already there in the Gallo-Roman era. Proof of this is its name, Aloxe, which is derived from Alussa (the land of the god Alus), and also the discovery of coins and a tomb dating from that period. It was here that the Roman road from Marseilles divided, with one route leading to Trèves and the other to Autun. Later, several kings — Charlemagne, Henri II and Louis XIV — owned land in Aloxe. There are allusions, in particular, to the first of these celebrated owners. The most renowned white wine in Aloxe still bears his name — Corton-Charlemagne; and the coat of arms of the commune still displays an eagle, recalling the time in 775 when Charlemagne, then aged 33, made a gift of some of Corton's vineyards to the members of the abbey of Saulieu, as compensation for their monastery being pillaged by the Saracens. The monks were certainly very appreciative, for even at this time Corton produced an excellent wine, much relished by the emperor, who took supplies with him on long journeys and regularly served it to his guests.

Two tasting cellars

After Charlemagne, the history of Aloxe-Corton becomes more obscure; in fact, for six centuries it was initially part of Echevronne and then of Pernand, no longer having its own independent existence. It was only in 1862 that it added to its name that of the best *cru* of the area — Corton.
Although very close to Beaune, a town that has grown considerably in recent years, Aloxe-Corton has barely changed at all. In 1962 it had more inhabitants than ever before: 275. In the past few years this figure has settled at around 250.
Aloxe-Corton possesses neither a restaurant nor an hotel, but it does have two tasting cellars which are visited by many tourists and advertised along *route nationale 74*. One belongs to the Château Corton-André,

and the other to a group of wine growers. The presence of these two cellars often leads to confusion, which does the village's reputation no good. At the château, the wine sold by La Reine Pédauque is often quite expensive, and hardly matches the splendour of its surroundings. The wine growers' cellar, on the other hand, although in more modest premises, offers wine of a very high quality. Owned by the commune, the cellar is run by seven independent wine growers: Robert Barberet, Pierre Bize, Louis Chapuis, Mme Masson, Max Quenot, Daniel Senard and Michel Voarick.

Mostly Grands Crus

The vineyards of Aloxe-Corton, totalling about 570 acres, lie on the slopes of a long hill which dominates the countryside. The summit, with a thicket of trees, is 1,275 feet high. The villagers claim that from the top you can actually see the snowy peak of Mont Blanc about five times a year. The grapes grown here are Pinot Noir for red wine and Chardonnay for white; generally they produce excellent results. The limestone soil at the top of the slope, which has been eroded over the years, is planted with Chardonnay. The Pinot Noir grapes are found lower down, on land that is reddened by iron oxide in the soil. Most of the vines situated on 'the mountain' can be classified as Grand Cru. Like Vougeot, Aloxe-Corton has only a small, limited number of Premiers Crus and *appellations de village*.

Corton-Charlemagne

Without any shadow of doubt, the most famous white wine in Aloxe-Corton is Corton-Charlemagne. Indeed, many consider it the finest white burgundy after Montrachet. This vineyard is situated high on the south side of the hill, and slopes gently towards the west, in the direction of Pernand-Vergelesses. Corton-Charlemagne

Louis Latour is the uncontested expert in Corton-Charlemagne. His wine combines vigour and finesse, and the good vintages, such as 1976, are irresistible. The bouquet is redolent of exotic fruits and often of honey. A sumptuous wine.

Although the quality is not at all bad, Bouchard Père & Fils' Corton-Charlemagne cannot be compared to that of Latour or Jadot. So the 1971 and 1973, tasted at the same time as other Corton-Charlemagnes, were disappointing. But the 1978, for instance, was again very good, with a certain exuberance and suggestions of fruit and honey.

Jaboulet-Vercherre has really taken great care with this wine from the Hospices, at great expense to himself. The taste of oak comes through strongly for some time and it is only after three or four years' maturing that the soft perfume and velvety taste become evident.

is also a Grand Cru of this commune. In the time of Charlemagne, red grapes were grown everywhere, as they were throughout the Côte, and apparently it was the emperor's wife who insisted that white grapes be planted. Charlemagne, a stout and cheerful man, who loved physical exercise, particularly hunting, appreciated good food and good wine. He was already quite old when he started to grow his legendary beard, but every time he drank, he would stain his beard with wine, scandalizing his courtiers and his wife, who looked on it as hardly proper for an emperor. Nagged incessantly, Charlemagne eventually gave in and issued instructions for red wine to be replaced by white, which would leave no trace on his beautiful white beard.

Relatively young Grands Crus

Despite their exceptional quality, these wines do not have a long history. Until the 19th century this vineyard was planted with Aligoté, a grape with no future, and it was the great grandfather of Louis Latour — today the largest owner in Aloxe-Corton — who had the happy idea of replacing the rustic Aligoté with the noble Chardonnay. So was born Corton-Charlemagne, a wine which nowadays is absolutely incomparable. In Burgundian terms, this Grand Cru is relatively young, about 100 years old. Aligoté has not, however, entirely disappeared from the area, for it was planted again in 1938.

Imperial bearings

Had it not been for the emperor's flowing white beard and Louis Latour's great grandfather, the celebrated Corton-Charlemagne would never have seen the light of day. The colour of a good vintage, pale yellow when young, has a beautiful golden glow, sometimes with glints of green when the wine is fully developed. Its

bouquet, in which some experts can detect a hint of cinnamon, has always seemed to me a harmonious mixture of fruit, oak and honey. The longer the wine develops, the fuller and more generous its perfume becomes. If you want to serve a bottle of relatively young wine, less than four or five years old, for example, you must open it at last half an hour before drinking it in order to give the bouquet time to expand. Its taste is a vigorous, lively and noble blend of fruit and oak, worthy of its imperial origins. Experts think that it can easily sustain 14° of alcohol.

Presidents and princes

The robust, mellow, rich qualities of a Corton-Charlemagne are not suitable as an accompaniment to certain dishes, particularly *hors-d'œuvre*, but I find it goes wonderfully with *foie gras*. I remember a meal at the *Restaurant Lameloise* in Chagny, where we started our meal with *feuilleté de foie gras frais* accompanied by a Corton-Charlemagne 1973; the wine and the *foie gras* complemented each other perfectly. Corton-Charlemagne, which also goes

Aloxe-Corton

Opposite page, above:
The cuverie of the château of Corton Grancey belonging to the Domaine Louis Latour. The buildings date from 1834 and were put up by the Grancey family, which never managed to make a profit out of wine-growing after Phylloxera struck in 1878. The buildings and vineyards were then bought by Louis Latour. The cuverie, which was altered in 1902, has not been changed since. The cellars hold about two million bottles.

Opposite page, below:
Aloxe-Corton at the foot of the hill of Corton.

Above:
The crossroads in Aloxe-Corton.

Right:
The tower of Château Corton-André.

Below:
The magnificent entrance gate to Château Corton-André. The château belongs to La Reine Pédauque, which runs a very large wine establishment in Aloxe-Corton.

During World War II, the occupying forces never managed to find Daniel Senard's cellars: the entrance had been hidden under a mound of earth which had been turned into a flower garden. After the war, Daniel Senard recovered his cellar intact.

The Domaine du Baron Thenard, with headquarters at Gevrey, produces a Clos du Roi which, even in mediocre years, can age for 12 years. Drunk too early, it is merely tolerable. A part of the vintage is bought by Remoissenet Père & Fils.

The Domaine Louis Chapuis in Aloxe-Corton owns about 25 acres of vineyard in the commune itself. The best red wine is probably the Corton Perrières (produced from 2½ acres of the 9¾ which the estate owns of Corton). Fine fragrance and taste, usually with a strong hint of oak.

The Domaine Chandon de Briailles owns 8¾ acres in Aloxe-Corton and a plot of old vines in Les Bressandes. This wine is often notable for its elegant, sensual bouquet and its balanced, subtle taste.

Daniel Senard makes a great wine from his 1¼ acres of Les Bressandes. It is pleasantly full-bodied, and the vigour of the taste does not conceal its elegance.

Charles Viénot surprised even the experts with his splendid Corton 1972: highly coloured, still lacking in bouquet, but supple, round and delicious.

In terms both of quality and quantity, Corton Grancey is the greatest of the Cortons, with a beautiful colour, elegant and lightly spiced bouquet, and strong, supple taste — and all this after being kept 10 years or more.

extremely well with lobster or salmon, was one of President Kennedy's favourite wines. During an official dinner given at the White House to celebrate the visit of the French Minister of Culture, a Corton-Charlemagne was served with *homard en bellevue*. At another banquet, given in honour of President Bourguiba of Tunisia, the *médaillon de saumon* was accompanied by this same wine.

In the Netherlands, Prince Bernhard also has a liking for Corton-Charlemagne, and Maison Patriarche Père & Fils has a framed letter, dated 9 March 1957, which says: 'I cannot thank you enough for your letter to say you are sending me 50 bottles of magnificent Corton-Charlemagne. It is a truly kind testimony of Burgundy's friendship, and I am deeply touched by this magnificent present'. At the lunch following the marriage of the then Princess Beatrix, *le médaillon de saumon royal* was accompanied by Corton-Charlemagne 1938, the year of the princess's birth.

Although Corton-Charlemagne enjoys an enormous reputation, some of the wines presented under its *appellation* are of an uncertain, even inadequate, quality. I have tasted some, for instance, which are very thin or very acidic, and others that have been too heavy or too thick. These differences arise from the varying locations of the vines: those in the sunniest positions provide the best wines — those that have earned Corton-Charlemagne its glowing reputation. The closer the vineyards are to Pernand-Vergelesses, the poorer the quality, although there are exceptions, and it must be said that this commune, too, produces a sublime Corton-Charlemagne (see page 95).

In my opinion, the two Corton-Charlemagnes to surpass all others are those from Louis Latour, who owns 22½ acres, and Louis Jadot, owner of 2½ acres. Bouchard Père & Fils, who have 7½ acres, also offer a very high-quality Corton-Charlemagne, as do the Hospices de Beaune, whose *cuvée* François-de-Salins deserves a special mention. For

some years this *cuvée* was bought by Jaboulet-Vercherre for astronomical prices: the 1982 fetched 120,000 francs per barrel of 228 litres.

Corton's various names

Although production of Corton-Charlemagne is relatively low at about 13,900 cases, on average, a year, its counterpart Corton Rouge is much more plentiful, with an average of 30,650 cases available; and a small amount of Corton Blanc is also made. Definition of a Grand Cru Corton is a complicated matter. The wine can, in fact, be sold under several *appellations*: Corton *tout court*, Corton followed by the name of the vineyard (for example, Corton-Bressandes), or even Château Corton Grancey. An authentic Corton may originate either from one small area simply called Corton, or from several areas of Grand Crus, so that this *appellation* can either pinpoint a precise vineyard or imply a group of different vineyards. But a Corton-Bressandes, for instance, must genuinely come from the place after which it is named. There are more than ten different vineyards belonging to the Corton group. The best lie northeast of the village and are named Le Corton, Clos du Roi, Renardes and Bressandes. But also from Languettes, Perrières, Pougets, Clos de la Vigne au Saint and Clos des Meix I have tasted delicious wines.

Château Corton Grancey

Château Corton Grancey is a wine which does not come from a single vineyard but from several Grand Cru vineyards belonging to Louis Latour. Long before the legislation relating to *appellation contrôlée* was introduced, he used to sell a selection of his better wines under that name, and he is legally authorized to continue doing so today. Indeed, because of this, Château Corton Grancey is a recognized name that Louis Latour uses for his Corton, and it

constitutes the largest output of Grand Cru in Burgundy, with an average of 70,000 bottles a year. This Grand Cru owes its name to a small château built just outside the village in 1749 by Antoine Jean Gabriel Bault. Some of Latour's wines are made in a *cuverie* behind the château and hundreds of thousands of bottles for dispatch are stored here in three cellar levels.

A happy blend

Corton Rouge is one of my favourite wines. I shall never forget the Château Corton Grancey 1962 which I drank 14 years after its vintage. It was served with *carré de veau* and I remember this meal as one of the best I have ever eaten. A fully developed Corton is a happy blend of the great wines of the Côte de Nuits and the Côte de Beaune. It combines northern vigour and southern suppleness, with truly marvellous results. Its dark colour, its generous bouquet with a hint of the fragrance of violets, its elegance, body and roundness, make it very rich but not too heady. It is a generous wine that makes one long for venison or a crackling log fire. For the fullest enjoyment it needs to age a long time; 10-15 years are considered necessary for it to reach maturity, when it becomes supple, mellow and full-bodied. When young, it can seem rather hard and fierce — impossible to judge properly. A wine grower told me that he makes his best Corton when the juice from the press is so acid as to be almost undrinkable. So you have to wait for the right moment to drink Corton, be it Grand Cru, Premier Cru or *appellation de village*. In 1976, I tasted seven different vintages of Aloxe-Corton Louis Latour: 1971, 1969, 1966, 1964, 1962, 1959 and 1955. Only the 1955 seemed really old and already a bit past its best. The other vintages were all excellent and had kept their vigour: the 1971, 1969 and 1966 were still overflowing with energy.

I would class a good Aloxe-Corton as one of the best commune wines in Burgundy. In a

Left:
Daniel Senard, mayor of Aloxe-Corton, and his son, Philippe. Their estate consists of 20 acres.

Below:
Hunting in the vineyards. In the background is the hill of Corton.

Another house which also produces a good Corton-Charlemagne — from its own vineyard — is Joseph Drouhin.

The life and work of wine grower Louis Chapuis from Aloxe-Corton, as told to his son Claude, forms much of the subject matter of the latter's book, Chapuis, Vigneron en Bourgogne.

As is the case with Corton Grancey, the name of the Faiveley family is added to the name Clos des Cortons (a Corton vineyard at Ladoix-Serrigny). This vineyard, which belongs exclusively to Faiveley, is made up of 7¼ acres. The 1970 was fleshy, good, but lacking in breeding.

The Domaine du Prince Florent de Mérode is the largest in Ladoix-Serrigny. The prince owns, amongst others, a large part of the premier Cru Les Maréchaudes and a plot of Clos du Roi. The wines, made by traditional methods, remain undeveloped for quite some time, but are notable for their sumptuous aftertaste.

Louis Jadot stores his Corton-Charlemagne in new oak vats. He clears his wine with milk, after a year of maturation. This special attention results in a wine with a very fine bouquet and a full-bodied taste of fruit and oak.

Aloxe-Corton

Côte de Beaune

simpler, more modest way, it resembles the great Corton mentioned by Voltaire in his letter to M. Bault of Château Corton Grancey: 'I need some of your good wine. I give enough good Beaujolais to my friends from Geneva, but secretly I drink your Corton myself.'

Crus of Aloxe-Corton

Grands Crus:
Corton
(followed by the name of a vineyard such as Bressandes, Clos du Roi, Renardes, Pougets, Perrières, Languettes, La Vigne au Saint, etc., and including Château Corton Grancey), Corton-Charlemagne, Charlemagne (not used).

Premiers Crus:
Les Valozières (part), Les Chaillots (part), Les Meix (part), Les Fournières, Les Maréchaudes (part), En Pauland (part), Les Vercots, Les Guérets.
At Ladoix-Serrigny:
Les Maréchaudes, La Toppe-au-Vert, La Coutière, Les Grandes-Lolières, Les Petites-Lolières, Basses-Mourettes.

The spelling of these names can often vary.

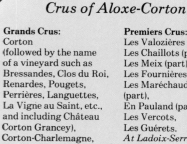

Chanson Père & Fils regularly produces a white Pernand-Vergelesses. With a plot in Les Caradeux, the firm makes a darkish yellow-green wine, with a faint bouquet and a round, quite fresh taste.

André Thiély cultivates 17¼ acres and produces some of the better white Pernand-Vergelesses. I tasted a delicious wine in his tiny cellar: fragrant, fruity, velvety and full-bodied.

Régis and Maurice Pavelot gave me a pleasant surprise with their Corton-Charlemagne 1975: an exquisite, elegant wine, with a lovely bouquet. Their white Pernand-Vergelesses was also very agreeable. They own 15 acres.

Les Fichots is a little-known Premier Cru. Maison Doudet-Naudin makes a wine which I found almost too heady, rather heavy and too alcoholic. I much preferred this company's Pernand-Vergelesses, especially the lighter vintages.

Roland Rapet cultivates almost 30 acres, which produce a range of good and very good wines. His plot in Basses-Vergelesses (3¾ acres) gives a wine that is round but not too full-bodied — a bit hard on the gums. There is a hint of terroir in the nose.

Maison Louis Latour has sold wines from Pernand-Vergelesses for a long time. I have tasted several vintages of the Ile des Vergelesses and have always felt the effect of the feu de paillé (see text). Beautiful colour, rather undeveloped bouquet.

Pernand-Vergelesses

*Below:
A Burgundy cellarman in working clothes.*

*Below right:
View of Pernand-Vergelesses from the Beaune direction. On top of the hill is the oratory dedicated to the Virgin.*

The chapel of Notre-Dame de Bonne Espérance was built in 1854 in thanks for the return to the Roman Catholic faith of an important Protestant lady. On the first Sunday of every August the annual village fête, which includes a handball tournament, takes place on the field behind the chapel.

Pernand-Vergelesses is a small village hidden in a lush and peaceful valley which nestles at the foot of the hill of Corton. There is a well marked road from Beaune, whereas the road from Aloxe-Corton is rather narrow, with no hoardings to attract the tourist, and almost invisible from the *route nationale*. Visitors, however, are warmly welcomed. The wine growers here do not put on airs, like some of their colleagues in other communes — on the contrary, they are usually very patient and understanding with anyone showing interest in their wines. The villagers are friendly and helpful, with a sense of community typified in 1975 when 20 vineyard workers put in an extra 1,600 hours to help their sick neighbours. Furthermore, their wine growers' association is one of the most active in the whole of the Côte d'Or.

Travelling players

Pernand-Vergelesses is the small Burgundian village to which Jacques Copeau brought his troupe of travelling actors in 1926. The rehearsals of the 'Copiaux', as they were christened by the locals, took place in an old *cuverie*. Their performances, heralded by a drumroll, were given all over the region, generally in village squares.

For a long time the inhabitants of Pernand-Vergelesses were nicknamed 'Les Moutelles'.

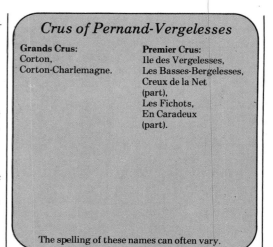

The Domaine Dubreuil-Fontaine owns a good 1¾ acres of Ile des Vergelesses, which usually produces an excellent wine, deeply coloured and with a certain finesse both in fragrance and taste.

The largest owner in the Ile des Vergelesses, Domaine Chandon de Briailles, is not based at Pernand-Vergelesses, but at Savigny. Its 10-acre vineyard produces a very good wine, full-bodied but with plenty of finesse. It needs to be laid down for at least five years.

Although the Domaine du Baron Thénard has its headquarters in Givry, it is also represented in Ile des Vergelesses. In my opinion, it produces one of the mellowest and most solid wines in the vineyard. Remoissenet Père & Fils have exclusive rights.

Below:
Pierre Dubreuil (of the Dubreuil-Fontaine estate) has been the mayor of Pernand-Vergelesses for over 35 years. The name of this commune is derived from the words 'nand' ('spring') and 'perdre' ('to lose'), meaning 'the place where there is an underground spring'.

Bottom:
The bottles are prepared for sale at the Domaine Laleure-Piot. From almost 20 acres the estate produces very good wines, which include an attractive white Pernand-Vergelesses (made not only from the Chardonnay grape, but also from a small percentage of Pinot Blanc). Another recommended estate: Denis Pères & Fils. Pernand-Vergelesses also grows raspberries and blackcurrants, although André Thiély points out that they are gradually being replaced by vines.

Crus of Pernand-Vergelesses

Grands Crus:
Corton,
Corton-Charlemagne.

Premier Crus:
Ile des Vergelesses,
Les Basses-Bergelesses,
Creux de la Net
(part),
Les Fichots,
En Caradeux
(part).

The spelling of these names can often vary.

This is the name of a small, local freshwater fish, but according to Pierre Forgeot, *moutelles* is an obsolete word for haricot beans, a vegetable once eaten in large quantities by the people of Pernand-Vergelesses. Vines have long since replaced beans — and no one seems to have any regrets.

Red and white soil

The vineyards of Pernand-Vergelesses extend over about 495 acres, producing red and white wines. The soil has a red tinge where Pinot Noir grows, but is white and chalky where Chardonnay is planted. In Pernand-Vergelesses, the best vines for red wine are situated in the Ile des Vergelesses (about 22 acres) and the Basses-Vergelesses (42 acres). These are Premiers Crus, generally sold under the *appellation* Vergelesses, such as Vergelesses de Savigny-lès-Beaune, although in both cases the name of the commune has to be included.
The best-known vineyard is the Grand Cru Blanc Corton-Charlemagne, part of which belongs to the commune. Although far from being the finest, the Corton-Charlemagne I tasted in the village had many great qualities. Pernand also produces another white wine, which has much less breeding, but which is made rather pleasant by a little extra chilling. The production of red Pernand-Vergelesses averages about 30,000 cases a year, and the white about 5,550.

Straw fire

It is not easy to describe red Pernand-Vergelesses. The villagers compare it to a young girl dressed in lace, whereas Aloxe-Corton is regarded as more like a mature married woman. I do not find these comparisons apt; in my opinion, Pernand-Vergelesses lacks feminine softness, but is brusquely masculine. The taste of one of the noble reds, Ile des Vergelesses, is sometimes compared to a straw fire: it starts to burn fiercely but quickly dies down. Although not soothingly soft, nor with a very long aftertaste, Pernand Vergelesses is not a wine lacking in charm; sometimes it has more finesse than its neighbours from Savigny-lès-Beaune, and goes well with a good steak. Most red Pernand-Vergelesses stay fresh for a long time and can be laid down for many years.

Small estates

There are no large estates in Pernand-Vergelesses: each of the 30 wine growers of the commune owns only a few acres. Chanson Père & Fils owns 13¼ acres here, plus 6 acres of Les Caradeux, producing white wine. The largest estate in the area is the Domaine Dubreuil-Fontaine, with about 50 acres spread over five communes.
Until quite recently, Pernand-Vergelesses was practically unknown. Bought in bulk by a number of *négociants*, it was mixed with other *crus* and sold under the rather vague *appellation*, Côte de Beaune-Villages. But times have changed, and since the prices of other *appellations* have risen steeply, the merits of Pernand-Vergelesses have come to be recognized. Various *négociants* in Beaune, certain foreign importers and some private buyers are now interested in it. Moreover, this growing reputation has induced the growers to employ proper wine-making and bottling techniques. As a result, Pernand-Vergelesses is increasingly taking on the image of a good burgundy at a price that can still be afforded.
Lack of space has prevented our illustrating the label of the well-known Domaine Bonneau du Martray. This estate owns about 27 acres in Pernand-Vergelesses and Aloxe-Corton, made up of Corton-Charlemagne (19½ acres) and Corton (7½ acres). Comte Jean Le Bault de la Morinière sells these wines only in France. The Corton-Charlemagne is often served at the Élysée Palace.

Crus of Savigny-lès-Beaune

Premiers Crus:

Aux Vergelesses (including Bataillère),
Les Marconnets,
La Dominode, Les Jarrons,
Basses-Vergelesses,
Les Lavières,
Aux Gravains,
Les Peuillets (part),
Aux Guettes (part),
Les Talmettes,
Les Charnières,

Aux Fourneaux (part),
Aux Serpentières (part),
Les Narbantons,
Les Hauts-Marconnets,
Les Hauts-Jarrons,
Redrescuts (part),
Aux Clous (part),
Les Rouvrettes (part),
Aux Grands-Liards (part),
Aux Petits-Liards (part),
Les Petits-Godeaux (part).

The spelling of these names can often vary.

Savigny-lès-Beaune

The traveller leaving Beaune for Paris via the autoroute should take time to park in the rest area outside Savigny-lès-Beaune, to enjoy the magnificent view over the village and surrounding vineyards. This spot is so beautiful that, during the opening of the autoroute in 1970, President Pompidou stopped his car there. Savigny itself, with many unexpectedly picturesque sights, is well worth a visit. There is the church, with its 12th-century tower and a 15th-century fresco; two châteaux, one much larger than the other; and several old houses whose walls and doors are decorated with unusual inscriptions. There are 20 of these, and it is fun to look for them as you stroll around. One, for example, reads: 'If I remember rightly, there are five reasons for drinking: the arrival of a guest, pressing thirst, the future, and, of course, the quality of the wine and anything else you care to imagine.' It is quite obvious that the people of Savigny are extremely fond of their wine.

Favourite of popes

Another inscription, on a stone near the Petit Château, notes: 'The wines of Savigny are nourishing, theological, and banish depressions.' The use of the epithet 'theological' is astonishing. It probably stems from the fact that many popes have shown a liking for Savigny, much of it being drunk at the Vatican — and not only during Mass.

mass. One wonders whether the popes knew, however, that in the remote past, the villagers used to honour Dionysus in the course of their fertility rites.

The wine growers of Savigny have benefited effect that severe measures would be taken them have modified the traditional methods of cultivation. For instance, they were the first to plant their vines in straight rows, and they also initiated a new system of pruning, which is named after its inventor, Guyot. It was probably recognition of this progressive outlook that prompted the Association Technique Viticole de Bourgogne in 1960 to carry out wine-growing experiments in one of the Savigny vineyards.

Dormitory village

Once a bustling place, and today a peaceful spot, Savigny is gradually being transformed, and its close links with Beaune are likely to convert it quite soon into a dormitory village. In fact, I read a notice in the local newspaper from the police to the effect that severe measures would be taken against anyone making a noise or creating a disturbance on the public highway. Dog-owners were also warned to keep their animals quiet at night so as not to disturb their neighbours' sleep. The new arrivals are certainly not welcomed by all the older inhabitants of Savigny, who are worried about their land, having so far managed to keep their 1,000 acres of vineyards intact.

Left, above:
One of the famous inscriptions to be found in Savigny. Roughly translated, it reads: 'The wines of Savigny are nourishing, theological and banish depressions'.

Left, below:
A sphinx in the park of the Domaine Chandon de Briailles.

Below and opposite page:
Vintage scenes in Savigny-lès-Beaune. The village has 80 growers who have started their own wine fraternity, La Cousinerie de Bourgogne (see pages 26-27).

The Grand Château of Savigny has been totally restored and is now a motor museum.

Two other excellent wines are the Savigny-Lavières from Tollot-Beaut and the Savigny from Albert Lacroix (both red).

Clos la Bataillère, triangular in shape and situated in the centre of Vergelesses, probably gives the best Savigny wines. Albert Morot produces a wine that is seductively elegant. Unfortunately, the 1972 still had traces of carbonic gas.

Maison Doudet-Naudin is proud to produce old-style burgundies that are heavy, heady and slow to develop. Other wine lovers may appreciate this type of wine, but I find them too tiring. Guettes is no exception.

Clos des Guettes today belongs to the Swiss firm of Henri de Villamont. Less heady than that of Doudet-Naudin, it is nevertheless very tannic, well-coloured and full-bodied. The long cork indicates that this wine needs ageing for a long time.

As well as 11¼ acres in Savigny-lès-Beaune, the Domaine Chandon de Briailles has 6½ acres in Les Lavières. It is a very successful red wine, rather light in bouquet but with a firm taste.

Bouchard Père & Fils own about 10 acres in Savigny. Despite its rather high level of alcohol (13.5° in 1973), Les Lavières gives a very harmonious and clear wine with a rather fruity bouquet.

Clos des Guettes' 17¼ acres belong to Mme de Rendinger. Although the wine is vinified at the château, élevage and bottling are handled by Maison Hasenklever (Lionel Bruck). As a rule, this wine only takes on fruitiness and charm after ageing for several years.

Two types of vineyards

The vineyards of Savigny-lès-Beaune are divided by the little River Rhoin into two sections, north and south. There are marked differences between the two: the grapes from vineyards on the south bank of the river mature some eight days before those on the north side. Furthermore, the southern vineyards, such as La Dominode, Les Jarrons, Les Marconnets, etc. have a gravelly soil and yield light wines, whilst those to the north, including Les Vergelesses, Les Lavières, Clos des Guettes and Les Serpentières, have a clay soil which produce somewhat fuller wines.

Spontaneous and candid

Despite these differences, the *crus* of Savigny-lès-Beaune have certain characteristics in common which clearly indicate that they are from the same family. Truly powerful Savignys are rare, with the possible exception of those sold by Doudet-Naudin, a *négociant* based in Savigny-lès-Beaune, whose wines generally have a high level of alcohol and tannin. A good Savigny-lès-Beaune is not distinguished by it lightness, but by a very characteristic spontaneity. The bouquet is neither dazzling nor richly sumptuous, but has a comforting candour and assurance; there is also a taste of *terroir* in the nose and palate. As a rule it can be served young, but it improves with ageing.

Savigny-lès-Beaune produces an average of 112,550 cases of red wine a year. In addition it also produces 3,170 cases of white, a fresh wine which also has a hint of *terroir*.

Savigny, where some *négociants* have large, cool cellars, boasts a further asset: its sparkling wines, produced from white wine of the Hautes-Côtes.

Bernard Delagrange, in Meursault, owns about 11 acres, with virtually only one tenant. The Beaune produced by this vineyard wins prizes in competitions every year. The taste is pleasant and elegant, the bouquet quite delicate. bouquet quite delicate.

As its name suggests, Les Epenottes is situated next to Les Epenots, the famous Pommard vineyard. The Domaine Parent in Pommard owns vines in both vineyards. Despite a bouquet that rather lacks fruitiness, and a not very intense taste, this is a clean and pleasant wine.

For lack of space, the label of Beaune Cent-Vignes of the Château de Meursault (Domaine Patriarche) has not been reproduced here. I have had the pleasure of tasting it several times and liked it very much. The Premier Cru Beaune from the same estate slightly disappointed me.

Other good wines which are not mentioned elsewhere in this section: Beaune Premier Cru from the Château de Meursault (Patriarche Père & Fils); Beaune Clos du Roy from Tollot-Voarick.

Below:
Claude Bouchard (right) of Bouchard Père & Fils at a tasting in the company's cellars at Beaune.

Opposite page, above left:
Beaune, viewed from the top of the Montagne de Beaune. The best vineyards are to be found there.

Opposite page, above right:
Some bottles on display at Denis Perret, a wine shop in Beaune.

Opposite page, below:
Old houses in the centre of Beaune; in the background is the bell-tower of Notre-Dame.

Beaune

Beaune, the capital of Burgundy, is the geographical and commercial centre of the Côte d'Or. The town, which dates from 52 BC, was evidently one of Julius Caesar's camps. Historians do not agree about the origin of the name: some think it comes from 'Belen', the god of the Gauls; others see it as a debasement of 'Belisana', a name for the goddess Minerva. A third theory associates it with 'belna', a small villa.

Beaune acquired the status of a city in 1203, and became one of the favourite residences of the Dukes of Burgundy. In addition, it was the seat of the Burgundian parliament. Because of its strategic position and ducal connections, Beaune was the site of frequent battles and power struggles. Furthermore, like all towns in Europe at that time, Beaune was visited by numerous natural disasters, including fire, famine and plague. The last of these was the fire of 1401, which destroyed three-quarters of the town. The archives of Beaune, recalling those bygone days, scarcely constitute a happy catalogue of events.

The cellars of Beaune

Calm returned to Beaune later in the 15th century. The walls and ramparts which still surround it were built in the reign of Louis XI. Today, these serve as shops and cellars for various *négociants*. Bouchard Père & Fils, for example, is established in an old château in Beaune, while Chanson Père & Fils use the three floors of an immense fortified round tower or bastion, the inside temperature of which is ideal for storing wine.

The whole town of Beaune is built, moreover, on a subterranean network of galleries and passages which are a great tourist attraction. Hordes of visitors go round the fine old cellars of Joseph Drouhin, Calvet, Patriarche Père & Fils, Champy Père & Cie,

Beaune

Côte de Beaune

Jaffelin, Les Cordeliers, etc. La Reine Pédauque alone, for example, plays host to more than 200,000 people a year.

A model shop

Fascinating though the cellars may be, Beaune above ground is even more interesting. Having retained its historic monuments and buildings, the town centre is exceptionally picturesque, and Beaune is one of the prettiest little towns in France. Place Carnot, with its two cafés, is the favourite meeting place of visitors as well as local residents. This is the site, too, of Beaune's best wine shop, owned by Denis Perret. The grocery shop that originally occupied the first floor of a house on the corner of Place Carnot and Rue de Lorraine, has in recent years been replaced by this luxurious store — as an example to others of its kind. To shield the bottles from light, the windows are of smoked glass, and to avoid any variation in temperature, the shop is air-conditioned. Denis Perret is patronized by five important wine firms: Bouchard Père & Fils, Chanson Père & Fils, Joseph Drouhin, Louis Jadot and Louis Latour, and sells wines exclusively from these *négociants*, mostly *appellations* from the Côte d'Or. However, he also stocks wines from other regions under the Denis Perret label. Considering the quality of the products, prices are very reasonable.

The Hôtel-Dieu

No tourist should miss a visit to the Hôtel-Dieu, a part of the so-called Hospices de Beaune. Situated near Place Carnot, it was founded in the 15th century by Nicolas Rolin, chancellor to the Duke of Burgundy, Philip the Good, and husband to Guigone de Salins. On 4 August 1443, Rolin ceded all of his worldly possessions, acquired 'by the

Wine grower Robert Ampeau, with his son Michel, produces a firm, clear and elegant wine from his one acre of the Clos du Roi. Wines from good years can easily be kept for a decade.

The Maison Leroy, which specializes in old vintages, brought out a Beaune 1966 which I tasted 10 years after its vintage. It was light, with a reserved bouquet, and a faintly spiced, elegant, quite full and forthcoming taste. Ths wine could still age longer.

Clos des Mouches is the great speciality of Joseph Drouhin, who owns 32½ acres, half red, half white. The white is notable for its rather strong aroma of oak and burnt nuts: fleshy taste.

Beaune tout court is very popular. Paul Joseph Bocion, a négociant in Beaune, makes his according to traditional methods. It has a beautiful colour and is good and firm.

Bouchard Père & Fils sells a white Beaune and a red Beaune Premier Cru under the label Beaune du Château. The white is particularly pleasant (although the red is far from being bad). Limpid colouring, with a delicate yet lively, clean taste.

Beaune opened a museum of wine in 1947 in the old Hôtel des Ducs de Bourgogne. It is well worth a visit.

The sport-loving tourist will find a heated swimming pool in Beaune, as well as tennis courts at the foot of the ramparts.

Beaune is 'twinned' with three foreign towns: Bensheim in Germany, Krems in Austria and Malmédy in Belgium.

grace of God' in order to build a hospital providing comfort and medical care for the poor. The motives for this act of charity are perhaps called into doubt if you happen to subscribe to the view of Louis XI on this subject: 'Having impoverished and disinherited so many of his subjects, well might he beseech divine mercy by providing care and succour for these unhappy creatures.' Work on the Hôtel-Dieu, begun in 1443, was completed on 1 January 1451. The beds of that period, which were larger than ours today, held two or even three patients, and this had its advantages since the huge room was not heated.

The Last Judgment

The beds in the Hôtel-Dieu, which are still lined up on display in the great Salle des Pauvres (170 feet long, 47 feet wide and 52 feet high), were actually in use until 1948. They are arranged so that the patients could see into the chapel where mass was celebrated each morning. Furthermore, the patients were expected to recite the various liturgical offices throughout the day, along with the monks, thereby expressing more confidence in divine help than in medical science. Apart from the Salle des Pauvres and the chapel, the magnificent Hôtel-Dieu contains a museum, a splendid main courtyard, an ancient pharmacy, and a kitchen, now equipped with modern gadgets which stand next to the ancient spit used for roasting meat and game. The museum is especially interesting: there are tapestries, pieces of furniture and paintings, including the celebrated triptych of *The Last Judgment* by the Flemish artist Rogier van der Weyden. Painted between 1443 and 1445, it shows the influence of Van Eyck, and in it you can pick out portraits of several important people of the age: Nicolas Rolin and his son, Cardinal Rolin, Guigone de Salins, Philip the Good, Isabella of Portugal, and others. This precious triptych is carefully guarded; flashlight photographs, for example, are prohibited, in order to prevent further fading of the picture.

Since its foundation in the 15th century, the Hôtel-Dieu has enjoyed visits from many famous people, Louis XIV being the first of royal descent. In modern times, Elizabeth the Queen Mother of England was the first sovereign to sign the visitors' book at the Hospices, as did her daughter, Elizabeth II, during a private visit there in 1979.

The wines of the Hospices

The old Hôtel-Dieu no longer houses the sick, but there is still a home for the aged in a recently added wing. This group of buildings, known collectively as the Hospices de Beaune, enjoys a sizeable income from wine-growing. It owns 143 acres of vineyards, which have been amassed from gifts and legacies received over the centuries, and up to the present day. The distinguished benefactors, in making these gestures, doubtless desired to ensure a place in heaven, as well as to show gratitude and give practical help to the nursing sisters. Whatever their spiritual fate, they at least had the satisfaction of their names being commemorated on the *cuvées* sold at auction — François Blondeau, Hugues and Louis Bétault, François de Salins, and the rest. The total area of the Domaine des Hospices is slightly greater than that of Clos de Vougeot. The wines produced are sold by auction, and this sale is a traditional and famous event in Burgundy. The vines, all Premiers Crus of the Côte de Beaune, are divided up roughly as follows: about 64 acres in Beaune itself, 20 acres in Meursault, 17 acres in Aloxe-Corton, 13½ acres in Savigny-lès-Beaune, and 16 acres in Pommard and Volnay. The Hospices also owns some plots in Gevrey-Chambertin, Monthelie, Auxey-Duresses and Pernand-Vergelesses.

Charity auction

The medical staff of the Hospices is obviously not involved in wine-growing. The estate is run by a manager who selects and signs on the workers who tend the vines. Each man is in charge of one vineyard, with

the manager in overall control. The growers receive a monthly salary and an annual percentage from the wine sales; so it is in their interests to aim at a good vintage. Vinification of the must is carried out under the manager's direction in a specially equipped *cuverie* behind the Hôtel-Dieu. The grapes used by the Domaine des Hospices are always de-stalked and the wine is stored in new oak casks.

The auction of wines from the Hospices de Beaune has traditionally always taken place on the third Sunday in November. Some 600 228-litre lots are sold, for an average of about 17,000 francs each (in 1982). The total money taken at this auction makes it the foremost charity sale in the world. The very high prices reflect not only the genuine wish of the buyers to contribute generously to a good cause, but also to benefit from the prestige and publicity thereby received. The auction and associated events are a fine advertisement for the wine-growing industry of Burgundy, but also have practical value; the average price serves as a barometer for the wine market in measuring the level of interest, at home and abroad, in the new vintage. A successful sale of Hospices will certainly raise the price of burgundies, whereas a moderate sale will keep them stable or even lower them.

Les Trois Glorieuses

At the junction of several main autoroutes carrying traffic to and from Calais, Antwerp, Hamburg, Milan and Barcelona, Beaune attracts tourists all the year round, but they arrive in their largest numbers for the Hospices wine sale. For three days the hotels are full and you can only get around the town on foot. The calendar of events includes tastings, receptions and exhibitions. On Saturday evening there is a candlelight dinner at the Château Clos de Vougeot. On Sunday afternoon, the auction is held in the market, followed by a dinner in the bastion of the Hospices. Monday sees the Paulée de Meursault, an amply provided lunch for the wine growers themselves. This brings to an

Champy Père & Cie is probably the oldest wine merchant in Beaune. Its Beaune-Avaux has a lively, pleasant bouquet, a rather thin taste that is supple but a little too light for my liking; and a rather light colour too.

Bouchard Père & Fils owns all of Clos de la Mousse. The wine has a fragrance with a hint of truffles, and a delicately charming taste, despite the degree of alcohol. The Clos de la Mousse — a Premier Cru — covers 8¼ acres.

Jacques Germain, of Chorey-lès Beaune, owns about 15 acres in Beaune. I liked his Teurons very much; the taste was charming, complex, rather full-bodied but not too heavy. It could age five to seven years.

Clos des Mouches is one of the best Beaune Rouges. It has a lovely limpid colour, body and roundness. The aroma of this very fine wine is like that of morello cherries.

The label does not mention the fact that Clos des Ursules (about 5 acres), is an enclave of Vignes-Franches, a Premier Cru owned exclusively by Louis Jadot. Fine bouquet, aroma of mulberries, very tannic taste with a striking forcefulness.

Le Lycée Agricole et Viticole de Beaune, an excellent school for future wine growers, owns several vineyards, including a parcel of Les Champimonts. This wine, awarded the tastevinage label in 1971, has 13.5° of alcohol, and is highly coloured, very fragrant and quite full-bodied.

Top:
The auction at the Hospices de Beaune. The man in the centre is concentrating his attention on a match. By tradition a match is struck with each new bid. If this bid stands, a second match is struck and when it goes out the hammer falls and the wine in question is sold. The auctioneer waits until the very last moment when there is no more flame to be seen.

Above:
Georges Mathelie, cellarman at Bouchard Père & Fils, samples wine with a tastevin. The cellars of this famous firm are beneath the remains of the Château de Beaune. A few years ago new cellars were built underground next to the old ones. Director Claude Bouchard preferred this to moving to an industrial estate. The new cave has a million-bottle capacity.

end the three days of festivities called Les Trois Glorieuses.

These traditional celebrations tend to divert the visitors' attention from the other Beaune, a modern town with new blocks of impersonal flats, shopping centres and a rapidly expanding industrial zone. In 15 years the population of Beaune has nearly doubled, from 11,000 to 20,000 inhabitants, and this trend will certainly continue. The wine business and its offshoots may still provide work for many people, but booming industry has also created new employment. One specialized Beaune industry is the manufacture of plastic chips for casinos.

The largest wine-growing commune

The steady growth of Beaune has, fortunately, had little effect so far on most of the local vineyards, though the course of the A6 autoroute has nibbled away a section of the Premier Cru Les Marconnets. In any event, Beaune can probably stand losing some vineyard space more readily than other communes in the Côte d'Or, because of its vast extent. The vineyards cover about 1,480 acres, forming a 1¼-mile carpet of greenery on the gentle slopes of the Montagne de Beaune. The vineyards produce an average of about 132,200 cases of red wine and about 6,400 cases of white. It is interesting to note from these figures, however, that Beaune, the biggest wine-growing commune in the Côte d'Or, does not produce the largest quantity of wine, certain proof of its concern with quality. Another significant fact is that the largest owners are the *négociants* (including the Hospices) or people who do not live in Beaune. There are no more than a dozen local wine growers.

A frank and honest wine

Much has been written about the wine of Beaune. The first point to make is that long before the introduction of legislation about *appellation d'origine*, wine from other, less important villages was sold under the *appellation* Beaune. This was the wine that

led Erasmus to say that he would like to live in France, 'not to command her armies, but to drink the wine of Beaune'. M. Morelot, a specialist writer on vines and wines, was far more precise, giving Beaune top place among the wines of the Côte d'Or, commending its body, frankness, colour, vigour, bouquet and softness, all of them qualities further enhanced by long ageing. In my opinion, a red Beaune is an honest wine, inspiring confidence, a wine that rarely disappoints and nearly always affords anticipated pleasure. Even though its character is not easy to describe, it is emphatically a true burgundy because of its Pinot Noir aroma. The wine balances nicely between heavy and light, its perfume is not exuberant, and the equilibrium seems good. Only rarely is one shocked or surprised by a red Beaune, but nevertheless it can provide great enjoyment. In the 19th century the taste of Beaune was described by Jullien as 'the most sincere of Burgundy'.

Differences between north and south

Not all red Beaunes are like one another: as elsewhere, they differ in keeping with the methods of wine-making employed, and these tend to vary according to the individual estate or village. Quality also depends on the soil composition of the vineyard, which gives each wine its specific characteristics. Thus, the central section of Beaune, bordered by *route nationale 470*, produces a wine often lighter than that from vineyards farther north. In the south, Clos des Mouches, Les Vignes-Franches, Les Avaux, Les Boucherottes and Clos de la Mousse, to name but a few, yield more delicate wines than the northern vineyards. Even so, the latter, for the most part Premier Crus, are generally considered to be the best, and enjoy a high reputation. Thus, Les Grèves, with its universally known Vigne de l'Enfant Jésus, Les Fèves, Les Cent Vignes, Les Marconnets, Clos du Roi, Clos de l'Ecu, Les Teurons and Les Bressandes are all very famous vineyards.

Bouchard Père & Fils is the largest owner of Beaune Premier Cru, with over 110 acres. Its Teurons does not have the finesse of Jacques Germain's Domaine de Saux, but with its superb elegance and pleasant bouquet, is of a very high quality.

Louis Jadot owns about 1½ acres of Beaune Theurons. This wine, with its powerful bouquet, is fruity, fleshy and full-bodied.

Albert Morey and his son live in Chassagne-Montrachet and own 3¼ acres of Les Grèves. A clean wine, agreeably supple, with a bouquet of some delicacy.

La Vigne de l'Enfant Jesus, a plot of Les Grèves, is exclusively owned by Bouchard Père. It covers 9¾ acres. The wine it produces has a rich colour, with a powerful bouquet and taste. It is only after a long period that it becomes 'like the infant Jesus dressed in velvet'.

The Domaine Albert Morot, under the capable direction of Guy Chopin, produces wonderful wines. Its Cent-Vignes, for example, has a rather fruity bouquet and a taste that is neither too thin nor too heady. The quality can vary.

Beaune Cent-Vignes is the best wine from the Domaine Besancenot-Mathouillet, which owns just over 27 acres (part of which is worked under the métayage system). The estate owns 7½ acres of Cent-Vignes, which produces a dark-coloured, fleshy and often slightly fruity wine.

Because there are so many Premier Crus from Beaune, it is very difficult to make a single choice, and this is further complicated by the fact that certain vineyards belong to several communes, and that some have similar-sounding names: thus, Clos du Roi, Les Bressandes and Les Marconnets all extend over several communes; and there is a Clos des Mouches as well as a Close de la Mousse, while next to Les Theurons is Les Teurons.

Côte de Beaune

Because of the small quantity produced, white Beaune is a rare wine. Simultaneously light and vigorous, it is less full than a Meursault. An even greater rarity is Côte de Beaune (without a village name). It was created for the lesser vineyards in Beaune, but one can also offer declassified Beaunes under this *appellation*. In red or white, it is generally a fairly light wine. A red Côte de Beaune which I enjoyed very much was the elegant Clos des Pierres Blanches of Michel and Yves Rossignol in Volnay. A pleasant example of white Côte de Beaune is the wine from Beaune's Lycée Agricole et Viticole, which has its own vineyards.

Chanson Père & Fils owns most of the 10 acres of Les Fèves. This is a rather elegant wine, with some breeding and a delicate bouquet. Despite its rather high level of alcohol (13.5°), it is a well balanced wine.

Clos de l'Ecu, at the top of a small hill, belongs to Jaboulet-Vercherre. This Premier Cru is a powerful Beaune, with a deep colour, a fruity, sensual bouquet, a robust taste and a lingering aftertaste.

Chanson owns just about 75 acres in Beaune, of which 9¼ acres are in Clos des Marconnets. This wine has a rather complex character: lightly fruity nose, very pale colour and a rather harsh taste; even the early years are somewhat hard.

Côte de Beaune

Opposite page:
The magnificent courtyard of the Hôtel-Dieu.

Above:
The bell-tower of the Notre-Dame church.

Left:
Visitors at Patriarche Père & Fils.

Below left:
Tourists waiting in the rain to visit Maison Patriarche.

Below right:
The great salle des malades *in the Hôtel-Dieu.*

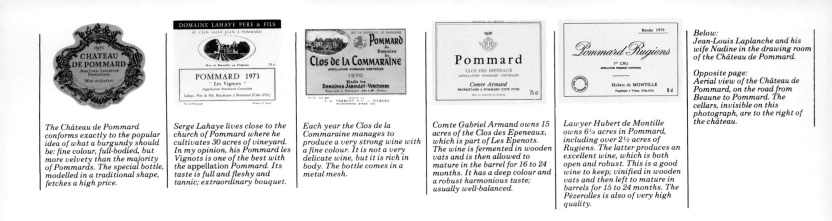

The Château de Pommard conforms exactly to the popular idea of what a burgundy should be: fine colour, full-bodied, but more velvety than the majority of Pommards. The special bottle, modelled in a traditional shape, fetches a high price.

Serge Lahaye lives close to the church of Pommard where he cultivates 30 acres of vineyard. In my opinion, his Pommard les Vignots is one of the best with the appellation Pommard. Its taste is full and fleshy and tannic; extraordinary bouquet.

Each year the Clos de la Commaraine manages to produce a very strong wine with a fine colour. It is not a very delicate wine, but it is rich in body. The bottle comes in a metal mesh.

Comte Gabriel Armand owns 15 acres of the Clos des Epeneaux, which is part of Les Epenots. The wine is fermented in wooden vats and is then allowed to mature in the barrel for 16 to 24 months. It has a deep colour and a robust harmonious taste; usually well-balanced.

Lawyer Hubert de Montille owns 6¼ acres in Pommard, including over 2½ acres of Rugiens. The latter produces an excellent wine, which is both open and robust. This is a good wine to keep; vinified in wooden vats and then left to mature in barrels for 15 to 24 months. The Pézerolles is also of very high quality.

Below:
Jean-Louis Laplanche and his wife Nadine in the drawing room of the Château de Pommard.

Opposite page:
Aerial view of the Château de Pommard, on the road from Beaune to Pommard. The cellars, invisible on this photograph, are to the right of the château.

Pommard

Côte de Beaune

Pommard is a pleasant village near Beaune, dominated by the square bell-tower of its church and the many advertising hoardings proclaiming the quality of its vineyards. The origins of this commune go back a very long way. At the beginning of the Christian era the Gauls built a temple there dedicated to Pomona, protecting goddess of fruit. In 1005 the village came to be known as Polmarium, which was corrupted by various stages to the present name. Modern Pommard is very unlike the village of old, but it is possible to find — parallel to the main street — a number of picturesque lanes no wider than about 13 feet, through which it is impossible to drive a car.

The legendary cross of Pommard

Pommard was once an important posting stage and the inns were used by travellers who had to ford the Vandaine between Beaune and Chagny. Before the construction of a bridge in 1670, the ford was the only way of getting across the river. This crossing, however, was much feared: carriages became bogged down in the mire or even overturned. The ford was marked by a cross which was known as the Croix de Pommard, the memory of which has become so embedded in the popular consciousness that the phrase, 'You haven't reached the Croix de Pommard yet', is still used to warn someone that his troubles are not yet over. The cross itself, restored in 1958, is now sited on one side of the road from Beaune to Chalon.

The river and its problems

Although the ford across the Vandaine no longer exists, the river still poses other problems. Its course takes it straight through the village, often causing serious flooding in bad weather. In August 1975, for instance, the swollen river badly damaged two newly surfaced roads and flooded several cellars. One local figure, Serge Lahaye, whose cellar was damaged, remarked bitterly to me that this had happened three times in 20 years. The local authorities have taken a number of measures, such as passing a section of the river through a culvert and constructing overflow outlets in the streets, to ensure that future damage from flooding will be limited. It is hard to say whether these new measures will prove sufficient, since the flooding of the Vandaine is not solely due to bad weather, but also to the geographical situation of Pommard and deforestation of the surrounding hills. The Epenots vineyard, for instance, owes its name to the pines which were there before vines were planted. The deforested land can no longer hold the rain water which then pours right down into the village. The one solution to the problem would be to replant the hills with trees and reduce the area of the vineyards. It is unlikely, however, that such a drastic measure will ever be taken: the vineyards are not ready to retreat before the rain!

The Premiers Crus

The vineyards of Pommard extend over about 850 acres, a much smaller area than that cultivated in the last century, when, in 1826, there were 1,750 acres of vineyards. This acreage, however, included the areas producing *vin ordinaire*, which have now completely disappeared following the introduction of the legislation governing *appellations d'origine*. As in the case of Beaune and Volnay, none of the wines produced by a Pommard vineyard has been judged worthy of the status of Grand Cru. Nowadays, the wine growers of Pommard will tell you that all their Premiers Crus are of similar quality, although certain vineyards do produce wines which are indisputably better than others. Thus, everybody knows that the best wines of

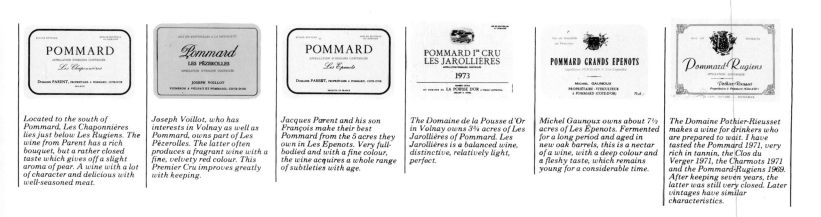

Located to the south of Pommard, Les Chaponnières lies just below Les Rugiens. The wine from Parent has a rich bouquet, but a rather closed taste which gives off a slight aroma of pear. A wine with a lot of character and delicious with well-seasoned meat.

Joseph Voillot, who has interests in Volnay as well as Pommard, owns part of Les Pézerolles. The latter often produces a fragrant wine with a fine, velvety red colour. This Premier Cru improves greatly with keeping.

Jacques Parent and his son François make their best Pommard from the 5 acres they own in Les Epenots. Very full-bodied and with a fine colour, the wine acquires a whole range of subtleties with age.

The Domaine de la Pousse d'Or in Volnay owns 3¾ acres of Les Jarollières of Pommard. Les Jarollières is a balanced wine, distinctive, relatively light, perfect.

Michel Gaunoux owns about 7½ acres of Les Epenots. Fermented for a long period and aged in new oak barrels, this is a nectar of a wine, with a deep colour and a fleshy taste, which remains young for a considerable time.

The Domaine Pothier-Rieusset makes a wine for drinkers who are prepared to wait. I have tasted the Pommard 1971, very rich in tannin, the Clos du Verger 1971, the Charmots 1971 and the Pommard-Rugiens 1969. After keeping seven years, the latter was still very closed. Later vintages have similar characteristics.

Pommard come from Les Rugiens, near Volnay, and from Les Epenots, or Epeneaux, in the direction of Beaune. But I have also tasted very good wines from Les Jarollières, Les Arvelets, Les Chaponnières, the Clos de la Commaraine and from the Château de Pommard.

A strong, full-bodied wine

The people of Pommard were reputed to be especially fond of dancing. Indeed, it is said of the women of Pommard that their first pregnancy only lasts three months! There is little likelihood that these aspects of local life are due to the wine, but it is true that the wine of Pommard is endowed with a number of outstanding qualities. It is a strong red wine, fuller-bodied than Beaune. Frequently the colour is a fine, deep red, but with a fairly unsubtle bouquet which may occasionally suggest leather, ripe plums or blackcurrants, or even chocolate. In general, I find that Pommards tend to taste strong but lack depth, purity and subtlety. But because of its strength and robustness, the taste is full and rich. Its full-bodied qualities and its alcoholic strength make it a suitable companion for all kind of game. Describing his own Pommard, Gérard Potel mentioned how well it went together with a good pheasant.

A wine to keep

Pommard needs to be kept a long time before it really comes into its own. It is often thought, incorrectly, that red burgundies do not have to age. Although this may be the case with certain wines, it is absolutely untrue of Pommard. Ordinary Pommards should be left for a minimum of three years, while the Premiers Crus should be given between five and eight years. Only time will give the wines that fine maturity which allows them to display their real virtues. But a Pommard remains a Pommard and rarely becomes supple. You might perhaps compare it to a retired general, whose civilian clothes

Crus of Pommard

Premiers crus:

Les Rugiens, Les Epenots,
Clos de la Commaraine,
Clos Blanc, Les Arvelets,
Les Charmots,
Les Argillières,
Les Pézerolles,
Les Boucherottes,
En Saussilles,
Les Croix Noires,
Les Chaponnières,
Les Fremiets, Les Bertins,
Les Garollières,
Les Poutures,
Les Clos Micot,
Le Refène,
Clos du Verger,
Derrière-Saint-Jean,
La Platière (part),
Les Chanlins-Bas (part),
Les Combes-Dessus (part),
La Chanière (part).

The spelling of these names can often vary.

Other good Pommards are: the Pommard from the Domaine Buisson-Battault in Meursault (from ¾ acre): the Pommard from the Domaine Jean Joliot in Nantoux (from 2½ acres).

Pommard

Opposite page, above
A strange image from the
Château de Pommard, a house
full of curious things.

Opposite page, below:
View of a Pommard slope. The
hills behind the village are
barren and vulnerable to
erosion.

Left:
The houses often conceal
beautiful gardens.

Below:
Jacques Parent on the balcony
of his house. Owner of 37 acres,
he cultivates them with the help
of his son François.

Pommard has no local tasting
centre, but there is a cellar that
serves fondue bourguignonne as
a speciality. This cellar, however,
has been closed for some while,
since it did not have proper fire
protection: rather odd, since
there happens to be a fire-
extinguisher factory in
Pommard.

The old buildings of Pommard
are floodlit during the tourist
season.

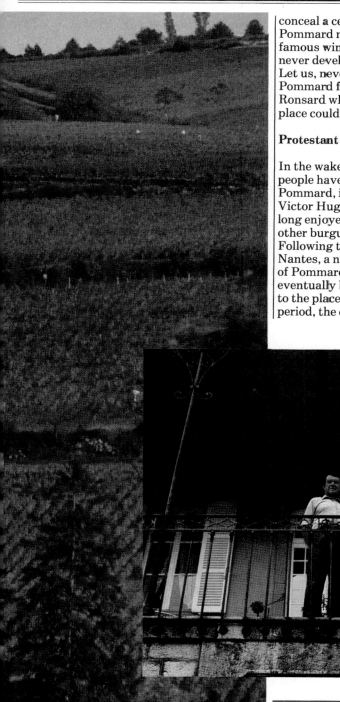

conceal a certain military stiffness. A Pommard never achieves the quality of other famous wines of the Côte d'Or, since it will never develop their grace and distinction. Let us, nevertheless, appreciate the wine of Pommard for what it is in the spirit of Ronsard who marvelled '. . . that such a small place could give birth to such a great wine!'

Protestant propaganda

In the wake of Ronsard, many distinguished people have expressed their admiration of Pommard, including Henri IV, Louis XV and Victor Hugo. Outside France, the wine has long enjoyed a reputation higher than that of other burgundies, for a very good reason. Following the revocation of the Edict of Nantes, a number of Protestant inhabitants of Pommard were forced to emigrate and eventually began to import their native wine to the places where they had settled. At one period, the demand for Pommard increased so swiftly that a number of merchants profited from the demand by selling other wines under the name of Pommard. Pommard has remained a very popular wine, particularly in America; in 1970, for instance, the massive purchases of Pommard for the American market caused the price of the wine to rise to unwarranted levels. This popularity also caused a certain amount of dishonest dealing, such as that reported by Arlott and Fielden in their book: an American importer was accused of selling a much cheaper Gevrey-Chambertin under the label of Pommard. That period of madness now seems to be over and I was told by Jacques Parent that he had been obliged to accept the return of a large part of his Pommard 1972 from his American client, since the wine had become virtually unsaleable because of its excessive price.

Nothing extraordinary

The high standing of Pommard in the trade means that it appears on the lists of most *négociants*, some of whom are also owners of vineyards and cellars in the locality. Unfortunately, the commercial value of Pommard has encouraged a number of wine growers to increase the quantity of their production at the expense of quality. Indeed, the general run of Pommards are of a very moderate quality and, in spite of their high price, it is not easy to find good bottles among them. I have tasted many that were undistinguished, either too acid or too alcoholic, and lacking any real quality. For this we have to turn to the Pommard Premiers Crus.

Château de Pommard

Although certain Pommards can be disappointing, there are others which have become great wines, thanks to the competence and care of their growers. Among these is the Château de Pommard, which comes from the most extensive vineyard in Pommard, covering 50 acres. It is also the largest single continuous vineyard

in the whole Côte d'Or belonging to the same family. The numerous advertising hoardings on the walls indicate that the château sells a considerable part of the vintage directly to visitors and tourists.

It was not without some misgivings, then, that I agreed to taste a number of vintages with the proprietor Jean-Louis Laplanche. However, I now have a number of the château wines in my own cellar and have found them very pleasing indeed, since they conform closely to all the qualities expected of a good Pommard. One of the secrets of

this quality is the age of the vines, at least 80% of which are more than 25 years old. Each year the estate is visited by between 50,000 and 60,000 people who can admire the pretty château and its fine cellars as well as tasting the wine. The château itself is of relatively recent construction and took over its present, important rôle from an older, smaller building, the Châteaux Micault. This has also been in the possession of M. Laplanche and his charming wife since 1965, and they have recently undertaken the restoration of this fine old building.

Château de la Commaraine

Another beautiful estate in Pommard is that of the Château de la Commaraine, the property of Michel Jaboulet-Vercherre. The walls of the château are entirely covered by Virginia creeper, while the building is flanked by a magnificent garden of huge rhododendron bushes on one side and by an extensive vineyard, the Clos de le Commaraine (10 acres), on the other. Anyone who has enjoyed the privilege of being invited to the château will know how warm the welcome is there. M. Jaboulet-Vercherre receives his guests in his private drawing room and may invite them to lunch in a small panelled dining room. I can still remember how the bouquet of a *coq au vin* made with Pommard was enhanced by the wine that we drank with it: a magnum of Clos de la Commaraine 1966. Although traditions are very important at the château (the cellar dates from the 12th century and vinification is carried out according to time-honoured methods), the house of Jaboulet-Vercherre now uses modern techniques — for instance, in its new vinification centre by the Paris-Lyon *autoroute*.

Opposite page, above:
The distinctive bell-tower of the church of Pommard. In the foreground can be seen the château of La Commaraine, its walls covered with Virginia creeper, the property of Jaboulet-Vercherre.

Opposite page, below left:
An old gateway gives on to a courtyard of the Château de Pommard around which are the buildings housing the barrels.

Opposite page, below right:
The arms of the Château de Pommard.

Left:
This old press, dating from the 16th century, is exhibited in the restored reception room at the Château de Pommard.

Below:
Filling the barrels. Each year Pommard produces on average 116,700 cases of red wine with at least 10.5° of alcohol (Premier Cru 11°).

Other Premiers Crus

The Clos de la Commaraine, along with Les Epenots and Les Rugiens, heads the Premiers Crus. Both Les Epenots and Les Petits Epenots are located almost on the boundary with Beaune, and the wine from the two vineyards can perhaps be better classified as Epenots. Just to show that one should not always trust the name of a place, Les Petits Epenots often produces a more impressive wine than Les Epenots, though with the exception of the lower part of the vineyard situated right against the boundary with Beaune. Acquired by the Maison Patriarche, this part produces a rather light wine. In general, however, Les Epenots yields a wine that is round, soft and pleasant to drink, but which should not be kept for too long.

Les Rugiens, both Hauts and Bas, are situated to the south of the village and produce a wine which, thanks to the iron in the ground (Rugiens stems from *rouge*), is much more robust and strong than the others. A good Rugiens, with its characteristic taste of *terroir*, only starts to open out after two years in the barrel and a further two in the bottle. Most of Les Rugiens Premiers Crus, the best, are from Les Rugiens-Bas; the wines of Les Rugiens-Hauts, not all of which are classified as Premiers Crus, are of lower quality. Yet the labels never mention the difference!

A gentle giant

Michel Gaunoux is considered by many wine experts to be the finest wine grower of Pommard, along with Jacques Parent and Comte Armand; and it was at the Gaunoux property that I was privileged to taste an exceptionally fine Rugiens. When I arrived, a number of the owner's German friends were already sampling his Rugiens 1962, and I was invited to take part in the tasting. I was then able to see how well the wine had matured, 14 years after its vintaging. Its bouquet was fat, rich and firm, its colour deep yet bright, while the taste was marked by a subtlety from which all trace of initial hardness had disappeared. It was a wine that could almost be described as a gentle giant, hiding its strength under a velvet cloak. In spite of the beautiful weather, which was especially fine and warm that day, the taste of that Pommard made me long for a mid-winter's day, snow outside, a great log fire inside, and an excellent game dinner.

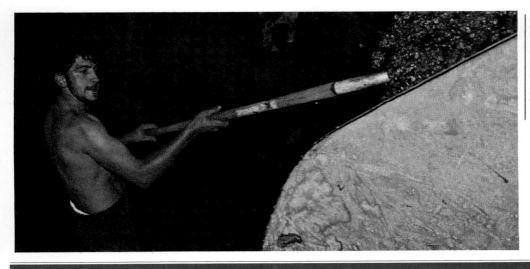

Volnay

Côte de Beaune

Leaving Pommard, the *route nationale 73* leads us to Volnay. Unlike most of the villages of the Côte d'Or, Volnay looks out over its vineyards and can be seen from a considerable distance. There is a magnificent view from its houses over the vine-covered slopes and the plain of the Saône. The unique geographical position of Volnay has inspired the local saying: 'In spite of Pommard and Meursault, Volnay will always remain the highest.' The siting of the village also encouraged the Dukes of Burgundy to build a château there from which, according to historians, they could enjoy the beauty of the countryside, the purity of the air and the excellence of the wines. This château was entirely destroyed in 1749 and no longer exists, but fortunately the countryside, the air and the good wine have survived. The little square by the church is especially picturesque.

The crossbowmen of Volnay

In addition to its wine and its château, Volnay could also boast a company of crossbowmen who, at the time of the Dukes, were the élite corps first of the Burgundian army and later of the army of the King of France. To test and improve the skill of the bowmen, an annual competition was started in 1393 during which they had to shoot down a parrot. The winner, who was crowned 'king', was excused for a whole year from work in the vineyards, and from military fatigues and billets. Little now remains of the past: the 14th-century church, a 15th-century chapel and a few old houses. But the wine has lost none of its glory.

Royal partiality

The annals of Volnay contain numerous references to the glory of its wine. History recounts that wine from Volnay was already sought after in Italy during the 6th century. It was Volnay that was served at the coronation of Philippe de Valois in Reims in 1328. The king was so impressed with the wine that, several years later, he visited Volnay with Duke Eudes IV to renew at greater length his acquaintanceship with the wine that had so pleased him. When the king left, Duke Eudes made him a present of over 4,000 gallons of Volnay which were no doubt gratefully consumed during the many festivities of the royal court.
Louis XI was also a great admirer of Volnay; after his conquest of Burgundy, he confiscated the whole of the 1477 vintage and had it transported to his château of

Régis Rossignol (a very common family name in Volnay) lives near the route nationale and owns 7½ acres in Volnay. His wines, somewhat acid when young, have a deep colour and become gentler with keeping.

After the death of Louis Glantenay in 1980, the estate (21 acres) was taken over by his son Bernard, who frequently produces a charming, supple and elegant wine. Not quite of the highest rank, but delicious all the same.

I have tasted a very characteristic Volnay in the beautiful cellars of the Maison Raoul Clerget at Saint-Aubin; its bouquet was especially delicate and fine. Though lacking great distinction, it was nevertheless excellent.

The Clos des Ducs vineyard, property of the Marquis d'Angerville, is located close to the northern part of the village. Fine colour, delicate bouquet and a subtle, multifaceted taste.

Plessis-les-Tours. No doubt he was only too aware of the popular belief that Volnay was a great inducer of happiness.

Another French king who was very fond of Volnay was Louis XIV, while after the coronation of Louis XV, it was Volnay that was served, together with Beaune and Pommard. The Volnay of those times, however, was very different from that we know today. Bossuet's cheerful promise to his nephew of a meal of oysters and Volnay confirms the fact that between the 14th and the 18th centuries the wine was much lighter in colour than it is now. During that period it had the 'partridge-eye' tawny-gold colour, which was especially sought in fine wines. This colour was obtained by a short period of fermentation, during which the must only came into brief contact with the skins. The wine was then drunk during its first year and was not allowed to age. It was only after the French Revolution, in response to the taste of Dutch and German connoisseurs, that wines were produced with a deeper colour which could be kept longer. It was at that period, too, that the last white vines disappeared.

Feminine grace

Although the wine of Volnay has acquired greater colour and body since the 18th century, it still remains anything but dull and heavy. The Volnay of the Côte de Beaune can be compared with the

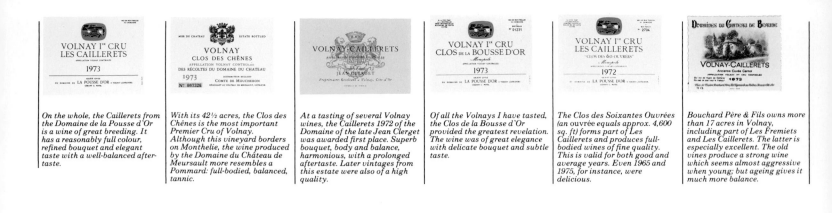

On the whole, the Caillerets from the Domaine de la Pousse d'Or is a wine of great breeding. It has a reasonably full colour, refined bouquet and elegant taste with a well-balanced after-taste.

With its 42½ acres, the Clos des Chênes is the most important Premier Cru of Volnay. Although this vineyard borders on Monthelie, the wine produced by the Domaine du Château de Meursault more resembles a Pommard: full-bodied, balanced, tannic.

At a tasting of several Volnay wines, the Caillerets 1972 of the Domaine of the late Jean Clerget was awarded first place. Superb bouquet, body and balance, harmonious, with a prolonged aftertaste. Later vintages from this estate were also of a high quality.

Of all the Volnays I have tasted, the Clos de la Bousse d'Or provided the greatest revelation. The wine was of great elegance with delicate bouquet and subtle taste.

The Clos des Soixantes Ouvrées (an ouvrée equals approx. 4,600 sq. ft) forms part of Les Caillerets and produces full-bodied wines of fine quality. This is valid for both good and average years. Even 1965 and 1975, for instance, were delicious.

Bouchard Père & Fils owns more than 17 acres in Volnay, including part of Les Fremiets and Les Caillerets. The latter is especially excellent. The old vines produce a strong wine which seems almost aggressive when young; but ageing gives it much more balance.

Volnay

Côte de Beaune

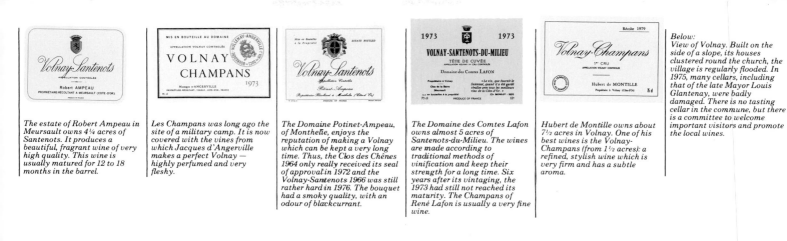

The estate of Robert Ampeau in Meursault owns 4¼ acres of Santenots. It produces a beautiful, fragrant wine of very high quality. This wine is usually matured for 12 to 18 months in the barrel.

Les Champans was long ago the site of a military camp. It is now covered with the vines from which Jacques d'Angerville makes a perfect Volnay — highly perfumed and very fleshy.

The Domaine Potinet-Ampeau, of Monthélie, enjoys the reputation of making a Volnay which can be kept a very long time. Thus, the Clos des Chênes 1964 only really received its seal of approval in 1972 and the Volnay-Santenots 1966 was still rather hard in 1976. The bouquet had a smoky quality, with an odour of blackcurrant.

The Domaine des Comtes Lafon owns almost 5 acres of Santenots-du-Milieu. The wines are made according to traditional methods of vinification and keep their strength for a long time. Six years after its vintaging, the 1973 had still not reached its maturity. The Champans of René Lafon is usually a very fine wine.

Hubert de Montille owns about 7½ acres in Volnay. One of his best wines is the Volnay-Champans (from 1½ acres): a refined, stylish wine which is very firm and has a subtle aroma.

Below:
View of Volnay. Built on the side of a slope, its houses clustered round the church, the village is regularly flooded. In 1975, many cellars, including that of the late Mayor Louis Glantenay, were badly damaged. There is no tasting cellar in the commune, but there is a committee to welcome important visitors and promote the local wines.

Chambolle-Musigny of the Côte de Nuits. It exhibits the same feminine grace, though perhaps with a shade less breeding. Camille Rodier notes: 'The wines of Volnay are remarkable for their elegance, their smooth taste, perfect balance and delicate bouquet. After the wines of Musigny, they are the finest in the whole of Burgundy'. The strong bouquet of the Volnays often suggests the scent of violets or of budding wild flowers.

Differences of vinification

A Volnay cannot be described in general terms; there are differences of both class and character between many of the wines. As already stressed, the quality of a wine is dependent on a number of factors: type of vine, age of the plants and the method of vinification, among many others. Some growers prefer to produce a wine which is light and fragile, clear in colour, while others make wines that need to be kept a long time before reaching maturity, simply by subjecting the must of the grape to a long period of fermentation.

For example, I have tasted a Volnay Caillerets Clos des Soixante Ouvrées 1964 at the Domaine de la Pousse d'Or which reminded me of all kinds of wine, except Volnay; it was strongly coloured and had considerable body. I have also been told by Régis Rossignol, owner of a small vineyard, that he prefers a stronger, tannic Volnay — effects he tries to achieve in his own wine. And even though he occasionally admits to wanting to produce a lighter, more supple wine, he always goes back to his old methods when the time comes for vinification. His friends would much prefer him to carry on in this way.

Three types of subsoil

Another factor with a strong influence on the character of a Volnay is the composition of the subsoil. In this respect, the slope can be divided into three bands which run parallel to route nationale 73. The highest band starts just below the village and includes the vineyards closest to Volnay. The subsoil of this band is very chalky. In the Clos des Ducs, which belongs to the Marquis d'Angerville, for example, the proportion of calcareous soil is as high as 50%. The vines therefore tend to produce a wine which is delicate, often light in body, although fairly alcoholic.

The second band stretches along either side of the route nationale and includes land with a high iron content; the percentage of chalk in this area is never higher than 25%. The rocky subsoil is covered by a relatively thin reddish layer of topsoil. Here are to be found the most famous vineyards of Volnay: Les Caillerets, Les Chevrets, La Pousse d'Or and Les Champans. These all yield wines of a fine colour, a bouquet which can be very strong, and a rich, complex taste.

The low-lying land of the final band produces wines which are less fine. The vines here grow in deep, damp earth and yield wines that lack body. While most of the vineyards located on the upper part of the slope are Premiers Crus, the lower ones rarely enjoy that status.

A wine-growing marquis

The commune of Volnay has about 555 acres of vineyard which have the right to the appellation d'origine contrôlée Volnay and Volnay Premier Cru. These are divided between 70 owners. The whole population of Volnay (460 inhabitants) makes a living from the vine, except for the two families who own the two small shops in the village. Volnay, like every wine-growing village, has its own élite of cultivators. One of them, the Marquis Jacques d'Angerville, uses cellars located close to the old ducal château. The Marquis owns 35 acres of vines, which include the whole of the Clos des Ducs (6 acres), about 10 acres of Champagne (the greater part) and several smaller plots of Les Fremiets, Les Caillerets and other Premiers Crus. With the exception of his Fremiets, which has been marketed for several years by the house of

Pinot, Jacques d'Angerville sells his own wines. Unlike other owners, who take little or no interest in their vineyards, the Marquis plays an active part in their running. He supervises personally all the business of the vineyards and takes the important decisions himself. During the important operation of vinification, for instance, it is he who decides whether to remove the stalks or not and in what proportion. He also supervises the fermentation process, determining the temperature and length of time the wine should stay in the vat. The vinification methods he uses are the traditional ones: the fermentation vats are made of oak and each year some of the casks are renewed. The wine may remain in the cask for one to two years, according to the quality of the vintage. It is always filtered at the bottling stage. This careful attention to detail produces a wine which is much in demand throughout the world and one which frequently appears on the wine lists of the best restaurants.

A Volnay from Meursault

Jacques d'Angerville (a calm, thoughtful man of considerable erudition) also owns 2½ acres of Les Santenots in Meursault, in addition to his Volnay vineyards. This yields a white wine which is sold under the *appellation* Meursault-Santenots. There is also a red wine called Volnay-Santenots which, although it comes from Meursault, can bear the name of its neighbour. Curiously enough, there does seem to be a preference on the part of the Meursault wine growers for red varieties in Les Santenots and a preference for white on the part of those from Volnay. The reason for this curiosity was explained to me by Jacques d'Angerville: in a commune dedicated to the production of red wine, the growers only need to produce white wine for their own consumption, while the reverse is true for a white wine commune. Personally, I prefer the red Volnay-Santenots to the white

Meursault-Santenots. The first is usually a very good wine, while the latter is often too full-bodied.

The Domaine de la Pousse d'Or

Describing the wines of Volnay a hundred years ago, a local poet singled out those of the Pousse d'Or as being 'diamonds set in gold'. Even today, this name still enjoys a position of rare distinction among the wines of Volnay; the vineyard is now the heart of the Domaine de la Pousse d'Or, which has been increasingly successful during the past few years.

The difference in spelling between Bousse d'Or and Pousse d'Or dates from 1967 and came about following a decree which forbade an estate to bear the name of an individual vineyard, if the latter, as was the case of La Pousse d'Or, included wines from other vineyards. The Domaine de la Romanée-Conti (of which La Pousse d'Or previously formed part) is the exception which proves the rule. La Pousse d'Or is currently under the supervision of a well-qualified man, Gérard Potel, whose family owns the majority of the shares in the vineyard. In addition to its holdings in Volnay (32 acres), La Pousse d'Or also owns 10 acres in Santenay and about 2½ acres in Pommard. All these vineyards are classified as Premiers Crus and are remarkable for the exceptional quality of their wines.

A vineyard of quality

Situated close to the main road and the vineyard of La Bousse d'Or, and opposite the old chapel of the cemetery, the Domaine de la Pousse d'Or can be seen from a long way off. Gérard Potel and his family live in a beautiful large house, which has been decorated with great taste. It houses a remarkable collection of paintings, water-colours and drawings which would be the envy of most serious collectors. The Clos de

la Bousse d'Or (5¼ acres) produces annually an average of 9,000 bottles of wine which would be a credit to any vineyard. I was especially impressed by its qualities during an unforgettable tasting in the cellars of the house. Of all the red wines of the Côte d'Or, the Bousse d'Or is, in my opinion, undoubtedly the finest; its delicate qualities are as pleasing to the nose as to the palate. I tasted several vintages, including that of 1973, which was a fairly damp year in Burgundy. Gérard Potel told how he had managed to obtain a wine of fine colour, bouquet and taste, in spite of the weather conditions. The lighter unfermented wine (the barrels where the skin had had very little fermentation time with the must) was used to make rosé, and only the finest barrels were reserved for the Bousse d'Or. The Clos de la Bousse d'Or is, in my opinion, as near to a perfect wine as can exist in this village: the apotheosis of a true Volnay.

Les Caillerets

I have tasted a number of other wines besides that of the Domaine de la Pousse d'Or. Indeed, the opposite of that supremely elegant wine seems to me to be the Volnay Caillerets Clos des Soixante Ouvrées, with its strength and richness. Produced by an enclave of 6 acres in the vineyard of Les Caillerets, the Clos des Soixante Ouvrées was the best wine of the whole vineyard in 1975; an average of 10,000 bottles a year are produced. Les Caillerets is situated in the middle band of the Volnay vineyards and is therefore on land which is characterized by a topsoil with high iron content, rarely more than 1 ft deep, over a bed of granite immediately underneath. The Domaine de la Pousse d'Or also owns 6¾ acres in Les Caillerets which yield a wine of great breeding, but one ageing much more rapidly than that of the Clos. A good Caillerets is still one of the strongest wines of Volnay and it is sometimes justifiably described as being

Opposite page, left:
Gérard Potel, the director of the Domaine de la Pousse d'Or, carefully examines the colour of one of his wines.

Opposite page, right:
Bottles of Volnay Clos des Ducs, one of the most distinguished wines of Volnay.

Left:
The entrance to the old cellars of Clos des Ducs, property of Marquis Jacques d'Angerville.

Below:
Gérard Potel, his wife and their daughter in their drawing room. The present vineyard employs five people and dates from 1964. It produces an average of 55,000 bottles a year.

More bottled wine is sold in Volnay than in Pommard, a situation which has existed for a long time.

To the south of the village a statue dedicated to Notre-Dame des Vignes indicates the spot where the Prussian invasion was halted in 1870. A thanksgiving procession takes place every year after the harvests.

Another Volnay that needs to be mentioned is the Volnay Clos des Chênes from Joseph Drouhin, usually with a fairly deep colour, rather firm and of very good quality.

'too big' for the commune. Les Caillerets (including Caillerets-Dessus) has a total area of more than 42 acres divided between numerous owners. It is in this vineyard that Bouchard Père & Fils produces its 'Ancienne Cuvée Carnot', the vinification of which is controlled with great care. The Caillerets produced by Jean Clerget is also a wine of exceptional quality. The renown of this vineyard is emphasized by the local dictum that the person who has no vines in Les Caillerets does not know the true worth of the wine of Volnay.

The vineyard of Les Mandennes has been restored to cultivation by Louis Deschamps, the veteran wine grower of Monthelie. His Monthelie is both supple and fresh, with a long-lasting aftertaste.

Michel Deschamps, the son of Louis, is president of the wine-growers' association. His wine can be excellent: deep-coloured and robust in good years, lighter in less successful years.

The maiden name of Mme René Thévenin was Monthelie, hence the name of the vineyard. Some 7½ acres, including part of the Premier Cru Meix-Bataille, produce a successful wine which needs to be kept three or four years. It often displays great similarity to a good Volnay.

Comte Robert Suremain owns about 17 acres of old vines at Monthelie. Although it is fairly limited, the quality is high and this elegant Monthelie ages well. The good vintages need to be kept for at least 10 years.

Jacques Parent of Pommard owns 7½ acres at Monthelie, which produces a wine that is more agreeable and lighter than his Pommard. Though not exceptional, it is pleasant and has character.

With Chanson Père & Fils, Ropiteau is one of the rare houses to produce a Monthelie. The Clos des Champs-Fulliot is a delicious, elegant and agreeably harmonious wine.

Monthelie

According to one past historian, the name of Monthelie comes from 'Mont-Oloye', a Celtic expression designating a high point of the road. This explanation would seem to be borne out by the local geography, for Monthelie is indeed sited on a hill up which climbs the main street of the village.

It is worth pointing out here that the name of Monthelie is incorrectly spelt in a number of books (including those by Lichine, Schoonmaker, Yoxall and others); the 'e' of the second syllable is silent and should not, therefore, bear any accent.

Monthelie, nowadays a modest village of 200 inhabitants, once enjoyed a position of great importance in the form of certain sovereign rights granted in 1078 by Duke Hugo I to the monks of Cluny. Two centuries later and until the middle of the 18th century, the inhabitants of Meursault were obliged to attend mass in the church of Monthelie because the church of Meursault was falling down and the chapel of the château was not large enough to hold such a congregation. The estate was then supposed to have been acquired by a pharmacist from Beaune who claimed to have discovered all kinds of therapeutic qualities in the local wine, but the existence of this great estate was definitively ended by the Revolution.

More wine than bread

The beginnings of the cultivation of wine at Monthelie are unknown. History does, however, recount that there were vineyards in the commune by 1475, which was when the local inhabitants started to cultivate the lands of the monks of Cluny. A former mayor, Comte Robert de Suremain, showed me the original deed, which is on a roll of parchment measuring about 17½ ft in length, granting these concessions. Two old sayings evoke the problems of the monks and wine growers in making the vines grow on the inhospitable land of Monthelie. The first notes that the village is 'a wine-growing area, but without water and arable land'; the second claims that 'in Monthelie, the poultry die of hunger during the harvest'. There was wine enough, then, at Monthelie to quench the thirst, but too little bread to satisfy the appetite.

Limited expansion

The wine of Monthelie is not widely known because relatively little is produced. During the past few years, however, a number of new vineyards have sprung up; yet the total area in cultivation is not more than 330 acres producing an average of 38,000 cases of red, and about 780 cases of a light white wine which has a tendency to become maderized. In general, new vineyards do not produce wines of high quality, but those of Monthelie seems to be the exception to the rule. On two occasions Louis Deschamps has been awarded a first prize for his Monthelie produced from a recent vineyard situated in Les Mandennes. This wine was considered even superior to the Premiers Crus.

There is a high degree of cooperation between the local wine growers, 17 of whom have recently built themselves a small tasting cellar, Les Caves de Monthelie, where 15,000 bottles are sold annually.

Similarities to Volnay

The price of the wines of Monthelie have for a long time been close to those of Volnay. At the end of the 19th century, Dr Lavalle wrote that the quality of the fine wines of Monthelie almost equalled that of the wines of its neighbour; and certainly Monthelie and Volnay are not only neighbours but are also very similar to each other. The wines of Monthelie are undoubtedly a little less fine than those of Volnay, but they do have the same light consistency. Despite their very feminine character, though, the wines of Monthelie are fairly full-bodied and age well. I have tasted a Monthelie 1969 at the property of the Comte de Suremain which had still yet to open out and which seemed

The Potinet-Ampeau estate is the owner of 27¼ acres, of which about 7½ acres are in the commune of Monthelie. This vineyard produces a wine which is usually allowed two years to mature in the barrel and a further two years in the bottle, at least for the red. The Monthelie is generally full-bodied with a clean taste.

Opposite page, centre:
New barrels represent a considerable investment, especially for a small vineyard. Ageing barrels are therefore carefully maintained and repaired.

Opposite page, below:
After the harvest, the containers which are used to transport the grapes are carefully cleaned. Here, they can be seen piled up pyramid-form.

Below:
View of the Château de Monthelie, the property of Comte Robert de Suremain.

Inheritance involves such a dividing up of the vineyard that the heirs, not wishing to cultivate a small vineyard which could not conceivably pay for itself, prefer to sell their part and leave the area. In 1976, one hectare (2.47 acres) at Monthelie could fetch 200,000 French francs.

As in the majority of the wine-growing communes of the Côte d'Or, flooding is relatively frequent at Monthelie. According to grower Louis Deschamps, whose own cellar was completely flooded in 1975, such a disaster happens every seven or eight years. Since 1976, the commune has taken certain measures to guard against flooding.

even harder than the 1971 I had tasted immediately before. It was only after it had been swirled around my glass for several moments that it began to open out. The Comte told me that a good vintage Monthelie should be well aired after it has been in the bottle for a long time, rather as a long unoccupied bedroom needs to have the windows thrown open before being used again.

Notable vineyards

It would be natural to expect the most notable vineyard of Monthelie to be that of

Les Duresses, a Premier Cru partly located in the commune of Auxey-Duresses, about 2½ acres of which are owned by the Hospices de Beaune. In fact, the distinction belongs to two vineyards close to Le Clos des Chênes of Volnay: Les Champs-Fulliot and Sur Lavelle. Ropiteau is one of the rare houses where I have tasted a Monthelie Champs-Fulliot. Very agreeable and well-balanced, this wine had more body than a Duresses of the same house. I drank it first with a tender saddle of lamb and later with a mild Brillat-Savarin cheese; in each case, the wine complemented the food perfectly.

The Domaine Buisson-Battault in Meursault owns well over 12¼ acres, of which about 10 acres are in the commune itself. The wines are excellent, even the simplest Meursault, Charmes, Genevrières and Goutte d'Or.

Louis Jadot usually produces a stylish Meursault with a fine, limpid colouring with green tints and a delicate perfume of ripe fruit. The taste tends to be rich with a spicy flavour. A very well-balanced wine. The Meursault-Blagny from Latour is always enjoyable.

Louis Latour, best known for his Corton-Charlemagne, also makes a very good Meursault. The wine is often fruity with a well-rounded taste and aroma. Satisfying, sometimes slightly spicy aftertaste.

The Château Meursault 1973 was the first vintage made by the Maison Patriarche of Beaune after buying the château, the vineyard and the trade mark 'Comte de Moucheron'. Well perfumed, fruity, with a taste of oak, since the new wine is stored each year in new barrels. Recent vintages have also been excellent.

The Domaine Jacques Prieur owns about 34½ acres on the Côte d'Or, of which 8¾ acres are in Meursault. Clos de Mazeray produces both white and red wines. I prefer the white which can be very fruity and have a fresh, supple taste.

The Marquis d'Angerville owns about 2½ acres of Les Santenots. From them he produces a fruity white wine, which is also notable for its freshness and grace.

Meursault

It is not necessary to spend very long in Meursault to see that it is a very important wine-growing village. Its narrow, winding streets could almost have been laid out in the uncertain footsteps of those suffering from an excess of its fine wines. Nor was it by chance that the film director Gérard Oury chose this typically French wine village as the setting for his great comic film, *La Grande Vadrouille*. A number of the hilarious adventures of Louis de Funès, Bourvil and Terry Thomas take place in the town hall, a high building with glazed tiles which stands on the ruins of a once-imposing château. Opposite, the church is especially notable for its 15th-century tower, the spire of which is one of the highest in the whole of

Burgundy (187 ft). There is a local legend that it was built by the fairies. On the church square is the Hôtel du Chevreuil, a somewhat decayed establishment which used to be famous for its cuisine and *cuisinière*, Mère Daugier.

The Château de Meursault

Meursault, which is a relatively large village with about 1,750 inhabitants, boasts some fine buildings and two châteaux as well as its town hall. The château, which can be seen from *route nationale 74*, was built in attractive white stone during the 17th century on older foundations. It was owned for a long time by the late Comte de

Moucheron and was eventually offered for sale in 1973. Among the possible purchasers were a group of Japanese who were seen one day actually counting the vines! The château, however, remained in French hands and was bought by André Boisseaux, of Patriarche Père & Fils. The main building had been uninhabited since 1940, but that and the outbuildings have now been entirely restored. Today, the numerous visitors to the château can see a fine collection of paintings in the salons and an impressive number of objects and bottles set out in the magnificent cellars. The new owners have turned the park in front of the château into a vineyard. This change brought protests from an ecological society in Puligny-Montrachet,

The Domaine Matrot of the hamlet of Blagny produces both red and white wines. The white Meursault-Blagny comes from an area of 4½ acres and has a less rich, flatter flavour than the usual Meursault, but it is a pleasant wine. This is also true of the red Blagny La Pièce sous le Bois.

The Domaine Matrot produces high-quality wines from its 37 acres. The best of the white wines is probably the Meursault-Charmes which, in good years, has an almost luxuriant perfume and taste: produced from 3 acres.

In 1955, Ropiteau entirely replanted its 4 acres of Les Poruzots. This holding produces a very elegant, strong wine, with a very distinctive taste. Even finer is the Genevrières, produced from just under 2½ acres.

Les Genevrières is one of the best Meursaults of Bernard Michelot. He owns 3¼ acres and makes a wine which is distinguished by its strong but subtle taste and its light, almost timid bouquet. Michelot also produces a Charmes and Perrières, both excellent.

Other good Meursaults not mentioned elsewhere come from the following estates: Potinet-Ampeau (Monthelie); Pitoiset-Urena; Michelot-Garnier (Clos St Félix); Ballot-Millot; Auguste Morey-Genelot; Marquis de Monteclair; Léon Ozga; Millot-Battault; Jean Monnier; François Jobard.

and not without some justification, since the fine trees of the park were replaced by vines planted in land of only mediocre quality which does not even qualify for the *appellation* Meursault.

Disappearance of the tasting centre

Apart from Beaune itself, Meursault attracts more visitors than any other village of the Côte. In summer, the 'Grappe d'Or'

Opposite page:
Les Tessons vineyard, Meursault. The commune is twinned with Rüdesheim in Germany and with Leignon in Belgium. L'Hôpital de Meursault is a district in the village where there is a factory making tractors for the vineyards.

Below:
André Ropiteau in his father's wonderful library. He runs the Domaine Ropiteau-Mignon (87 acres), to which the house of Ropiteau Frères (the property of Chantovent) has exclusive rights. Half the vines on the estate are situated in Meursault.

camping site, which is on a hill near the centre, teems with tourists — especially Belgian, Dutch and German — who have come to Meursault to taste its wines. For many years, Meursault enjoyed the benefits of a tasting centre, the *Maison de Meursault,* which was located in the neighbouring hamlet of l'Hôpital de Meursault (where a leper colony had been founded in 1180). The wines for the *Maison de Meursault* were made available by 40 wine growers who each provided one barrel every year. The *Maison de Meursault* was finally closed because the growers eventually preferred to sell their wines from their own cellars and also because the wine of Meursault became so well known that collective publicity became pointless. It is worth noting the high number of advertising hoardings in Meursault which publicize direct sales from the grower who also bottles his own wine. This is especially true in the street which leads in the direction

of Puligny-Montrachet. The *Maison de Meursault* has now become an ordinary restaurant.

The Paulée de Meursault

At least once a year, every village of the Côte enjoys a period of celebration at the time of the wine harvest, but at Meursault there is also a special feast, the Paulée de Meursault, which is always held on the third Monday of November, thus bringing to an end the period of festivities known as the Trois Glorieuses of Burgundy.

The Paulée was originally intended as a feast to bring together the owners and the workers at the end of the harvest period. A pig would then be slaughtered and the flesh fried quickly in a frying-pan (*poêle*), from which utensil the feast undoubtedly got its name. In 1932, Comte Lafon decided to organize a great banquet for wine growers, press and clients, to promote the sale of Meursault wine. There were 35 guests at that first Paulée and all the growers present had to bring their best bottles. The following year, the feast was attended by 90 guests; nowadays, there are 400, the maximum number which can be held in the main banqueting hall of Meursault. The wine growers, *négociants* and their clients are obviously given priority as guests, but the number of places is limited and these have to be reserved at least six months in advance. The Paulée is always a very substantial banquet, naturally with wines in abundance. In 1974, for example, the menu was: *terrine de canard au poivre vert, suprêmes de lotte Joinville, jambon au Meursault, faisans à l'ancienne,* cheeses and Meursault in plenty. Tradition dictates that all the guests, but especially the growers, bring the wine; so much is brought that the tables groan under the weight of the bottles. Every year, too, at the Paulée, a literary prize is awarded to a well-known author. The prize, very suitably, consists of 100 bottles of Meursault, donated, each year, by one of the growers.

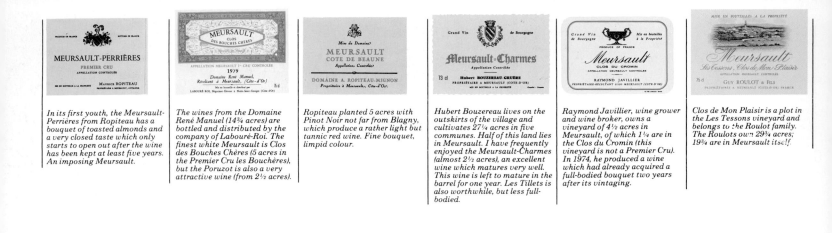

In its first youth, the Meursault-Perrières from Ropiteau has a bouquet of toasted almonds and a very closed taste which only starts to open out after the wine has been kept at least five years. An imposing Meursault.

The wines from the Domaine René Manuel (14¾ acres) are bottled and distributed by the company of Labouré-Roi. The finest white Meursault is Clos des Bouches Chères (5 acres in the Premier Cru les Bouchères), but the Poruzot is also a very attractive wine (from 2½ acres).

Ropiteau planted 5 acres with Pinot Noir not far from Blagny, which produce a rather light but tannic red wine. Fine bouquet, limpid colour.

Hubert Bouzereau lives on the outskirts of the village and cultivates 27¼ acres in five communes. Half of this land lies in Meursault. I have frequently enjoyed the Meursault-Charmes (almost 2½ acres), an excellent wine which matures very well. This wine is left to mature in the barrel for one year. Les Tillets is also worthwhile, but less full-bodied.

Raymond Javillier, wine grower and wine broker, owns a vineyard of 4½ acres in Meursault, of which 1¼ are in the Clos du Cromin (this vineyard is not a Premier Cru). In 1974, he produced a wine which had already acquired a full-bodied bouquet two years after its vintaging.

Clos de Mon Plaisir is a plot in the Les Tessons vineyard and belongs to the Roulot family. The Roulots own 29¾ acres; 19¾ are in Meursault itself.

Origins of the village name

According to Pierre Forgeot, the primitive form of the village name was 'murasalt', meaning a high, fortified camp. Other etymologists have claimed, however, that it derived from 'muris saltus', meaning the distance which can be jumped by a rat. This hypothesis, allegedly based on the fact that the red vines are only separated from the white by that distance, seems very far-fetched. The wine-growing area covered by white varieties is considerably more extensive than that of the red. The latter are planted principally at the southern and northern extremities of the commune. The quantities of the wines produced show how much more important the white is in Meursault: on average 170,000 cases, as opposed to some 9,700 cases of red.

Blagny

There are three sorts of red Meursault: Meursault Rouge *tout court*, Volnay-Santenots (see page 114) and Blagny. The name of Meursault does not appear on the bottle labels of the last two. Blagny is a group of houses situated on the side of the slope to the south of Meursault and very close to the boundary with Puligny-Montrachet. A tiny island of trees and stone in the surrounding green ocean of vines, this hamlet is near the quarries which provided Chancellor Rolin with the paving stones for the 50 steps of L'Hôtel-Dieu in Beaune in 1441.
Red Blagny is produced by a number of Premiers Crus with picturesque names: 'La

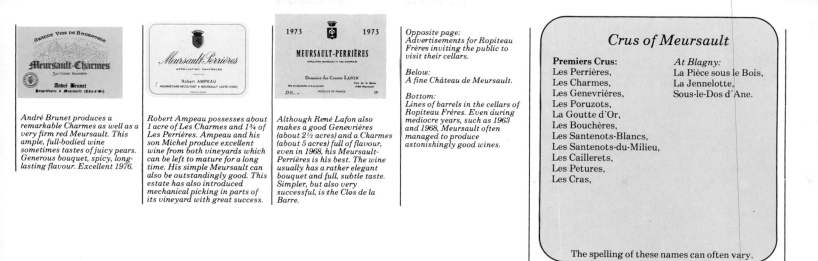

Crus of Meursault

Premiers Crus:
Les Perrières,
Les Charmes,
Les Genevrières,
Les Poruzots,
La Goutte d'Or,
Les Bouchères,
Les Santenots-Blancs,
Les Santenots-du-Milieu,
Les Caillerets,
Les Petures,
Les Cras,

At Blagny:
La Pièce sous le Bois,
La Jennelotte,
Sous-le-Dos d'Ane.

The spelling of these names can often vary.

Pièce sous le Bois' or 'Sous le Dos d'Ane'. The number of owners is relatively low; for example, there are only four for the whole of 'La Pièce sous le Bois'. Red Blagny is a rather hard, rough wine. Its bouquet, which could justifiably be called 'savage', lacks delicacy. Mme Matrot, of the vineyard which bears her name, told me: 'Blagny is a wine you either like or you don't. But those who do tend to remain faithful to it.' There is also a white Blagny bearing the legal *appellation* of Meursault-Blagny. Since part of the vineyards of Blagny are located in Puligny-Montrachet, that commune also produces a red Blagny; I particularly like the one from the Domaine Leflaive at Puligny.

Soft and well-bred

Although red Meursault, which is produced in tiny quantities, does not enjoy much of a reputation, the white can keep company with the most distinguished, and it is to its white wine that the commune owes its fame. It would be hard to disagree with the local saying that 'he who drinks Meursault neither lives nor dies foolish'. In addition to its beautiful golden colour, white Meursault, naturally rich in glycerine, has a soft, round taste which still retains a high degree of freshness. A faint odour of nuts and spicy flavours can often be detected in its very fruity bouquet. The really good vintages often suggest ripe grapes or peaches which have been gathered on hot days. The breeding and grace of Meursault make it an ideal companion to a *poulet à la crême* and all freshwater fish, especially pike. I can also recommend sweetbread braised *au Meursault* and other dishes with veal.

A wine to keep

In spite of its soft and pleasant qualities, Meursault is still strong enough to age well. The oldest Meursault I have tasted dated from 1885. Notwithstanding its great age, I was as much taken by its freshness as I was charmed by its amber colouring, its slightly spicy bouquet and velvety taste. In 1976 I had the opportunity of tasting a number of Meursaults whose age ranged from 6 to 15 years. They had all retained their freshness and, surprisingly enough, the oldest of them, a Meursault Sainte-Anne 1961 from Patriarche Père & Fils, seemed still so young that it would have been impossible to guess its age; indeed, it could easily have been taken for a 1970 or 1972. The Meursault-Genevrières 1963 from Les Hospices de Beaune was similarly surprising: after being kept for 15 years it had lost none of its mettle. I also much enjoyed the fresh Meursault Les Poruzots 1970 from Ropiteau Frères.

Considerable differences

A tasting session in the shady cellar of Bernard Michelot, the good-natured president of the local wine growers' syndicate (there are about 65 vineyards in the commune), showed how different the numerous *crus* of Meursault can be. Bernard Michelot offered me four Meursaults 1975 straight from the barrel. He began with one from the lower part of the slope which he took first from an older barrel and then from a new one. The latter was a markedly more forthcoming wine. I then tasted a Meursault from a vineyard above the Premiers Crus, which seemed rather light. Finally, M. Michelot produced a wine from a vineyard located below the Premiers Crus, which was at first hard to distinguish from a Premier Cru. However, the Meursault-Charmes which I tasted last gave me the chance to establish a pecking order for the wines. In fact, one really needs to experience such a tasting to understand the amazing diversity of the wines of Meursault. Even among wines of a similar type, the differences of style, taste and breed can be considerable.

Six white Premiers Crus

The finest white Premiers Crus of Meursault are all located to the south of the village, on the long slopes of a hill which stretches as far as Puligny-Montrachet and ends with the famous vineyard of Montrachet.
In order of acreage, these premiers Crus are: Les Charmes, Les Perrières, Les Genevrières, La Goutte d'Or, Les Bouchères and Les Poruzots. Each of these Premiers Crus produces a distinct and well-defined wine, except perhaps for La Goutte d'Or and Les Bouchères where the differences are less marked. I would personally place these two at the bottom of the list; they produce strong, full wines, with an agreeable taste, but with a less elegant bouquet than the others. I would award the fourth place to Les Charmes, which I have heard compared to 'a

jolly Burgundian, richly dressed, with the gift of making friends easily.' This is usually a fat, fleshy wine, with a slight taste of spices. The name of the wine has lent itself easily to use in jokes, for which wine growers have a particular fondness; for instance, 'the charms (Charmes) of Mme X are frozen or damaged by hail, those of Mme Y have already bloomed, but those of Mme Z have just been harvested . . .'

The three greats

The Premier Cru of Les Poruzots is almost unknown because it is so small, only 10

acres. Despite its lightness in comparison to the others, I would still place it in third place; its grace, elegance and freshness amply compensate for that weakness. Les Genevrières is, however, a worthy second. This wine, very different from Les Charmes, takes its name from the junipers (*genévriers*) which used to grow on the land now occupied by the vineyard. In character, it can perhaps best be described as resembling a serious, reserved intellectual, whose company is sought for his conversation. Generally speaking, a Meursault-Genevrières is a finer wine than Les Charmes; its taste, which is stronger than its bouquet, has a soft, rich

Opposite page, above left:
The menu of the 42nd Paulée de Meursault.

Opposite page, above right:
The imposing cuverie of the Domaine Jacques Prieur.

Opposite page, below:
Tasting in the cellars of the Château de Meursault.

Right:
Cleaning out the cuverie.

Below:
View of Blagny.

The hamlet of Blagny owes its existence to the cult of Belenus, a sun god who also had a temple at Belna, present-day Beaune. The name of Blagny is derived from Bela Magny (or Maison); the village boasts a 15th-century chapel with a bell made in Argentina.

Meursault   Côte de Beaune

flavour, in which there are faint traces of other tastes, including an aroma of nuts. Les Genevrières can age in a very special way, like the 1966 of Chanson Père & Fils, the taste of which evoked impressions of moss and undergrowth. Could this, I wonder, be the taste of the juniper berries which had formerly grown on the land of the vineyard? Les Perrières, which takes its name from a former quarry, makes a very worthy top of the list. The qualities of this Premier Cru can only be expressed in superlatives. Of all the wines of Meursault, it is the fullest, the most sumptuous, the longest and altogether the most complete. This superb wine has a bouquet which often suggests toasted almonds. After tasting this Meursault, one can easily understand why Cardinal de Bernis, the ambassador of Louis XV to the Holy See, would only celebrate mass with a good vintage Meursault, saying: 'I would not like my Creator to see me pulling faces at the moment of communion.'

The Domaine du Duc de Magenta owns 12½ acres at Auxey. The whites, which are fruity and possess high vinosity, are among the best of their kind. The reds are very distinctive and balanced.

I have tasted the white Auxey-Duresses of Michel Prunier with a sole meunière at the restaurant La Crémaillère. They have a fine straw colour, good fresh bouquet and a distinct, strong taste. The red can be very tannic.

I prefer the red wine of the Clos du Moulin aux Moines to the white of the same vineyard. Roland Thévenin, owner of 14¾ acres in the commune, produces a good though not great wine.

Bernard Roy, who is probably the most progressive grower in Auxey, uses apparatus which he himself built. His strong Duresses often only reveals its true class after some ten years (although I have found the wine of certain years rather disappointing).

Robert Ampeau, with 2½ acres, is also established at Meursault and his 1972 red, for example, had the softness of white Meursault, with an agreeable bouquet and a taste of soil and tannin.

The Maison Leroy owns 5 acres at Auxey. The red usually needs to be kept for a very long time and only begins to open out after several years. This wine usually has a lot of character and is rarely too heavy. The white is also perfectly acceptable.

Auxey-Duresses

Located on the ridge of a valley running into the Hautes-Côtes de Beaune, Auxey-Duresses occupies a strategically important position. The roads from Meursault, Beaune and Pommard all meet there, and the little main street twists its way between the houses. The Gauls built fortifications on the neighbouring heights, and at one time the village boasted a château. Nowadays, only the Moulin aux Moines and the church evoke a sense of the past. The mill, formerly owned by the monks of Monthelie, was acquired by Roland Thévenin in 1962. The tower of the church is a classified monument, while inside the church is a triptych of the Flemish school (end of the 15th century) representing the life of the Holy Virgin.

Change of name

Modern Auxey-Duresses, with its 350 inhabitants, is a calm and peaceful village. The main signs of life are to be found at the wine business of the Maison Leroy and at the restaurant, *La Crémaillère*, which serves regional dishes, notably *quenelles de brochet à l'auxeyroise*, in a neo-classical setting. The village was formerly known as Auxey-le-Grand (to distinguish it from the neighbouring hamlet of Auxey-le-Petit) but, in 1924, in keeping with the current fashion of the Côte, the name of the most distinguished area within the village — les Duresses — was added to Auxey. Only later was it realized that the new name was not a very wise choice, since it was much harder to remember than the old one and foreigners found it hard to pronounce.

A little known wine

Auxey-Duresses has suffered the further handicap of not producing a great deal of wine — only about 38,550 cases of red and approximately 12,750 cases of white; consequently the merchants mix most of their Auxey-Duresses with wine of other *appellations*, which can then be sold under the general *appellation* of Côte de Beaune-

Villages. Very little genuine red Auxey-Duresses therefore finds it way onto the market. White Auxey-Duresses, even less well known, is generally sold under the very basic *appellation* Bourgogne — a wasted opportunity. A number of growers, hoping for better days (i.e. better prices) keep their white wine too long in the barrel, with sometimes disastrous consequences; I have tasted white wines kept in the barrel for two years which were yellowish in colour and so mediocre as likely to be unsaleable even as white Bourgogne. Because of these drawbacks and the natural desire to increase profitability, many growers have replaced their white vines with red, hoping in this way to enhance the name of Auxey-Duresses. They are unlikely, however, to be successful in the foreseeable future, since the local wines still lack body and other essential qualities.

It would be wrong to assume, however, that a white Auxey-Duresses is a mediocre wine. On the contrary, a well vinified vintage may possess excellent qualities: the softness and vinosity are almost worthy of a Meursault, but bouquet and taste are more neutral, weaker than those of the better known whites. Even so, the very reasonable price can still make it an attractive wine for connoisseurs.

Hard but strong wines

The white vineyards adjoin those of Meursault. The red, facing southwest, are close to Monthelie and enjoy more sun. This is where the Premiers Crus are located, and it includes the best known vineyard — Les Duresses — about 37 acres, extending into Monthelie; the Hospices de Beaune own about 1 acre which produces a wine bearing the name of Cuvée Boillot on the label. As its name suggests, Les Duresses produces a wine which tends to be hard when young but strong enough to age well.

Le Val, which is classified as Premier Cru in certain sections only, produces a finer, more fragrant wine than that of Les Duresses. Its

30 acres are divided between five owners. Although the red wines of Auxey-Duresses vary from vineyard to vineyard, they have certain qualities in common; the most obvious of these is their firmness, especially when young. They therefore need to be kept for many years if they are to acquire some of that balance and suppleness which is normally expected of a good red burgundy.

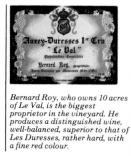

Bernard Roy, who owns 10 acres of Le Val, is the biggest proprietor in the vineyard. He produces a distinguished wine, well-balanced, superior to that of Les Duresses, rather hard, with a fine red colour.

Crus of Auxey-Duresses

Premiers crus:
Les Duresses,
Les Bas-de-Duresses,
Clos du Val
(or Climat du Val),
Reugne (including
La Chapelle)

Les Grands-Champs,
Les Escusseaux,
Les Bretterins
(including La Chapelle).

The spelling of these names can often vary.

Auxey-Duresses

Right:
View of Auxey-Duresses. The village has 425 acres of vineyard in cultivation.

Below:
The Domaine du Moulin aux Moines, the property of Roland Thévenin.

Roland Thévenin controls more than half the business in Saint-Romain. His wine is sold through Poulet Père & Fils in Beaune. The white Saint-Romain is often quite lively in taste and matures surprisingly well.

The Maison Louis Latour markets almost all white appellations of the Côte d'Or, including Saint-Romain. The wine, golden with hints of green, often has a rather light bouquet and a very fresh taste, full with a flavour of ripe fruit.

The Domaine Thévenin-Monthelie (no relation to Roland Thévenin) owns 34½ acres, of which about 20 are in Saint-Romain (17½ white and 2½ red). The white can be extremely delicious, with a fine, restrained strength; it is rather like a minor Meursault. The red is coarser and less long-lived.

Red Saint-Romain has a very special fruity taste reminiscent of cherries. This rather heady wine is produced by Roland Thévenin. When kept, it takes on a light, agreeable bouquet.

Saint-Romain

The road to Saint-Romain, a small village some miles from Auxey-Duresses, is so narrow that two cars can hardly pass each other and the local bus has difficulty in getting through. The commune consists of two villages — Saint-Romain-le-Haut, perched on a rock, and Saint-Romain-le-Bas down in a valley — and has only 320 inhabitants. As in most small villages, Saint-Romain has to rely on a single all-purpose shop, which serves as dairy, grocer, baker and newsagent. Meat is sold by a travelling butcher who visits the village on a particular day. There is only one café and tourists are rare. Yet Saint-Romain, which is a very picturesque village, possesses a 12th-century church with a Romanesque tower, a slightly sloping nave and a beautifully carved 16th-century pulpit. Not far from the village are caves which were inhabited in the Bronze Age.

'Mon Village'

Of the total 5,000-acre area of Saint-Romain, only a small part is planted with vines. The commune *appellation* consists of about 330 acres, which produce an average yield of 12,900 cases of red wine and about 11,100 of white. These amounts are not large enough to interest the merchants of Burgundy; for this reason, more than half the total production of Saint-Romain is marketed by the local grower and merchant, Roland Thévenin, who used to be the mayor of Saint-Romain. Roland, who now lives in Santenay, first began to ship Saint-Romain under its own name in 1947, the year it acquired its own *appellation*. At the Dijon fair of 1962, he introduced Saint-Romain under the name of 'Mon Village'; for a long time since then, this term has been synonymous with that of Saint-Romain. Wine labels, brochures and the now-vanished billboards at the entrance to the village have all carried it.

Delicate whites

The red wines of Saint-Romain lack the noble qualities of the more famous wines of the Côte de Beaune; yet they are, in fact, very agreeable to drink, with an earthy taste sometimes similar to that of fresh, ripe cherries. Roland Thévenin describes them as 'virile, reckless yet urbane'. The whites of Saint-Romain are rather more memorable, but are not easily saleable. Though less full than the whites of Meursault or Puligny-Montrachet, they are still very fruity and fresh, and go extremely well with the famous snails of Burgundy. Roland Thévenin has compared their delicate qualities to those of a 16-year-old girl.

Le Charmois is the name under which the Maison Clerget markets its white and red wine from the Pimont. I find the white generally excellent, with a full taste, a strong hint of terroir and an agreeable aftertaste. The red somehow lacks depth.

In addition to being a grower (15 acres), Camille Fornerot tends a nursery of young vines. His white Premier Cru La Chatenière has a characteristic taste of nuts. He also makes a good red Saint-Aubin.

The red Saint-Aubin Les Frionnes is, in good years, a robust, lively wine with a strong scent of oak in the bouquet and taste. I also enjoy the white enormously: it is finer and deeper than the ordinary Saint-Aubin.

The estate of Jean Lamy produces on the whole very good wines which have received several awards from the Chevaliers du Tastevin. Hubert Lamy — on the other side of the same street — also produces a Saint-Aubin which is usually of high quality.

The Domaine Roux Père & Fils includes 8½ acres of Saint-Aubin. Its red Saint-Aubin is often supple with a characteristic earthy taste. Besides this very agreeable wine, the red La Pucelle is certainly to be recommended.

Opposite page above: The arms of the ancient barony of Saint-Romain.

Opposite page below: One of the 'Mon Village' hoardings which used to point the way to Saint-Romain.

Centre: The château of Gamay.

Below: Harvest scene.

Saint-Aubin

Saint-Aubin, like Saint-Romain, is located away from the Côte proper; its vineyards border those of Chassagne-Montrachet. Since it is at a relatively high altitude, its climate is drier and colder (with more snow in winter) than that of Chassagne. This is a typical wine-growing village and 90% of the population make a living from wine or from related occupations. The streets are narrow and the houses old. The only interesting monuments are the church (in which the skeletons of plague victims were discovered and which is now being restored) and a tree, the Peuplier de la Liberté, planted in 1848. The commune of Saint-Aubin includes the hamlet of Gamay, where the Seigneur du May settled on his return from the Crusades and introduced a grape then unknown in Burgundy. Only after the grape, Gamay, had been cultivated for some time was it realized that although it produced a lot of wine, the latter was of very mediocre quality. The cultivation of Gamay was therefore prohibited in the Middle Ages; but in modern times the variety has taken very well in the Beaujolais. The château of Gamay still exists, but is in private hands and is not open to the public.

An adventurous project

The vineyards of Saint-Aubin consist of around 593 acres (of which 388 acres are Premiers Crus). The total acreage has therefore doubled since the mid-1970s. One of the most adventurous projects in this

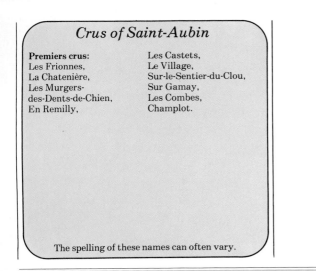

Crus of Saint-Aubin

Premiers crus:
Les Frionnes,
La Chatenière,
Les Murgers-
des-Dents-de-Chien,
En Remilly,

Les Castets,
Le Village,
Sur-le-Sentier-du-Clou,
Sur Gamay,
Les Combes,
Champlot.

The spelling of these names can often vary.

expansion was the restoration of the vineyard of Pimont, high above Chassagne-Montrachet. Until a few generations ago, the wine from this vineyard is supposed to have enjoyed a reputation almost equal to that of Montrachet, though for various reasons this did not last. Maurice Clerget, director of Maison Raoul Clerget, which ships almost one-third of all local wine, decided to restore the vineyard to its former glory. He has therefore replanted entirely the 30 acres of Pimont, a part of which is located in Chassagne. Total production of the commune is about 27,800 cases of red wine and 10,300 cases of white.

A flavour of nuts

Although the white Saint-Aubin does not sell very well and often has to be down-graded to a simple Bourgogne, it certainly deserves a mention. It is agreeable, very fruity, with high vinosity and suppleness. The taste and aftertaste occasionally possess a very special nutty flavour which can also be found, though less strongly, in the red Saint-Aubin. The latter is a fairly charming, pleasant wine, a rather exceptional fact in one of the more modest Côte d'Or communes where wines tend to be a bit rough. Another feature of red Saint-Aubin is usually a lot of *terroir* in its taste. The best known Premier Cru, both for its red and white wines, is Les Frionnes.

Below:
Maurice Clerget inspects his young plastic-covered plants at Le Pimont, the vineyard recently restored to cultivation. The Clerget family, whose name (notably the Volnay branch) goes back to 1268, is one of the oldest families of Burgundy. This photograph was taken in 1976. The vineyard of Le Pimont, however, has become totally productive in the meantime.

Bottom:
In Burgundy, Gamay is both the name of a grape variety and a hamlet.

Le Montrachet of the Marquis de Laguiche is often light and delicate, very fine, and much more subtle than might be expected, though it has less taste and less bouquet than the other Montrachets. Nevertheless, it is a wine of much nobility. Drinking it is a great experience.

The Domaine du Baron Thénard produces a 'classic' Montrachet of a beautiful pale gold colour with green tints; it has a magnificent perfume and a deeply satisfying taste, which is both very distinguished and has high vinosity. This very well-balanced wine is marketed by Remoissenet.

The Montrachet from Bouchard Père & Fils can be an extraordinary wine, with a subtle, exciting perfume and an expansive, subtle taste. However, I have tasted wines from less successful years which have had rather less finesse.

The Domaine Jacques Prieur in Meursault owns 1½ acres of Le Montrachet (in Chassagne). This produces about 2,000 bottles annually. The wine is fragrant, subtle and of great breeding. Prieur also produces a good Les Combettes (from 3¾ acres).

The Domaine de la Romanée-Conti bought its 1¾ acres of Le Montrachet from three different owners during the period 1964-80. In the past year, 1.6 million francs have been paid for just under half an acre belonging to Roland Thévenin. An excellent, almost voluptuous wine with a magnificent perfume.

René Fleurot of Santenay is one of the small Montrachet growers, producing no more than 600 bottles a year. Neither the taste nor the bouquet are especially delicate, but the aftertaste is superb, almost spicy and very long-lasting.

Puligny-Montrachet

Although the village itself differs is no way from other wine-growing communes of the area, the name of Puligny-Montrachet is a symbol of excellence, for nowhere else in the Côte de Beaune has the Chardonnay grape been cultivated to such a peak of perfection. The layout of the village is, nevertheless, interesting; the streets, the squares and even the church appear to have been planned for an area more extensive than that of modern Puligny-Montrachet. The houses of Pommard and Volnay, built on top of one another, seem to suggest a declining population, while the surprising spaciousness of Puligny seems indicative of growth. This is not the case, however, since the censuses show that the population of the commune is dwindling. There were 1,200 inhabitants at the end of the 19th century, but now only 550. This fall in population can be attributed to the fact that the best vineyards no longer belong to the inhabitants of the village of Puligny, but have gradually become the property of vineyards located in other communes or of wine merchants whose main business is elsewhere. Of course, the renown of the Grands Crus of Puligny-Montrachet ensures that they are a highly desirable property.

The château of Puligny-Montrachet

Nothing remains in modern Puligny of the ancient Gallo-Roman settlement of Puliniacus; the only reminder of the past is a carved wooden eagle of the 8th century. The château, which is the only building of any consequence, is more recent, dating from the time of Louis XIV. For many years this was the home of Roland Thévenin, vine grower, poet and formerly a wine merchant in Saint-Romain, of which he was also the mayor. Roland restored the château to its former splendour, but he was eventually forced to leave it because of various problems. It cannot now be visited and the fine park is also closed to the public. The extensive collections of paintings, objects from the Napoleonic era and the portraits of men of many nationalities who fought in World War

I were all moved to Thévenin's beautifully appointed new home, the Château de la Cré, in Santenay-le-Haut. Puligny-Montrachet thus has little left of interest, since there is no wine-tasting centre either — an astonishing state of affairs, considering that it is one of the world's most famous wine-producing villages.

Chardonnay grapes instead of blackcurrants

The total wine production of Puligny-Montrachet consists almost exclusively of white wine, the quantity of which averages 100,000 cases. Near Blagny, on the borders of Meursault, a very small quantity (no more than an average of 3,600 cases) of red is also made. In the past, the red wine was produced from the Gamay grape, which was then much more abundant and easily saleable. Puligny was for years a staging post where horses were watered, and doubtless the wine that was sold to thirsty riders and coachmen helped to keep it on the map.
When it became apparent that the Gamay only yielded mediocre wines which could not compete with the better, cheaper wines from the Midi, the vines were replaced by blackcurrants. Until the outbreak of World War II, Puligny-Montrachet produced between 30 and 40 tons of blackcurrants annually. Since then, both the Gamay grape and the blackcurrant have been totally eclipsed by the white Chardonnay, and so high is the reputation of the white wines of Puligny that even the flat land around the village has been planted with vines.

Le Montrachet

Although the standard of some of the wines bearing the official *appellation* of the commune can sometimes vary considerably, that of the Premiers Crus and the Grands Crus is always exceptional. The magnificent quality of these vineyards has remained unchanged for several centuries. Located along a broad band to the west of the village, they might be compared to a symphony which begins *pianissimo* on the borders of

Meursault (Les Combettes and Les Referts, Premiers Crus) and ends *maestoso* with the Grands Crus Bâtard-Montrachet and Le Montrachet. The fame of Le Montrachet is world-wide; it produces a dry white wine which excels all the white wines of Burgundy and probably of the whole world. It is not surprising, therefore, that both Puligny and Chassagne have embellished their names by adding that of the famous vineyard which extends from one commune to the next: 10 acres in Puligny and 8½ in Chassagne. To avoid any confusion, Montrachet as a whole will be discussed in this section.

The bare mountain

The name of Montrachet conveys precisely the type of ground to be found in this vineyard, since it is derived from 'Mons Rachisensis', Mont Rachat, which literally means 'bare mountain'. Indeed, this vineyard is sited on a hillside with such poor, rocky soil that no other trees, nor even scrub, can grow there. At first sight, there is nothing especially memorable about the countryside of Montrachet and the uninformed tourist would scarcely give it a second glance, unless he happened to notice the dilapidated little gates over which the name of 'Montrachet' is displayed.
As is the case with all the very best wines, the important factors are those that are hidden or not immediately obvious, and Le Montrachet is no exception to the rule. The subsoil is of complex composition, but mainly calcareous; the drainage is perfect and the vineyard, since it faces south to south-east, receives maximum sunshine from dawn to dusk, thus producing satisfyingly ripe fruit. In 1962, the French government took a wise decision in building the A6 motorway through the vineyards of Beaune rather than through those of Le Montrachet, even though this involved costly rerouting.

Bouchard Père & Fils produce a Chevalier-Montrachet which needs to be kept for at least four years, preferably more. It has a fine bouquet, and a delicate, almost honeyed, taste.

The magnificent Chevalier-Montrachet of the Domaine Leflaive also has a vague flavour of toast in bouquet and taste. An exceptionally successful, beautifully balanced wine.

Les Demoiselles of Louis Jadot is one of the most exquisite wines in the whole of Puligny-Montrachet. It has a fine, limpid colour; the perfume is quite strong, the occasional hints in it of honey and oak can also be discerned, toned down, in the fine, soft taste.

Louis Latour also makes a Demoiselles, but of a lighter colour than that of Louis Jadot. It has a very fruity bouquet and a round, quite fresh taste. This wine is exceptional in quality.

Leflaive makes a Bâtard-Montrachet with a pretty colour and a rather reserved bouquet. The taste, on the other hand, with its flavour of toast, is both firm and strong; the aftertaste is extraordinary.

The Domaine Delagrange-Bachelet at Chassagne-Montrachet owns 2 acres in Bâtard-Montrachet. The wine is pale straw in colour, velvety, fruity and rich in perfume. Edmond Delagrange is one of the suppliers of La Tour d'Argent in Paris.

Below left:
Vincent Leflaive, one of the owners of the highly reputed Domaine Leflaive.

Below right:
Roland Thévenin in his former study at the Château de Puligny-Montrachet. His present study in Santenay much resembles this one, Napoleon's bust included.

Opposite page, below left:
The Château de Puligny-Montrachet seen from the park. The château cannot be visited.

Opposite page, below right:
A typical scene in a Puligny courtyard. The village is twinned with Johannisberg in Germany.

Three important owners

For more than three centuries and until the French Revolution, Le Montrachet belonged almost completely to the single family of Clermond-Montoizon. Today, this vineyard is divided between a dozen owners, some of whose holdings can virtually be measured in square yards, while others consist of no more than an acre or two. Half of Le Montrachet, however, belongs to three large estates: the **Domaine Marquis de la Guiche,** the Domaine du Baron Thénard and the Domaine du Château de Beaune (Bouchard Père & Fils).

The Domaine Marquis de la Guiche has owned 5 acres in Puligny for many years and the yield is marketed entirely by Joseph Drouhin. The grapes are pressed at Chassagne-Montrachet where they are the responsibility of manager Jean Colin; the must is then vinified and the wine made by Drouhin himself.
The Domaine du Baron Thénard owns 4¾ acres in Chassagne. The wine is vinified at Givry where the estate owns extensive cellars, and Remoissenet Père & Fils handle the major part of the sales.
The Domaine du Château de Beaune (or Bouchard Père & Fils) holds a mere 2¾ acres

Albert Morey and his sons live in Chassagne and own half an acre of Bâtard-Montrachet. Their wine has a strong bouquet; it is relatively full-bodied and has a tendency to be heavy and flabby. The aftertaste is excellent.

The Domaine Lequin-Roussot (Santenay) has been awarded several gold medals in Paris for its Bâtard-Montrachet. The winning of these awards is doubtless due largely to the fact that the vines (three-quarters of an acre) are more than 50 years old. It is a very perfumed, agreeably balanced wine with a prolonged aftertaste.

Pierre Ramonet of the Domaine Ramonet-Prudhon recommends that his Bâtard-Montrachet should be drunk with foie gras, lobster or a gratin of crayfish. It is a beautiful light colour, with a strong and subtle taste, and an aftertaste of toast.

Half the vineyard of Bienvenues-Bâtard-Montrachet belongs to Leflaive, who produces a nicely balanced wine, finer and lighter than that from Bâtard-Montrachet, but with considerable qualities. It has a strong taste and a delicate perfume.

One of the most important customers for the Bienvenues-Bâtard-Montrachet of Ramonet-Prudhon is Alain Chapel, master chef; this is one of the greatest compliments which can be paid to a vineyard. The wine has a fine bouquet, light, soft and rich, with a very prolonged aftertaste.

Robert Carillon owns no more than a quarter of an acre of Bienvenues-Bâtard-Montrachet, but he produces an exceptional wine. It is straw-coloured with green tints, and has a very agreeable bouquet and delicate taste, though lacking a little in delicacy.

in Puligny. It is worth noting that this is the only wine merchant owning an appreciable part of this vineyard.

In praise of Le Montrachet

The praises of Le Montrachet have been loudly sung over the centuries. In the opinion of Alexandre Dumas, this wine should be drunk 'on one's knees with head uncovered'. For Jean Colin, former mayor of Chassagne, 'Le Montrachet, a miracle of creation, is one of those marvels which console us for the setbacks of this life. Legend has it that God only rested after he

had created Le Montrachet.' Indeed, this fine wine has never lacked admirers. Someone once wrote: 'The amber colour of Le Montrachet has a very special warmth, for this wine is supposed to absorb more sun than others. Its soft, rich taste caresses the palate and its bouquet, like a religious cantata resounding through the vaults of a Gothic cathedral, shows both strength and gentleness.' Referring to a good vintage Montrachet, Dr Lavalle wrote, 'You can never pay enough for it.' In other words, Le Montrachet is an exceptional wine.

Almost decadent

It is almost impossible to find the words to do justice to this wine, and words alone can often do little more than convey vague impressions or sensations. The most detailed appreciations and authoritative books are less eloquent than the taste of a single mouthful. My own very first tasting was a revelation: the wine was masterly and so exquisite that it almost seemed decadent. Its incomparable fruitiness contained subtle flavours of almond and honey; and its abundant richness and roundness reminded me of the words of Frank Schoonmaker: 'Le

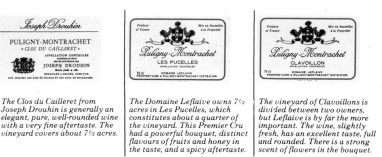

The Clos du Caillaret from Joseph Drouhin is generally an elegant, pure, well-rounded wine with a very fine aftertaste. The vineyard covers about 7½ acres.

The Domaine Leflaive owns 7½ acres in Les Pucelles, which constitutes about a quarter of the vineyard. This Premier Cru had a powerful bouquet, distinct flavours of fruits and honey in the taste, and a spicy aftertaste.

The vineyard of Clavoillons is divided between two owners, but Leflaive is by far the more important. The wine, slightly fresh, has an excellent taste, full and rounded. There is a strong scent of flowers in the bouquet.

André Ramonet (who works under both his own name and that of Ramonet-Prudhon) bought about three-quarters of an acre of Le Montrachet jointly with his father in 1978. The strip lies between those of de Laguiche and Bouchard. It produces a majestic wine.

The Domaine of the Duc de Magenta owns 2½ acres of the Clos de la Garenne. This wine has light green tints, a bouquet characterized by the scent of flowers, a delicate, delicious taste, high in vinosity, a little acid and a flavour of toast.

The Domaine Bachelet-Ramonet in Chassagne-Montrachet owns about 1½ acres of Bâtard-Montrachet in the Puligny sector. Excellent wine with a subtle richness, which benefits from keeping. The estate includes just over one-quarter of an acre of Bienvenues-Bâtard-Montrachet.

Montrachet is not a wine: it is an event.' Subsequent tastings confirmed my first impressions. Once again, however, it has to be emphasized that not all the wines of Le Montrachet are alike; these few acres produce wines which can be very different, according to the grower. Broadly speaking, the owners of the larger plots make the best wines because they have enough grapes to allow them to eliminate the bad ones, thus ensuring good vinification. In addition to the three above-mentioned owners, a note should also be made of the Domaine Jacques Prieur of Meursault, which owns 1½ acres of Montrachet, and the Domaine de la Romanée-Conti, of about the same size. I would just proffer one piece of advice. If you ever have the chance of buying a Montrachet of any estate, snap it up immediately. It is not something which will happen very frequently, since the annual harvest of only 2,600 cases, on average, is too small to satisfy the innumerable admirers of the wine.

Bâtard-Montrachet

There is, nevertheless, some comfort for those who fail to obtain a bottle of Le Montrachet itself. Firstly, even the very good village restaurant, which is called *Le Montrachet*, does not always carry the wine on its list. Secondly, the other Grands Crus are very seldom inferior in quality to Le Montrachet and their prices are much more accessible. One of these, the Bâtard-Montrachet, is located just below Le Montrachet. This vineyard of 29 acres also continues from Puligny into Chassagne. It produces about 4,700 cases on average of a fuller wine than Le Montrachet; it is, however, less round, less elegant, and with a less persistent aftertaste. I find that it has a characteristic tone, variable in strength, of finely toasted white bread, a flavour which can be found again in the Chevalier-Montrachet. Like the genuine Montrachet, the Bâtard-Montrachet only really opens out when kept for five years or more. The most important owner is the Domaine Leflaive

with 4¾ acres. The rest is extensively subdivided.

Bienvenues-Bâtard-Montrachet

This Grand Cru, which is really an extension of Bâtard-Montrachet, owes its name, at least according to legend, to the fact that the lord of the village made a gift of it to the local poor, a gift which was 'bienvenu' — very welcome. The Bienvenues-Bâtard-Montrachet, half of which belongs to the Domaine Leflaive, is totally within the commune of Puligny and consists of 5¾ acres yielding a very small harvest: about 1,450 cases. It is lighter than the Bâtard-Montrachet and develops more quickly; in spite of its grace, however, it tends to lack depth. Its bouquet, which can be rich, often has a flavour of honey. The price difference between these two *crus* can often be as high as 10%. Like the Domaine Leflaive, the Domaine Ramonet-Prudhon of Chassagne-Montrachet also makes excellent Bienvenues-Bâtard-Montrachet.

Chevalier-Montrachet

The Grand Cru Chevalier-Montrachet consists of 17¾ acres, and is thus almost as big as Le Montrachet. Situated above the latter, it produces an almost equally good wine. A carefully vinified Chevalier-Montrachet is a wine of rare distinction, perfect balance and only slightly lighter and less round than Le Montrachet. It also has a strong, characteristic bouquet, honey-flavoured with a hint of toast. The approximately 2,000 cases of Chevalier-Montrachet fetch higher prices than those of the other white Grands Crus, except, of course, Le Montrachet itself. The most important owners of this vineyard are Bouchard Père & Fils, with 5¾ acres, and the Domaine Leflaive with 4¾ acres. The Chevalier-Montrachet also includes an enclave of 2½ acres, known as Les Demoiselles, which is divided between Louis Jadot and Louis Latour. This enclave should not be confused with the Premier Cru of the

same name which borders on the Chevalier-Montrachet; to avoid any misunderstanding, the Premier Cru Les Demoiselles is now known as Le Cailleret. There are, of course, countless jokes on the subject of the Chevalier and his Demoiselles and the birth of the Bâtard . . .

The other crus

In addition to these four Grands Crus, Puligny-Montrachet also includes several Premiers Crus; although these are less elegant, they are still wines of high quality. La Cailleret produces full-bodied, supple wines, which have a certain elegance and improve with age. This vineyard includes the Clos du Cailleret, of which 7½ acres are exploited solely by Joseph Drouhin. The Domaine Leflaive owns 7½ acres in Les Pucelles which produces a wine almost of Grand Cru standard, with a very fruity taste which has a flavour of honey. This same estate cultivates almost the whole of the Clavoillons to produce a fragrant well-rounded wine. Les Folatières is a relatively recent Premier Cru, light and fine, like the wine of Le Champ-Canet. The Clos de la Garenne produces a rich, velvety, subtle wine. Les Combettes, close to Meursault, produces soft and rich wines, with strong bouquets, which are similar to those from the neighbouring commune. These wines were originally sold by the growers of Meursault, who were owners of Les Combettes, as Meursault-Combettes until the passing of the law governing *appellations d'origine*. There are also a number of less well-known Premiers Crus and the simple Puligny-Montrachet, which can be very variable in quality. Of the many I have tasted, some were heavy and flat, while others were full, delicate and with undeniable distinction in both bouquet and taste. I can only underline once more that the most important factor in the quality of such wines is the professional conscience of the owner or of the merchant who sells them.

Etienne Sauzet established a considerable reputation for his Les Combettes. His widow and grandson own 3½ acres which produce a wine notable for its elegant, balanced taste. The perfume opens out rather slowly.

Jean Virot, the manager of the Domaine Leflaive, finds that his Les Combettes has much in common with a Meursault. The wine, which soon becomes agreeable and balanced, does not need to be kept long. It has a rather full taste and an oak-flavoured bouquet.

In one competition, Les Combettes of Robert Carillon was placed first among all the wines of Puligny-Montrachet, even ahead of a Montrachet. I thought it excellent with a strong taste in which it was possible to trace flavours of ripe fruits and nuts.

The simple Puligny-Montrachet of Louis Latour is an exceptional wine which has all the qualities that might be expected of a Latour, including roundness of taste and bouquet. Although it has relatively little breeding, it is well-balanced, almost sensual.

Like Louis Latour and the Domaine Leflaive, Henri Boillot of Volnay produces an excellent Puligny-Montrachet. The bouquet is interesting, almost intellectual, and the rather sensitive taste sometimes suggestive of spices.

The Domaine Roux Père & Fils at Saint-Aubin cultivates only 1 acre at Puligny-Montrachet, but produces a marvellous wine from this holding: the 1972 was awarded a gold medal at Mâcon in 1976. It has a fine colour with green tints; exuberant, very fruity bouquet; distinctive taste, intense yet delicious.

Right:
Harvest time at Puligny-Montrachet.

Below right:
An old door to the holding in Le Montrachet of Baron Thénard, one of the biggest owners of this famous vineyard.

Crus of Puligny-Montrachet

Grands Crus:
Montrachet,
Chevalier-Montrachet,
Bâtard-Montrachet,
Bienvenues-
Bâtard-Montrachet.

Premiers crus:
Le Cailleret,
Les Combettes,
Les Pucelles,
Les Folatières (part),
Clavoillons,
Le Champ-Canet,
Les Chalumeaux,
Les Referts, La Garenne,
Sous-le-Puits,
Hameau de Blagny.

The spelling of these names can often vary.

The estate of Albert Morey and his sons Jean-Marc and Bernard consists of 37 acres. Their white Chassagne-Montrachet is excellent, with its light perfume and an agreeable flavour.

Raoul Clerget of Saint-Aubin owns a number of large, gloomy cellars at Chassagne. I tasted a good red Chassagne-Montrachet there (with a hint of oak in the taste and bouquet) as well as the white Chenevotes, a stylish, limpid wine.

In a tasting at the premises of Delagrange-Bachelet, I hesitated between his Morgeot and his Caillerets. I finally decided that I preferred the former because of its fine perfume, its fleshy taste and high vinosity. The estate owns 2½ acres of Caillerets and 2¾ acres of Morgeot, from a total of almost 25 acres.

Pierre Ramonet and his son André share the wine of the Domaine Ramonet-Prudhon. Pierre sells under the name of the estate itself, while André uses his own name. It is a strong Morgeot, with plenty of flavour and perfume.

In 1974, the Domaine du Duc de Magenta made a Clos de la Chapelle which, without chaptalization, was only 11.5° proof. There are greenish tints in the colour, a little 'greenness' in the taste, and an aftertaste of toast. Later years also produced good wines.

Wines from the Albert Morey estate have often received awards, including his Caillerets. This is a wine which always requires patience. A full taste, strong bouquet and great suppleness.

Chassagne-Montrachet

From the Montrachet vineyard, on the edge of Puligny, the village of Chassagne-Montrachet can already be seen less than a mile away; but to reach the village itself from Puligny, you have to cross the *route nationale 6*, which is the old road from Paris to Lyons. The layout of Chassagne suggests the structure of a mobile: the village consists of a number of districts linked by fairly long streets. The most important building is the banqueting hall, which is a large, square edifice whose light colour makes it stand out from the houses of the vineyard workers.

Opened in 1967, and financed by the local council, this hall is used for marriages, wine-tastings, and for the meetings of the very active village associations such as the Sports Society, the Music Society, the Firemen's Society, etc.

As is the case with most of the wine-producing areas, the population of Chassagne-Montrachet is declining: in 1940, the village had 1,100 inhabitants; in 1968, 505, and now just over 450. The majority of those who leave the area to live elsewhere are young people.

A violent history

Nothing seems likely to disturb the calm of present-day Chassagne-Montrachet, but the history of the village is full of incident, and occasionally of violence. At the end of the 15th century, for instance, Jean de Chalon, Prince of Orange, decided to lend aid to Mary of Burgundy, daughter of Charles the Bold, then engaged in a campaign against Louis XI. The Prince of Orange began by killing the king's representative in Dijon. The murder provoked the fury of the king

Côte de Beaune

who ordered the prince to be hanged and all his towns, villages and châteaux burned. After several engagements with the royal armies, Jean de Chalon retreated to Chassagne. He did not stay there long, however, and was forced to flee when Louis XI sent his Swiss mercenaries to Burgundy. The prince abandoned Chassagne to the invaders who then proceeded to commit the most terrible atrocities. In 1478 they set fire to the village and many of the inhabitants were burned to death or horribly injured. Since then, the inhabitants of Chassagne have been popularly known as the *mâchurés*, or the 'bruised ones'.

A quarry of pink stone

Chassagne was already a wine-producing village at that period; it has even been claimed that the first vines were planted there in the 3rd century. If true, it took a long time for the cultivation of vines to become significant, since Chassagne remained very much an agricultural village, with meadows and cornfields. The 740 acres of modern vineyards only began to be cultivated around the middle of the 19th century. Chassagne also benefited from the exploitation of another resource — its stone quarries. For at least 500 years, the hills of

Chassagne had been quarried for a pink stone which, when polished, looks very much like marble, as does the hard limestone of Comblanchien. The stone has been extensively used in the houses and church of Chassagne. The quarries are still worked, but employ only about 10 people. Samples of the polished stone can be bought in the little boutique, *Pierre de Chassagne*, which is located on the church square.

Les Ruchottes, at the top of the slope, belongs to the Domaine Ramonet-Prudhon and yields a wine of similar distinction to that of Les Pucelles of Leflaive at Puligny. Pierre Ramonet compares the qualities of this very delicate wine to those of a young girl.

The Criots-Bâtard-Montrachet of the Domaine Delagrange-Bachelet is one of the two wines produced by this Grand Cru in relatively large quantities. It is elegant in character, sumptuous in taste and lighter than the Bâtard-Montrachet.

The Domaine Albert Morey consists of 37 acres, of which 8½ produce a Chassagne-Montrachet with an agreeable taste and bouquet. Another excellent red Chassagne is that of André Ramonet (Prudhon).

In addition to his white wine, Louis Carillon, a Puligny grower, also makes a good red Chassagne-Montrachet. With a fine colour, this wine is fruity, fairly light and with a long-lasting taste.

The Domaine Bachelet-Ramonet owns almost 28 acres, mainly in Chassagne-Montrachet. The wines are very stylish and of high quality, like the white La Romanée (¾ acres), Ruchottes (1 acre) and Caillerets (1½ acres). The reds are also delicious, such as the Clos St Jean (3 acres).

There is usually a strong though subtle taste of terroir in the red Clos de la Chapelle. This wine from the Duc de Magenta is also very well balanced.

Truffles and bats

In addition to wine and stone, Chassagne-Montrachet also produces something rather curious and increasingly rare: truffles. In the past, they were plentiful in the surrounding woods; Jean Colin, former mayor of Chassagne, recalls that there was a harvest of about 100 lbs of truffles in 1951. M. Colin is also the owner of a superb truffle, weighing just over 10 oz, which he has preserved in alcohol. The woods are also full of mushrooms and wild and medicinal herbs. Chassagne is famous, too, for another curiosity, namely bats, which are to be found in great numbers, even among the vines, where it is very difficult to distinguish them from the reddish earth. One final note on Chassagne: it is a village — and there cannot be many — with no café, no bar and no restaurant!

More red than white

In 1981 there were about 735 acres of vineyard in production, which were divided roughly as follows: 28 Grands Crus, 392 Premiers Crus and 315 of simple Chassagne-Montrachet. Thus the quantities of fine wine and those of the commune wines are almost equal, which is a very satisfactory state of affairs. Unlike Puligny-Montrachet, red wine has an important role to play here and its annual production is, in fact, higher than that of the white. The annual production of red averages about 84,000 cases a year, while that of white is about 59,000 (this figure does not include the white Grands Crus, but the quantity of these is hardly significant). Another distinguishing characteristic, rare in Burgundy, is that this wine-growing commune, in which there are 20-25 growers, includes a high number of large estates, many of which own more than 24 acres. The absence of small holdings has also contributed to the depopulation of the area.

Criots-Bâtard-Montrachet

The best vineyards of Chassagne are planted with white vines and produce the three Grands Crus: Montrachet, Bâtard-Montrachet and Criots-Bâtard-Montrachet. The two former, which are partly in Puligny, were discussed in the previous section. The third, the Criots-Bâtard-Montrachet, is located completely within the commune of Chassagne. This vineyard is situated in an extension of Bâtard-Montrachet and consists of only about 4 acres — the tiniest and rarest of the Grands Crus. The word 'Criots' is almost certainly derived from *cailloux* (pebbles), which are often to be found in good wine-growing soil. The Maison de Marcilly and the Domaine Delagrange-Bachelet are the main proprietors of this Grand Cru, each with 1¼ acres from which they each produce an annual quantity of about 670 cases. The rest of the vineyard is divided between three or four owners, and the small number of grapes which they can harvest sometimes means that they cannot carry out vinification on their own. I have tasted a Criots-Bâtard-Montrachet at the property of Edmond Delagrange at the same time as a Bâtard-Montrachet of the same vintage. They seemed very similar to each other, but the Criots appeared more elegant and less full-bodied; it had a beautiful yellow straw colour, a then still discreet perfume and a mouth-filling, almost juicy taste.

The Premiers Crus

Of the many white Premiers Crus I have tasted, some were elegant and light, while others were rich and strong. The fact that a wine comes from a particular vineyard is not necessarily a guarantee of quality since, as already mentioned, each grower has his own methods of cultivation, vinification and maturing. One of the few constant factors is location: the vineyards higher up the slopes produce lighter wines than those farther down. Le Cailleret and Les Ruchottes (also known as Les Grandes Ruchottes) are perfect examples of this principle. The best known of the white Premiers Crus, Le Morgeot, includes wine from a hamlet of the same name consisting of an old deserted abbey and its outbuildings. Several estates and *négociants* produce a white Chassagne-Montrachet Morgeot. I liked this strong-tasting wine for its liveliness and strength. One of the best Morgeots comes from the Ramonet-Prudhon estate. The Duc de Magenta produces a greenish Morgeot of great purity under the name of Clos de la Chapelle. This vineyard of 10½ acres, located behind the abbey, belongs to the great-grandson of Maurice MacMahon, Duc de Magenta, second president of the Third Republic.

Noble blood

Even though its white wines are still excellent, I feel that Chassagne-Montrachet heralds a decline in the long line of great whites. I sometimes envisage the wine quality as a broad curve which starts at Auxey-Duresses, sweeps upwards through Meursault, reaches its peak at Puligny-Montrachet and starts its slow descent at Chassagne-Montrachet. The downward curve might even be said to begin with Le Montrachet itself, the part located in Puligny being considered superior. Obviously this is just a personal theory but, in my opinion, the majority of the white wines of Chassagne-Montrachet, despite their similarities to the other Grands Crus, do not achieve the same sublime perfection. Both Puligny and Chassagne are incontestably of noble blood, but if Puligny is a duke, then (recognizing that there are exceptions) I would give Chassagne the title of count.

The Domaine Ramonet-Prudhon owns about 1¾ acres in the Clos Saint-Jean. This vineyard, some of which is quite old, yields a wine which is at first slightly forbidding, but eventually exhibits a fine bouquet and a lot of breeding.

In the 15th-century cellars of the Château de la Maltroye, Marcel Picard produces a light and elegant red Chassagne Clos de la Maltroye, in addition to his very good white wine.

The Clos de la Boudriotte of Ramonet-Prudhon is by far my favourite red Chassagne. It has a fairly intense colour and a superlative bouquet with surprising distinction: altogether a subtle wine of great breeding.

This red Morgeot 1973 (13°) was produced by the Domaine Prieur-Brunet at Santenay. It was agreeable, full-bodied, with a certain vigour in the aftertaste; the bouquet was still somewhat timid.

A difficult choice

When ordering wine in a restaurant, I would never hesitate to take even an unknown white Chassagne-Montrachet; however, I would be much more careful in choosing a red, where the differences of quality are far greater. I have tasted six Chassagne-Montrachet 1972 reds of various provenance in one day: only one was really good. This was a red Clos de la Chapelle of the Domaine du Duc de Magenta. It had considerable character, a certain rough quality, and a slightly peppery flavour. Well structured and deeply coloured, it was a pleasure to drink. The saying is that red Chassagne-Montrachet is dressed in a velvety cloak, and indeed a certain softness cannot be denied. However, it rarely becomes a truly accessible wine, seeming to remain somewhat guarded. You cannot expect a dashing perfume or generous taste. Its strength recalls certain wines of the Côte de Nuits, especially Nuits-Saint-Georges; but this rather superficial resemblance is only an echo rather than a true reflection of those wines.

Perfect synthesis

There are, nevertheless, some delicious examples of red Chassagne, well balanced and of incomparable individuality. The Clos de la Boudriotte of the Domaine Ramonet-Prudhon seemed to me to be the best of all the reds produced in the commune. It comes from a plot which covers just over 2½ acres of the Premier Cru of the same name, which is located to the south of the village, half-way between Chassagne-Montrachet and the abbey of Morgeot. I found this wine very impressive indeed. Its magnificent bouquet suggested an exquisite mixture of wild flowers and ripe fruit; its taste could not be faulted, being distinguished yet at the same time reserved. It was, in my opinion, a perfect synthesis of a Bordeaux and a burgundy.

Famous restaurants

I have tasted other wines on the estate of Ramonet-Prudhon, which is considered the best of Chassagne-Montrachet. M. Pierre Ramonet and his son André cultivate 42 acres, and their wines appear on the lists of the most famous restaurants in the world: *Bocuse, Troisgros, L'Auberge de l'Ill, La Villa Lorraine* and *Comme chez Soi*. The biography of Alain Chapel, by Fanny Deschamps, contains a long account of a meeting between the master chef and Pierre Ramonet. Ramonet-Prudhon also produces an exceptional red Chassagne — the Premier Cru Clos Saint-Jean — not to be confused with the Clos Saint-Jean of Bouchard Aîné. I must also mention the Clos de la Maltroye, an interesting Premier Cru which belongs to the château of the same name. All this goes to show that red Chassagne must be selected with the greatest care.

Below:
View of the chai of the abbey of Morgeot, which has belonged since 1967 to the Domaine du Duc de Magenta. The technical manager is Paul Gauthey. During the summer of 1975, Philippe de Magenta was visited by the Begum Aga Khan and the Duchess of Orléans.

The name of Chassagne or Chassaigne is very common. It is derived from the Latin cassina, which means 'little house'. Chassagne normally has 500 inhabitants, but this number is doubled at harvest time.

A kind of stone obelisk from Chassagne-Montrachet was set up at Amersfoort in Holland during the festivities there in 1976.

Although most of the wine-producing communes of the Côte d'Or are only simple, rustic villages, Santenay might almost be described as fashionable, for it has a casino which is very popular during the summer months; employing 40 people, it is by far the largest single business concern in Santenay and its large profits are of considerable benefit to the village. Strangely enough, the casino does not owe its existence to wine but to water, since Santenay is the site of a number of springs with therapeutic properties.

The nymph of Santenay

Sentennacum, located at the crossing point of a number of roads, was already famous for its springs in Roman times. Among those who subsequently sung their praises was Pierre Quarré, a doctor of Charolles, who enthusiastically described 'their miraculous effects' and wrote of 'the nymph of Santenay'. A century later the water was deliberately polluted by its owner and the peasants of the surrounding countryside were deprived of its healing effects. A short time afterwards, nature rectified the situation when a second spring, smaller than the first, appeared a few hundred yards away and the local inhabitants began to use the water again — though secretly. In 1890, it became necessary to sink a well to a depth of nearly 300 ft; several years later, another one, 200 feet deep, was sunk. These two springs still continue to yield waters with very different properties: one relieves liver disorders while the other alleviates rheumatism, sciatica and skin ailments. The water is very unstable and cannot be transported or bottled, so that anyone wishing to take advantage of its curative qualities is obliged to stay in one of the large houses in Santenay designed to accommodate patients. Some of these residents, however, were probably drawn to the town for the sake of its wine. There is a story told of one gentleman who suffered

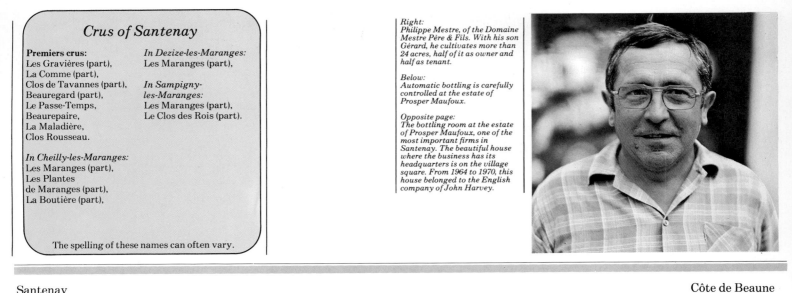
from liver attacks. The waters cured his complaint so effectively that he was able to start drinking wine again: but he drank so much that he fell ill again and had to start taking the waters, and so it went on . . .

A home for retired railwaymen

The presence of the waters and the casino attract large numbers of tourists to Santenay and the village now boasts a modern hotel of 60 rooms, the *Santana*. Unfortunately, there is no good restaurant in Santenay. Before World War II, however, Santenay attracted even more tourists than it does now and then had a 100-room hotel. After the war the hotel no longer seems to have been profitable and the building was sold to the French Railways and converted into a rest home for retired employees. Its replacement, the *Santana*, was opened in 1979. Thanks to its new accommodation facilities, Santenay has every appearance of developing into a notable spa.

Three villages

The old hotel, the springs and the casino are all situated in Santenay-le-Haut, one of the three villages which make up the commune. This village was formerly inhabited by vineyard workers, but nowadays the wine is made in Santenay-le-Bas, which is home for most of the 1,000 commune labourers and their families. The third village, Saint-Jean, is now only a hamlet, although evidently more important in the past. There are few historical monuments in these parts, but Saint-Jean possesses a pretty little church which is a pleasant mixture of Romanesque and Gothic. At Santenay-le-Bas there are two châteaux of great historical significance, which now belong to growers. Philip the Bold stayed in the château which bears his name and is today owned by M. Pidault. The latter has entirely restored the château and carries out his own vinification here, including vintages from his large Mercurey vineyard (about 250 acres). The second

château, which is very large, once belonged to the Romanée-Conti estate. Its immense cellars — among the finest in the Côte — can hold more than 4,000 barrels, but the present owner, René Fleurot, only cultivates about 27 acres, which is not nearly enough to fill those dark, empty spaces.

A majority of large estates

Some years ago, the Institut National des Appellations d'Origine made a number of changes to its list of Santenay vineyards. This resulted in about 975 acres of *appellation* production being registered, of which about 345 are of the Premier Cru *appellation*.
The Maison Prosper Maufoux, which is right in the centre of Santenay, became much larger in 1972. In conjunction with a leading grower, it planted more than 66 acres, the Domaine Saint-Michel, on land bought either in the Premiers Crus vineyards or on a plateau overlooking the commune. Although the vines are still relatively young, they yield a wine of encouraging quality. The Domaine Saint-Michel is not the only large holding in Santenay, for there are about 25 plots of more than 24 acres. The annual production is about 127,600 cases of red wine and only 1,850 of white. Unlike Chassagne-

Montrachet, the red is considerably more important than the white, the latter being much inferior to those of the more renowned communes of Chassagne-Montrachet, Puligny-Montrachet and Meursault.

Neighbouring communes

Most of the Santenay vineyards belong to people who live in the village or in Chassagne. However, several growers from neighbouring communes, such as Rumigny, Cheilly-les-Maranges, Dezize-les-Maranges and Sampigny-les-Maranges, also own land there. The three last communes are entitled to use their own *appellations*, but the amount of wine they produce is so small and the names so little known that it is usually sold under the *appellation* Côte de Beaune-Villages. Even in 1979, which was a year of especially abundant harvests, Cheilly, Dezize and Sampigny only produced a little over 4,500 cases under their own names. This very low level of production is clearly discouraging, and the growers of these three communes have therefore turned their attentions to plots of land in Santenay, not only to increase their income but also to gain recognition. Such incursions have not been especially welcomed by the growers of Santenay, because the land bought by the

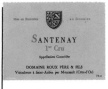

The Domaine Roux Père & Fils of Saint-Aubin owns 4½ acres of Santenay Premier Cru, divided between La Comme, Beauregard and Beaurepaire. I remember the wine for its dark, intense colour, its raspberry perfume, its suppleness and lightness.

Like the Domaine Lequin-Roussot, the Domaine Prieur-Brunet produces a very good white Santenay. The Petit Clos Rousseau was very full-bodied and had an oak taste: it might be described as a poor man's Corton-Charlemagne.

Although the vines of the Domaine Saint-Michel (which belongs partly to Prosper Maufoux) are still young, the wine has a deep red colour, and a pleasing bouquet and taste; this is very characteristic of the wine, which in time becomes very agreeable.

Although the name of Clos du Haut Village is mentioned on the label, this vineyard, the property of the Domaine Lequin-Roussot, is not a Premier Cru. However, its fine bouquet and excellent taste make it a wine of far superior quality to those with commune appellations.

In spite of its slightly off-putting name, the Santenay-Maladière from Prieur-Brunet fairly bursts with health. It is supple, with an earthy taste which leaves a slightly bitter but soft flavour. Although it has little breeding, it is strong and good.

The Domaine Mestre owns 26 acres, of which 5 are in Les Gravières. Philippe Mestre was awarded a gold medal in Paris for this wine which left me with a particularly comfortable, relaxed feeling.

inhabitants of the neighbouring communes does not produce very good wine. The growers from Dezize form an exception to this rule, cultivating their holdings very conscientiously. Since the inferior wines are often sold at considerably lower prices than those of Santenay, the market is upset and the reputation of the village adversely affected.

A wine that needs patience

While the red wines of Chassagne-Montrachet appear less immediately agreeable than the other reds of the Côte d'Or, those of Santenay lack spontaneity; they are discreet, retiring wines which may sometimes surprise by a certain astringency, but signally lack some depth, finesse and body. The popular saying that 'Santenay has the soul of Volnay and the body of Pommard' hardly seems valid. If, fancifully, one were to compare Santenay with an individual, I would visualize a rather slender, conservatively dressed man whose humble origins still betray themselves in spite of his education. Even on weekends and holidays he would tend to wear a waistcoat and tie. When meeting people he gives the initial impression of being somewhat reserved; only on better acquaintance does he start to

loosen up. Santenay conveys just this impression of reticence; it appears to lack the generous charm of a true burgundy. But do not write it off completely on that account; patient cultivation reveals its real and appreciable qualities.

Good Santenay has a fine, deep colour, a lively bouquet with a suggestion of almonds and strawberries, a strong taste with an earthy, rustic quality and a slight bitterness. It is certainly not a light wine to be drunk young, but the good vintages will develop very well if left to age. Once ready for drinking, it should be allowed time to breathe, since it opens out only very slowly. For this reason, it is often said that the last glass of a Santenay is the best.

East of the church tower

It is claimed in Santenay that the best vineyards are located to the east of the church tower — in other words, those situated between Santenay and Chassagne-Montrachet. It is there that can be found the most characteristic Santenays; in the western part of the area a slightly lighter, flatter wine is usually produced. Les Gravières is the best known, with its enclave, Le Clos de Tavannes, which borders on Chassagne-Montrachet. This vineyard

produces one of the most robust wines of Santenay: very little breeding, but strong and firm. More than others, it must be allowed to breathe for a time before serving, as, for instance, this wine from the Domaine de la Pousse d'Or which at first tasted very closed and hard, but gradually softened and became more agreeable after contact with the air. Just above Les Gravières is La Comme which, like most vineyards on the upper parts of the slope, produces a wine which is the lightest in all Santenay, with a bouquet that is both more elegant and more sumptuous. One grower referred to a Santenay La Comme as 'perfumed' during a tasting; and the less successful vintages have an odour of faded roses. Like all the good Santenays, La Comme needs to be kept for at least four years or, in the case of a good vintage, even longer.

Passe-temps

There are also two other Premiers Crus to the east of the church tower which are inferior to the others, namely Beauregard and Le Passe-Temps. Unfortunately, the château which goes with the vineyard of the same name — the Château du Passe-Temps — is more impressive than its wine. This vineyard is supposed to owe its name, which means 'pastime', to its location: situated near the village, it used to belong to a number of growers who, instead of staying home when the weather was bad, went to work there to pass the time. Other Premiers Crus, such as La Maladière (formerly the site of a lepers' hospital) and the Clos Rousseau, produce wines which are often very good.

A different pruning system

Careful inspection of the vines of Santenay will show that the method of pruning them is different from that generally practised on the Côte (with the exception of Chassagne-Montrachet). Whereas the Guyot system is used elsewhere, Santenay uses the system en cordon de Royat. There is a fundamental difference between the two methods: the

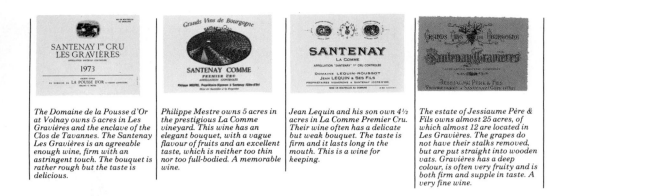

The Domaine de la Pousse d'Or at Volnay owns 5 acres in Les Gravières and the enclave of the Clos de Tavannes. The Santenay Les Gravières is an agreeable enough wine, firm with an astringent touch. The bouquet is rather rough but the taste is delicious.

Philippe Mestre owns 5 acres in the prestigious La Comme vineyard. This wine has an elegant bouquet, with a vague flavour of fruits and an excellent taste, which is neither too thin nor too full-bodied. A memorable wine.

Jean Lequin and his son own 4½ acres in La Comme Premier Cru. Their wine often has a delicate but weak bouquet. The taste is firm and it lasts long in the mouth. This is a wine for keeping.

The estate of Jessiaume Père & Fils owns almost 25 acres, of which almost 12 are located in Les Gravières. The grapes do not have their stalks removed, but are put straight into wooden vats. Gravières has a deep colour, is often very fruity and is both firm and supple in taste. A very fine wine.

Guyot system replaces the main branch bearing the fruit-yielding branches every year, while the Royat method only takes out the young shoots. The vines of Santenay and Chassagne last longer but are exhausted more quickly because made to work harder. The subsoils of these communes, though relatively richer than those of the others, does not favour root growth, hence this system of pruning is used to stimulate the vines into yielding a deeper, more subtle wine. This method also has another advantage: the vine is more resistant to frost, which can be responsible for a considerable amount of damage at Santenay, where the winters are often very cold.

Individualistic growers

The growers of Santenay, more than those of other communes, have a distinctly individualistic streak. Since the local growers' syndicate failed to reach agreement in 1976 on the election of a president, each member has tended to act very much on his own behalf. No collective publicity brochure has been published since 1974. On a more personal level, this individualism was brought home to to me when one grower only agreed to allow me to visit him provided I did not go to see his brother! Despite this, however, there is generally good understanding between the growers, who are

Below left:
The château of Passe-Temps and
its vineyard.

Below:
Instruments used by Philippe
Mestre to gauge the alcohol
content of his wine. In the
foreground is a tastevin for
examining the wine.

Bottom:
Ullaging in the cellars of the
Maison Maufoux.

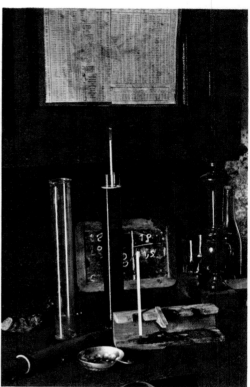

Santenay

always happy to discuss their experiences and to help one another. Philippe Mestre, one of the most important local figures, is especially involved with village affairs. I met him by chance one July day when, after months of dry weather, it was raining. Instead of simply welcoming the change of weather, M. Mestre was looking at his watch. As a municipal councillor, his main concern was how long the rain was going to last, so that he could calculate exactly how much help would have to be given to growers who had been principally affected by the drought.

Nurserymen and growers

The Domaine Mestre Père & Fils pays special care to the quality of its wines, and I have found some of the best of Santenay there. The Domaine Lequin-Roussot, which is 200 years old, is also especially attentive

The spring water of Santenay is very similar to that of Baden-Baden in Germany. It contains a high percentage of lithium, which makes it especially suitable for treating cases of nervous depression. In a sense, therefore, the water and wine of Santenay have exactly the same therapeutic qualities.

The water of Santenay is so salty (100 grammes of salt per bottle) that in 1749 someone suggested extracting salt from it, but this project was never carried out.

Santenay is twinned with Bacharach in the Mittelrhein region of Germany.

The estate of Bernard Bachelet & Fils in Dezize-les-Maranges owns 47 acres, including land in Santenay. The Santenay is often very successful, with a fine colour, fruity bouquet and very full taste with a suggestion of fruit and nuts. The Dezize-les-Maranges is also very pleasant.

to the vinification and fermentation of its wines. The estate comprises about 37 acres, and the two sons of Jean Lequin, René and Louis, are always looking for ways of making better wine. They have even started a nursery for vines which, although it may not represent a saving, does at least ensure that their plants are healthy and strong. More than half the young plants are weeded out before being replanted; and two-thirds of the young shoots were destroyed by drought in 1976. The Lequin brothers are typical of the growers of Santenay who are tireless in their efforts to improve the quality of their wines.

Below:
The Château de Chorey, one of the most beautiful estates of Chorey-lès-Beaune. It now belongs to François Germain. Dating from the 13th century, it was once partly destroyed and then rebuilt in the 17th century. The beams of the cuverie are carved with the dates of exceptional harvests, such as that of 28 August 1893.

Chorey-lès-Beaune has no fewer than four patron saints: St Lucien, St Hubert, St Vernier and St Vincent.

The records of Chorey mention that, in 1828, the wines of the commune were often used to 'improve' the wines of more famous ones.

Chorey-lès-Beaune produces an average of 45,800 cases of red wine and 165 of white under its own name.

The three communes of Les Maranges (see Santenay), whose wine is generally sold as Côte de Beaune-Villages, possess a total of 657 acres of vineyard, divided approximately as follows: Dezize-les-Maranges 198, Sampigny-les-Maranges 148, and Cheilly-les-Maranges 311. In the past, there was a Benedictine monastery in Dezize and the monks are known to have cultivated the vine.

The competence of a négociant can be clearly judged in the case of a wine such as the Côte de Beaune-Villages, which is made from a mixture of wines from several villages. The wine from Jadot had a beautiful colour. It was fleshy, having a lot of strength and a gentle, firm aftertaste. Louis Latour also produces an excellent Côte de Beaune-Villages which has a lot of style.

The Maison Joseph Drouhin often produces a fairly light Côte de Beaune-Villages, which is quite delicious and distinctive. Another good Côte de Beaune-Villages is the Clos Royer from Bouchard Père & Fils (from their own 2 acres in Ladoix-Serrigny).

The Domaine Tollot-Beaut & Fils owns about 22 acres at Chorey-lès-Beaune and some 27 acres in other communes, including Aloxe-Corton. The Chorey is excellent, with a robust and frank bouquet, an exceptionally good taste, and a fine deep colour.

François Germain and his family live in the Château de Chorey. The harvest from their own 30-acre vineyard is left to mature in the cellars of the château. Since 1976, they have also produced a red Chorey-lès-Beaune (from 2½ acres), which is a pleasant, good-quality wine.

Côte de Beaune-Villages

The *appellation* Côte de Beaune-Villages is a saviour for those communes of the Côte de Beaune which have problems in selling their red wines under their own name, either because their harvest is too small, their name too little known, or the quality of their wine not sufficiently high. This *appellation d'origine* is attributed to 16 villages which, however, have a right to their own *appellation* (if needed, their names can be completed by 'Côte de Beaune' in letters of equal size). The *appellation* Côte de Beaune-Villages is thus different from the *appellation* Côte de-Nuits-Villages, which comprises wines without individual identity. Of the villages which sell their wines under the *appellation* Côte de Nuits-Villages, only Fixin has the right to sell them under its own name as well.

For red wines only

The villages which can be grouped under the Côte de Beaune-Villages are the following (in alphabetical order): Auxey-Duresses, Blagny (near Meursault), Chassagne-Montrachet, Cheilly-les-Maranges, Chorey-lès-Beaune, Dezize-les-Maranges, Ladoix-Serrigny, Meursault, Monthelie, Pernand-Vergelesses, Puligny-Montrachet, Saint-Aubin, Saint-Romain, Sampigny-les-Maranges, Santenay, Savigny-lès-Beaune.
Despite the presence of Puligny-Montrachet, which is known principally for its white wine, the Côte de Beaune-Villages is applied only to red wines, whereas the Côte de Nuits-Villages also includes a few white wines. Aloxe-Corton, Beaune, Pommard and Volnay, the four great *appellations* among the red wines, cannot be demoted to Côtes de Beaune-Villages but only to Bourgogne. In the past, the quantity of Côte de Beaune-Villages used to vary considerably from year to year, since growers preferred to sell their wine in good vintage years under their own commune *appellation*. Thus, in 1971 only 45,600 cases were registered, as opposed to

156,400 in 1974. Production has now become stabilized at around 98,700 cases. The quality of Côte de Beaune-Villages — a typical *négociant* wine — is very variable.

Chorey-lès-Beaune

Chorey-lès-Beaune is one of the most interesting communes whose wine is sold under the *appellation* of Côte de Beaune-Villages and deserves individual mention.

There are about 40 wine growers in Chorey-lès-Beaune, a very old village, and all are very concerned with quality. The Domaine Tollot-Beaut, notably, produces a wine which is much sought after by the great restaurants. The 300 acres of vineyard at Chorey are located to the north of Beaune, some way from the foot of the slopes and to the east of the *route nationale 74*, except for a small plot located to the west, on the borders of Savigny-lès-Beaune.

Chalonnais

Because of the limited amount of wine it produces — less even than that of Chablis — the Chalonnais is undoubtedly the least known wine-producing region in the whole of Burgundy. It is sometimes called the 'region of Mercurey', although Mercurey does not enjoy a very widespread reputation. During the 18th and 19th centuries, the merchants of Beaune sold this red wine (like that of Givry) under the name of a commune of the Côte de Beaune. Just at the time that the laws governing the use of *appellation d'origine* came into force, World War I broke out, reducing even further the numbers of an already under-populated area, and few people were left to work in the vineyards.

Renewal

Times have now changed, and the Chalonnais is going through a period of prosperity. During the past 15 years, the quantity of Mercurey produced has grown by some 55,500 cases, and the vineyards of Rully are also expanding. The Chalonnais now provides the wine for much of the regional *appellations* Bourgogne and Bourgogne Passetoutgrains. Since Aligoté vines do very well in this area, the Bourgogne Aligoté de Bouzeron has also acquired a very high reputation. Finally, Rully produces a sparkling Bourgogne of remarkable delicacy.

An extension of the Côte de Beaune

Although the Côte of the Chalonnais is a direct extension of that of Beaune, the land is much more fragmented. Unlike the long stretches of vineyard which characterize the Côte de Beaune, the Chalonnais is broken into a large number of small wine-producing areas, and the four principal *appellations* — Rully, Mercurey, Givry and Montagny — are several miles apart.

I discovered this white Rully at Le Lameloise in Chagny. It had a limpid, almost platinum, colour, a fresh and fruity perfume, and a pleasant, characteristically refreshing taste.

The Delorme Domaine de la Renarde produces a red Rully of exceptional lightness and a very fresh white which is softer and richer than the red, but strengthened by a certain immaturity.

The Clos Saint-Jacques is a white wine from the Domaine de la Folie. This is a delicious Rully with a lot of strength and a characteristic taste. The very good red Rully from this estate, the Clos de Belle-Croix, has a black label. I usually find this wine to be very successful, although both red and white of 1980 and 1981 are disappointing.

The house of Faiveley used to produce a rather heavy red wine from its own 12½ acres in Rully. This wine has now become rather more lively, but it does vary in quality from year to year. The 1978, for instance, was far better than the 1979. The white Rully is attractive, distinctive and supple, with a light aroma of nuts.

The wines represented by these labels are only a few of the good wines of Rully. At Le Faugeron restaurant in Paris. I also found a very fine white Rully from the Domaine du Prieuré (owned by M. Monassier). The wine had a fairly strong bouquet of Chardonnay and a nice fresh taste.

Another delicious white Rully is the one from Chanzy Frères (Bouzeron). It usually has a clean, mouth-filling taste with a slightly nutty aroma.

Rully

It was no accident that my favourite restaurant in Burgundy, *Le Lameloise* at Chagny, recommends Rully as a fine *vin de table,* for the vineyards are about two and a half miles away. According to Pierre Forgeot, the village of Rully was built on the actual hillside in Roman times, but a plague epidemic in 1347 forced the villagers to build a new village, that of present-day Rully, at the foot of the hill. History now seems to be repeating itself, because the vineyards are once again climbing up the slope.

At the top of one hill about 100 ft high, Jean-François Delorme, a particularly energetic grower, has cleared some 44 acres for cultivation. He is not the only local grower to increase the area of his vineyards, and Rully is one of the rare wine-producing communes where it is possible to expand in this way. In good years, the annual harvest is, on average, 27,500 cases of red wine and 25,000

of white, but this yield will shortly increase to approximately 33,500 for both wines and no doubt this will increase in the future to almost 90,000 cases.

A white wine of quality

Jean-François Delorme, whose estate consists of about 75 acres, including 12½ in Givry and Mercurey, has a simple explanation for this rapid development; 'Since the prices of the other burgundies have risen so much, our wines are now well worth buying. Furthermore, the white wines of Rully are of high quality, especially the good vintages. Our red wines are not as good, but the vineyards are still relatively young, younger, for example, than those of Mercurey. But even if the red Rully is often too light, with too little body, it still has great delicacy.'

Noël Bouton, of the Domaine de la Folie, comprising 42 acres, is also an enthusiastic advocate of Rully and sells both his red and white wines to a number of leading restaurants.

Like cool marble

Although the red wine of Rully still lacks body, the white is an up-to-par burgundy. Made from the Chardonnay grape, it has a beautiful transparent colour, sometimes with greenish tints. The bouquet and the taste have certain recognizable characteristics, often evoking the cool, polished smoothness of marble. Its very dry, refreshing taste make this an excellent wine to be drunk as an aperitif and it goes very well with mussels, oysters, a terrine or cold meats.

It is generally recommended that a red Mercurey should be uncorked one hour before being served. This is especially applicable to the Mercurey of Paul Jean Granger, which is a very strong wine, needing to be kept five or six years.

Emile Voarick is the owner of almost 45 acres of the Mercurey appellation. I was not very impressed by his Mercurey 1972, with its disagreeable perfume, but I did find his Clos du Roy very pleasant. This is a distinctive, ingratiating wine which will certainly become more subtle with time.

The house of Faiveley owns 178 acres in Mercurey. In addition to its simple Mercurey, it also produces various 'Clos' wines. One of these is the Clos du Roy, a perfectly 'correct' wine (7½ acres), but I rather prefer the Clos des Myglands (17¼ acres) which often has a taste of wood and fruit. The white Clos Rochette (5 acres) is also a good wine.

Michel Juillot is one of the most competent growers of Mercurey. I have tasted several of his wines, including those bearing the 'Chante Flûté' validation; all of them were extremely good. His Clos des Barraults, which is located on the upper part of the slope, produces a wine of character, body and balance.

Other good Mercureys not mentioned elsewhere are produced by: Jacques Tupinier (14¾ acres, 2½ of which produces a delicious white wine): Michel Raquillet (19¾ acres).

Below:
In the foreground: grapes harvested at Mercurey. In addition to the vineyards within the commune of Mercurey itself, the appellation includes those in the neighbouring hamlets.

Opposite page:
A street in Mercurey. A number of wine-growing families have lived there for several generations. Unlike most of the communes in the Chalonnais, Mercurey does not have a wine cooperative.

Fifteen years ago, Mercurey produced over 160,000 cases a year. This figure has recently reached almost 180,000.

The wines with the 'Chante Flûté' validation are chosen from among the best of Mercurey. A 'chante flute' is a small plunging siphon used in Burgundy.

There are a large number of commemorative crosses around the village, notably in the places where Napoleon stopped.

Mercurey

The vineyards of Mercurey, about seven miles from those of the Côte de Beaune, grow on land with a subsoil like that of the Côte d'Or. The same grape, the Pinot Noir, is also used, which gives the red wines of Mercurey a family resemblance to those of the Côte and also places them in the same price range. It is apt that Mercurey should derive its name from Mercury, the god of commerce, to whom the Romans dedicated a temple here. Mercurey is the senior *appellation* of the Chalonnais, not only by reason of price and reputation, but also because the harvest is greater than that of Rully, Givry and Montagny together. There is a total of some 1,605 acres producing an average of 212,200 cases of red wine and 9,050 of white. The latter, which is produced from the Chardonnay, is grown on land which is unsuitable for the Pinot Noir.

Large estates

Mercurey is the only Chalonnais wine to be produced and marketed on a considerable scale, and a number of firms have invested heavily in local vineyard acreage. Five estates — Bouchard Ainé, Faiveley, Pidault, Protheau and Rodet — own more than half the vineyards, which obviously leads to a certain amount of jealousy on the part of the other owners. One of these estates, for example, made a purely speculative purchase of about 250 acres of partially cultivated land, for which it paid a much higher price than the current market value. Clearly determined to make its investment pay, the estate has given more attention to quantity than to quality. This policy has two unfortunate consequences: rising land values and falling wine prices.

The Chante Flûté

Mercurey also includes about 60 small producers with less than 2½ acres and a number of medium-size holdings. The former will probably disappear altogether, however, over the next generation. With the admirable aim of increasing the fame of Mercurey, the wine growers have formed a brotherhood, La Confrérie Saint-Vincent et des Disciples de la Chante Flûté de Mercurey which, since 1972, has organized a yearly tasting at which the red wines of the previous two harvests and the white of the last harvest are presented. The jury, composed of five experts from Mercurey and the surrounding area, takes its responsibilities very seriously, and selects only the best wines. In 1976, only 300,000 bottles were thus honoured by the jury. The selected wines are given a numbered label which bears the name of the producer, the vintage and the words 'Chante Flûté'. From experience, I can affirm that the bottles bearing this label are indeed exceptionally good.

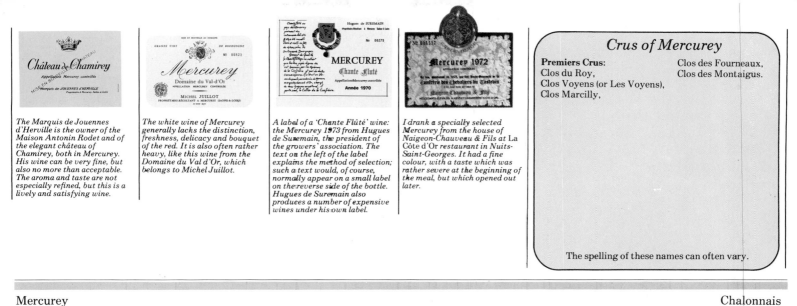

Crus of Mercurey

Premiers Crus:
Clos du Roy,
Clos Voyens (or Les Voyens),
Clos Marcilly,
Clos des Fourneaux,
Clos des Montaigus.

The spelling of these names can often vary.

A single street

The tasting cellar of Mercurey, which is another collective enterprise on the part of the owners, is one of the few attractions of Mercurey. The houses of this village of 1,500 inhabitants are strung out along a single road, on either side of which are the vines. *L'Hôtellerie du Val d'Or*, unprepossessing from the outside, has a small, well-lit dining room presided over by the owner, Jean-Claude Cogny. He offers a number of delicious specialities: *terrine de volaille, quenelles de brochet* and *coquelet au vin de Mercurey,* all of which I enjoyed enormously. He also serves many other delicious regional dishes.

Low yield per acre

The *appellation* Mercurey also includes wines from the neighbouring communes of Saint-Martin-sous-Montaigu and Bourgneuf-Val d'Or, although the latter is now considered part of Mercurey. According to an official decree of 1943, the following five vineyards have the right to the *appellation* Premier Cru: Le Clos du Roy, Le Clos Voyens (or Les Voyens), Le Clos Marcilly, Le Clos des Fourneaux and Le Clos des Montaigus. The wines produced by these vineyards are not necessarily the best, and it often happens that those which are not classified produce better wine. Red Mercury must contain at

least 10.5° of alcohol (11° for a white), the Premiers Crus and the wines which bear the name Mercurey followed by the name of a vineyard must have at least 11° (11.5° for whites). Another standard is worth noting: the yield, fixed at a maximum of 35 hectolitres per hectare, is the lowest in the Chalonnais, Mâconnais and Beaujolais, and the same as that of the communes of the Côte d'Or.

Le Belle Gabrielle

The fame of Mercurey is by no means of recent date; for centuries, it was one of the favourite wines of the aristocracy. It used to be said that there were three types of Mercurey: the first for people of high social standing, the second for their servants, and the third for washing their horses' hooves. Although red Mercurey has always been a wine with a lot of body, it was also a favourite among ladies, notably Marguerite de Flandres and the beautiful Gabrielle d'Estrées, mistress of Henri IV, who apparently preferred Givry. The growers of Givry and Rully recently tried to affiliate themselves to those of Mercurey, but the wines of these communes are so different that the project was abandoned.

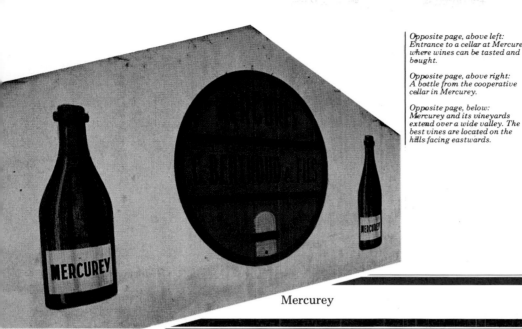

Opposite page, above left:
Entrance to a cellar at Mercurey where wines can be tasted and bought.

Opposite page, above right:
A bottle from the cooperative cellar in Mercurey.

Opposite page, below:
Mercurey and its vineyards extend over a wide valley. The best vines are located on the hills facing eastwards.

Left:
Sign on a wall in Mercurey. Although direct sales by wine growers to individuals are increasing, the négociants still control from 60% to 70% of sales to consumers.

Below:
There are a number of very attractive houses, such as the one illustrated here, in Mercurey (pop. 1,500). One of the chapels of the village church dates from the 11th century.

Hugues de Suremain enjoys describing his negotiations with the great American buyer, Frank Schoonmaker. On one occasion, Suremain extolled his own Mercurey 1961. Schoonmaker claimed it was too tannic, closely resembling a Bordeaux, and proceeded to recommend at least three ways of clearing the wine. Suremain replied that he would never subject his wine to any such process and advised Schoonmaker to wait for three years, when the wine, as Schoonmaker knew, would be much more expensive. Despite the American's protests, Suremain refused to give way. In 1976 the Mercurey 1971 had indeed lost its tannin.

Quite a few white Mercureys have a distinct taste of burnt almonds.

Twenty years behind

According to Hugues de Suremain, president of the wine growers' association, Mercurey owes its current reputation to being 'at least 20 years behind the Côte d'Or'. Working methods have remained very traditional. Fermentation is often allowed to go on longer than is strictly necessary and is still frequently carried out in cement vats. Chaptalization (addition of sugar to the must to increase alcohol content) is used very little. Finally, the wine is always left to age in oak barrels.

The price of Mercurey has tended to be lower, in the past, than those of the wines of the Côte d'Or, although they are not much cheaper at the present time. Hugues de Suremain told me: 'The crisis of the early 1970s hardly affected us, because we tried to keep our prices steady.' However, the Côte d'Or undoubtedly exerts a strong influence on Mercurey, since about 70% of its wines are sold by the *négociants* of Beaune or Nuits-Saint-Georges. As in the Côte d'Or, the wine is sold in casks of 228 litres instead of in the traditional 215-litre casks of the Chalonnais and the Mâconnais.

A great table wine

Although regions of Mercurey and the Côte d'Or have numerous points in common, the wines have their own distinct personalities. Those of Mercurey lack the breeding of their neighbours to the north, but they are characterized by generosity, perhaps brusqueness, by a sort of rustic elegance and a taste which is sometimes rough and tannic. Generally speaking, they age well and open out after two or three years of keeping.

Although never very gracious, the bouquet can be found very pleasing from the first scent; it evokes a variety of fruits, including blackcurrant, raspberry and redcurrant (while the bouquet of the Côte d'Or wines is more suggestive of flowers). But nothing is more subjective than one's appreciation of a perfume. As an example of this, there is the French oenologist who, in the presence of his colleagues, compared the bouquet of Mercurey to the smell of a 'fresh sausage sandwich'! The colour of Mercurey is a dark ruby red. All these characteristics make it a good, individual wine.

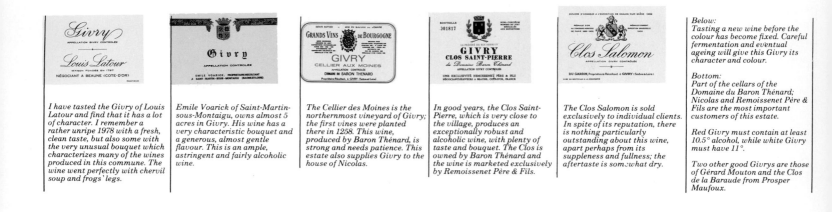

I have tasted the Givry of Louis Latour and find that it has a lot of character. I remember a rather unripe 1978 with a fresh, clean taste, but also some with the very unusual bouquet which characterizes many of the wines produced in this commune. The wine went perfectly with chervil soup and frogs' legs.

Emile Voarick of Saint-Martin-sous-Montaigu, owns almost 5 acres in Givry. His wine has a very characteristic bouquet and a generous, almost gentle flavour. This is an ample, astringent and fairly alcoholic wine.

The Cellier des Moines is the northernmost vineyard of Givry; the first vines were planted there in 1258. This wine, produced by Baron Thénard, is strong and needs patience. This estate also supplies Givry to the house of Nicolas.

In good years, the Clos Saint-Pierre, which is very close to the village, produces an exceptionally robust and alcoholic wine, with plenty of taste and bouquet. The Clos is owned by Baron Thénard and the wine is marketed exclusively by Remoissenet Père & Fils.

The Clos Salomon is sold exclusively to individual clients. In spite of its reputation, there is nothing particularly outstanding about this wine, apart perhaps from its suppleness and fullness; the aftertaste is somewhat dry.

Below:
Tasting a new wine before the colour has become fixed. Careful fermentation and eventual ageing will give this Givry its character and colour.

Bottom:
Part of the cellars of the Domaine du Baron Thénard; Nicolas and Remoissenet Père & Fils are the most important customers of this estate.

Red Givry must contain at least 10.5° alcohol, while white Givry must have 11°.

Two other good Givrys are those of Gérard Mouton and the Clos de la Baraude from Prosper Maufoux.

Givry

Givry is distinguished from the other wine-producing communes of the Chalonnais by its very rich past. Even as early as the 6th century, the village enjoyed a high reputation and from the Middle Ages onwards royalty, aristocracy and merchant class alike sang the praises of Givry wine. All modern growers will remind you that Henri IV was a great admirer of the wine, although this is not necessarily a tribute, since that monarch was noted more for his heavy drinking than for his fine palate. In the 18th century Givry was still considered as the wine-growing centre of the Chalonnais, a fact indicated by the immense size of the cellars of the Domaine du Baron Thénard, in which it was possible to store more than 2,000 barrels and nine huge casks with a capacity of hundreds of hectolitres. Givry's renown lasted until the end of the 19th century, when the local wines were much more expensive than those of Mercurey.

Threat to an appellation

This period of prosperity seems now to have ended, and Givry as a wine-producing commune runs a serious risk of vanishing altogether. This is not because the vines are sick or badly maintained, but because the expansion of the urban area of Chalon-sur-Saône is gradually eating into the land around Givry. It is clearly very hard for the growers to resist the attractive offers made by the property developers, and the area of land under cultivation for wine has recently diminished substantially. The *appellation* is thus caught up in a vicious circle, since falling production inevitably means a lowering of both reputation and price which, in turn, provokes further selling of land. Fortunately, however, there are still a number of wine growers with sufficient belief in Givry to do everything possible to safeguard the *appellation*. Louis Latour, for example, rents almost 5 acres of vines; the Du Gardin family, owners of the Clos Salomon, are extending their vineyards; and, at the instigation of M. Bordeaux-Montreux, the Domaine du Baron Thénard cultivates more than 50 acres, which is about a quarter of the total *appellation*. This estate is divided between three reputable vineyards: the Cellier aux Moines, the Clos Saint-Pierre and Les Bois-Chevaux.

The wine of Givry has often been compared to that of Volnay, yet the very distinct personality of the former makes this a misleading comparison. Its bouquet has often reminded me of the smell of a wet forest or, more prosaically, of damp woollen garments drying on a radiator. There is something veiled and indistinct in the taste of a Givry, yet it is precisely this quality of velvety vagueness which makes it so seductive. It is a wine that usually can be recognized easily at blind tastings. A good Givry is a round, rather alcoholic wine, which generally ages well.

As well as an annual production of about 47,800 cases of red Givry, the commune also produces 4,850 cases of white. I know only that which is produced by Baron Thénard, which has a soft, fresh, pure taste and is very agreeably flavoured. Unfortunately, this wine is not for general sale.

Were it not for Louis Latour, one of the most vigorous promoters of its wine, Montagny would certainly not enjoy its present reputation. Louis Latour produces a wine of very limpid colour, very dry taste, slightly fruity, and sometimes slightly green.

I tasted this Premier Cru at the cooperative wine cellar at Buxy, one of the largest producers of Montagny. Although not all the member growers of this cooperative produce good wines, the best are of appreciable quality.

Jean Vachet owns several acres in the commune of Saint-Vallerin, where he also carries out his own bottling. I now find his Montagny rather pleasant, especially the Premier Cru Les Coères. Another good Coères is that produced by Bernard Michel (same village).

Montagny

Montagny is the southernmost *appellation* of the Chalonnais and consists of only 754 acres of vines. As the name of the village hints, the land is fairly broken and the vineyards are scattered over hills of altitudes varying from about 800 to 1,300 feet. Most of the vineyards can be seen from Montagny itself, situated in the hollow of a valley. The only exception is the commune of Mont Laurent, situated near Buxy, which is included in the *appellation*, as are Jully-lès-Buxy and Saint-Vallerin. Formerly, the wine from these three villages was sold under the name of Côte de Buxy and for several centuries both red and white wines were produced. According to Jullien, the author already quoted, the white wine was slightly sparkling and, if bottled during the March following the harvest, would become as bubbly as champagne. Nowadays, there is only one Montagny, white and non-sparkling, produced from the Chardonnay.

A fresh mouth and a clear head

Although the wines of Montagny are only of secondary importance in the context of the whole of Burgundy — average production being 34,400 cases — they are still of considerable quality. In an article in the now-defunct review *Wine,* Michael Broadbent noted that a good Montagny was a fine, seductive wine which offered rather more for its price than a more classic white burgundy, although it would never, of course, attain the elegance of a Montrachet.

The wine of Montagny has a fine golden colour, tinted with green, a delicate bouquet, usually fairly reserved, and a very characteristic, exceptionally dry taste. A number of those I have tasted are high in alcohol and have a certain softness and richness, while others are more earthy and leave a spicy aftertaste. Some connoisseurs claim to be able to detect a taste of nuts but I

have never been able to trace it. One peculiarity of Montagny is the local legislation which allows any Montagny to call itself Premier Cru as long as it has a minimum of 11.5° of alcohol instead of 11°. The existence of this law risks devaluing the *appellation*, since the extra half-degree would, in all other parts of Burgundy, only justify the addition of the word 'supérieur'. But whether it has 11° or 11.5°, this wine remains equally agreeable to drink, and there is much truth in the local saying that 'Montagny keeps the mouth fresh and the head clear'.

The cooperative of Lugny St Genoux-de-Scissé is supported by about 200 wine-growers, who together cultivate about 2,225 acres. Their red Mâcon (Supérieur) is often fruity and easy to drink.

Every January the Perraton cup is awarded in Mâcon to the best white Mâcon harvested the previous year. The Prissé cooperative has often won the cup. Georges Duboeuf markets this wine regularly. The ordinary Mâcon-Prissé is also very good.

Piat has the sole right to use a very special long bottle, which is also used for this white Maçon. The wine, which is produced by the Viré cooperative, often has rather a lot of greenness, but is fresh, distinctive and very good.

Wine from Viré (formerly Viriaco) was known as early as the year 751. Hubert Desbois is the owner of the château of Viré, where he produces a fresh, earthy wine, which is marketed by the house of Prosper Maufoux.

Other good wines from Mâcon which are not mentioned in this or the following section include: Mâcon-Pierreclos from Guffens-Heynen (red); Mâcon-Uchizy from the Domaine Talmard; the Mâcons from the cooperative in Chardonnay (especially white); the Mâcon of the cooperative in Buxy (especially white); Château de Mirande, a Mâcon-Villages; the white Mâcon from Henry Lafarge in Bray.

Mâconnais

The Mâconnais, a large area between the Chalonnais and Beaujolais, is often regarded as that part of France where north meets south. Here the roofs of the houses become noticeably flatter, the terracotta tiles are rounded, and facades of buildings sprout galleries. The grapes ripen sooner than in the Chalonnais and, in general, harvests begin a week earlier than in the areas to the north. Although there are a number of large towns, making this the most densely populated wine-producing area of Burgundy, the Mâconnais seems to have escaped the worst disfigurations of the consumer society. Certain parts of the region still look as though they belong to another age, with their ancient villages, lovely little Romanesque churches, narrow, winding roads, green and peaceful meadows, pure air and marvellously fresh scent of unspoilt countryside. Large-scale tourism has not yet assailed the Mâconnais, and one can only hope that the region will preserve its native character and old-fashioned charm for many years to come.

Mâcon

The capital of this region is Mâcon. In Roman times it was already considered an important strongpoint, because of its strategically advantageous position on the banks of the Saône. It was also noted at that time for its workshops, which specialized in making bows and arrows designed for hunting in the vast, dense forest which covered the area. Cultivation of the vine in the area also dates from those early times. Ausonius, the 4th-century poet of Saint-Emilion, mentions vineyards in the region around Tournus and Mâcon.
Although the buildings of modern Mâcon are not especially notable for their beauty, the centre of the town, the fine quays along the Saône, the narrow streets and picturesque little squares still provide considerable interest. There are several reputable restaurants in the town, such as the *Auberge*

Bressane, with its very talented chef, and the Frantel restaurant, the *Saint-Vincent.* The dishes at the *Hôtel Bellevue*, where André Champagne is both owner and head chef, are perhaps slightly less distinguished, but nevertheless equally delicious. Mâcon is really a crossroads town, close to Bresse with its *appellation contrôlée* poultry, to the Charolais with its famous beef cattle, and to Lyon, third city of France and famous as a gastronomic centre.

A 33-day journey

Although cultivation of the vine was already known in Mâcon in Roman times, it was not until the 11th and 12th centuries that wine-growing expanded under the influence of the monks of Cluny. For several centuries, the wines of Mâcon were restricted to local consumption; they only became widely known after the 17th century, thanks to Claude Brosse. Finding it hard to sell his wine near home, this enterprising grower decided to take his wine to Versailles and prove its qualities to the court. So he set off with two casks on a cart, pulled by his strongest oxen. The journey north lasted 33 days; shortly after his arrival at Versailles, he happened to be attending mass in the chapel of the château, when Louis XIV made his entrance. Brosse, like the rest of the congregation, fell to his knees but he was so tall that even in that position he still seemed to be on his feet. After the service the king asked to be introduced to this man of such impressive stature. Claude Brosse then explained why he had journeyed to Versailles, and the king, intrigued, expressed a desire to taste this wine from Mâcon. Several sips were enough to convince him, and he declared the wine far superior to those of Suresnes and Beaugency, the Loire wines then drunk at court. Brosse had won his point and from that day his reputation was made. Everyone at court clamoured for his wine. Although he returned to his native town, he made several more journey to Paris

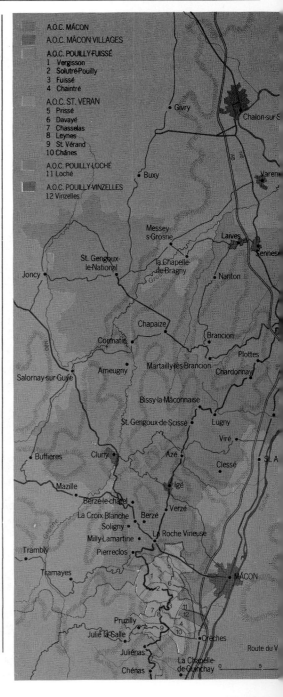

A.O.C. MÂCON
A.O.C. MÂCON VILLAGES
A.O.C. POUILLY-FUISSÉ
1 Vergisson
2 Solutré-Pouilly
3 Fuissé
4 Chaintré
A.O.C. ST. VERAN
5 Prissé
6 Davayé
7 Chasselas
8 Leynes
9 St Vérand
10 Chânes
A.O.C. POUILLY-LOCHÉ
11 Loché
A.O.C. POUILLY-VINZELLES
12 Vinzelles

Opposite page:
Map of the Mâconnais. There are more than 9,000 wine producers in the area.

Left:
The vineyards of Chardonay. The grape variety of the same name may have originated from Saint-Véran, where it has been known since the 17th century.

Below:
Two cellarmen of the Lugny cooperative. Cooperatives do especially well in the Mâconnais.

Bottom:
Lunch-time at the Maison du Mâconnais, where you can enjoy an excellent meal at a reasonable price. The Maison makes its own selection of wines from the region and its wine list is indeed remarkable.

Mâconnais

and eventually became a very wealthy man. This, at any rate, is the story; and even if not accurate in every detail, it is undeniably a splendid example of resourcefulness and individual self-promotion.

More white than red

During the age of the Sun King, the Mâconnais was principally known for its red wine, but today the region produces a preponderance of white. Out of 12,600 acres in cultivation, about 6,200 are planted with Gamay and a small area with Pinot Noir. The remaining 6,400 or so are planted with Chardonnay (except for a tiny area of Aligoté) which yield a white wine known for its high quality, due to the virtues of the very calcareous subsoil. Red Mâcon, however, sells much more successfully than white Mâcon, with the obvious exception of a great wine like Pouilly-Fuissé. For this reason, the growers now prefer, if the land is suitable, to plant red varieties. The Mâconnais includes a number of *appellations d'origine,* both regional *appellations* as well as the more reputable individual *appellations*, such as Pouilly-Fuissé, Pouilly-Vinzelles, Pouilly-Loché, Saint-Véran, which are the subject of later individual sections.

The Clos du Chapitre (about 5 acres) at Viré is a very well known vineyard owned by the Maison Jacques Dépagneux. The wine has a rather special bouquet, with a smoky perfume; it is a robust, solid, full wine with a slight reflection of green in the colour.

Joseph Drouhin is one of the négociants of Beaune who markets a Mâcon-Villages, followed by the name of a vineyard, here Laforet. The fine limpid colour is slightly tinted with green, the bouquet rather reserved and unripe, the taste distinctive and agreeable, with a suggestion of soft fruit.

Les Charmes (198 acres) is located on a wide plateau behind the cooperative of Lugny. This vineyard has a lot of old vines which produce an exceptional wine — refreshing, with a fine aroma and a strong, rich taste.

Les Genièvres is a clos of almost 20 acres located very close to Les Charmes at Lugny. The wine is marketed exclusively by Louis Latour, who keeps the wine in his cellars, allowing it to mature in wooden barrels. This is an excellent wine in its own individual way.

One of the best Dutch restaurateurs, Paul Fagel, features the white Mâcon-Clessé from Jean Thévenet. The wine is particularly remarkable for its fruity agreeable perfume and its fresh, nicely balanced taste.

The Château de Byonne has almost 7½ acres, two-thirds of which are planted with white and the other third with red. The very fresh white wine has green tints and a distinctive, slightly fruity perfume, with high vinosity. The wine is distributed by the Maison Chevalier & Fils.

Mâcon, Mâcon Supérieur, Mâcon-Villages

The wine-producing areas of the Mâconnais belong to numerous small family estates, but this division into small holdings has long been counterbalanced by the creation of cooperatives. Thus more than half of both white and red Mâcon is produced by 15 cooperative cellars. The many first prizes won by the wines from the cooperatives in local competitions prove that these wines are generally better than those produced by individual growers — contrary to what happens in most other wine-producing areas. In a number of vineyards, the cooperatives are considered a necessary evil, but in the Mâconnais, on the other hand, they are very highly regarded and enjoy the enthusiastic support of the wine growers. Working meetings are well attended, holiday excursions are organized and weekend visitors receive a warm welcome. In short, the Mâconnais has always supported new developments. In 1966, when the members of the Lugny cooperative were asked to vote on amalgamation with the cooperative of Saint-Gengoux-de-Scissé, 299 out of 300 approved the motion. The director of another cooperative assured me that in the Mâconnais they tend to talk not so much of 'I' as of 'we'.

Too many appellations

The largest cooperatives are those of Lugny-Saint-Gengoux-de-Scissé, Viré and Prissé. Their reputation, especially for white wines, is so high that it was at one stage proposed that communes such as Lugny, Viré and others should have their own *appellation d'origine contrôlée*. However, an inspector of the Institut National des Appellations d'Origine told me that the introduction of further new names was undesirable since there were already too many *appellations* in the Mâconnais and the addition of still more new names would only create additional

The Domaine du Lys, owned by Thorin, produces a fairly agreeable Mâcon-Villages, although it is a bit rough. The 1975 had a fresh, 'green' taste, with a flavour of earth and spices: the colour was very limpid, the bouquet good.

Opposite page:
This huge machine at the cooperative of Lugny siphons off the stalks after they have been removed from the grapes.

Right:
The Château de Viré in the village of the same name. Viré is one of the best-known appellations of Mâcon-Villages. Curnonsky, in his book, Cuisine et Vins de France, lists at least 163 recipes for which Viré is particularly suitable.

Below:
Arrival of the grapes at the cooperative of Lugny.

confusion among consumers. It is perhaps worth noting, too, that one recently created *appellation*, Saint-Véran, has not been as successful as expected, and this too may have discouraged further elaboration (see page 161).

Red and rosé Mâcon

The vineyards of the Mâconnais, like those of the Beaujolais, are planted with Gamay; but since the soil and subsoil are not alike, red Mâcon lacks the charm and suppleness of Beaujolais. However, although it may not be the most elegant of wines, red Mâcon is still better than the Bourgogne Grand Ordinaire, the most basic *appellation*. The northern part of the Mâconnais produces wines which are harder and rougher than those of the south. During numerous tastings of red Mâcon, I have felt that although the majority of the wines tend to be astringent, there are some others which, even when young, are almost as supple and perfumed as Beaujolais. The cooperative of Saint-Gengoux-de-Scissé produces some very successful wines in this category which often win gold medals. This region also produces a Mâcon rosé (which is marketed by Piat, among others), a fresh and agreeable wine which occasionally has an earthy taste.

White Mâcon and Mâcon Supérieur

The red Mâcon is produced chiefly in the north of the region, while the white is produced almost everywhere else. The wines from the more ordinary areas bear the *appellations* of Mâcon Blanc or Pinot-Chardonnay-Mâcon. This last *appellation* has tended to reinforce the widespread but erroneous idea that there is a grape variety called Pinot-Chardonnay. In fact, the *appellation* exists because, in theory, a Mâcon Blanc can be produced from either Pinot or Chardonnay, though it is almost always made from the latter.
A white Mâcon is a wine of great freshness, sometimes rather 'green' and often with a certain earthy taste. Some Mâcon whites

have a scent of spices and honey. They are usually drunk very young, but the best ones keep their freshness for about three years. White Mâcon must have at least 10° of alcohol and the red 9°. If either of these wines is 1° above these levels, it has the right to the *appellation* Mâcon Supérieur, though this is rarely claimed and the white wines in this category are usually sold as simple Mâcon.

Mâcon-Villages and Mâcon with a commune appellation

The *appellation* Mâcon-Villages is really identical to the *appellation* Mâcon Supérieur, but only applies to the white wines. To qualify for the former *appellation*, the legal maximum level of production is 50 hectolitres per hectare and the minimum degree of alcohol is 11° (0.5° more than for an ordinary white Bourgogne.) Unlike Mâcon Supérieur, however, the territory which can produce Mâcon-Villages is strictly defined and is limited to 43 of the best villages. As a rule, Mâcon-Villages is fuller and finer than Mâcon Supérieur and is a better wine. The Mâcon which is sold under the name of an individual commune, such as Mâcon-Viré, is really Mâcon-Villages but normally with

more character. This category includes reds as well as whites, but these are very much in the minority since the average production of reds never exceeds more than about 55,500 cases while that of the whites (including the Mâcon-Villages) can be as high as 994,000 cases or thereabouts. This latter figure is also substantially greater than the total production of Mâcon Blanc and of Mâcon Supérieur Blanc. The Mâcon-Villages wines should, therefore, be of great interest to buyers who are looking for a good bottle of wine at a reasonable price.

Left:
Advertising in Solutré. It was there that I heard the saying, 'Better to stick your nose into a glass of Pouilly-Fuissé than into your neighbour's business.'

Below:
A goatherd and her charges. Goat cheese and Pouilly-Fuissé go extremely well together.

Opposite page, left:
Marcel Vincent of the Château Fuissé.

Opposite page, right:
View of Fuissé.

Another distinguished Pouilly-Fuissé is the La Roche from Guffens-Heynen in Vergisson. I also quite like the Solutré from André Dauvigne.

The Clos du Bourg is located next to the church in the centre of Fuissé and belongs to Maurice Luquet. There he makes a full, fleshy, well-knit wine. The colour is generally clear and limpid, the perfume fine.

Although Louis Latour sells a very large quantity of Pouilly-Fuissé, the quality is irreproachable. It seems a little less fleshy than the others, perhaps because Louis Latour is also deeply involved in the production of the great white wines of the Côte.

The Château Fuissé produces outstanding wines, not only in exceptional years, but also in less favourable ones. Subtlety, character, refinement and balance are qualities which are always present. The best quality is to be found in the Vieilles Vignes.

Pouilly-Fuissé, Pouilly-Vinzelles, Pouilly-Loché Mâconnais

About seven miles west of Mâcon is a small area which produces wine which could be termed as liquid gold: Pouilly-Fuissé. The 1,384 acres of this *appellation* produce the best white wine in the whole of the Mâconnais and extend over four communes — Fuissé, Solutré, the greater part of Chaintré and Vergisson. The vineyard land is scattered at altitudes ranging from about 1,000 to 1,300 feet. The wine takes its name from Pouilly, a hamlet almost adjoining Solutré and Fuissé, which is a somewhat larger village. The two rocky outcrops of Solutré and Vergisson dominate the ocean of vineyards like two gigantic, petrified ships. The Roche de Solutré is particularly impressive; in 1866, an immense prehistoric ossuary was discovered at its foot, containing the bones of about 40,000 horses which must have been chased over the cliff by prehistoric hunters. Later, the Romans established a military camp at Solutré. It is also said that Vercingetorix once lit a fire there to serve as a rallying point for the Gallic tribes during their last struggles for independence. This event is commemorated each year on Midsummer Day by an immense fire of vines kindled on the summit of the Roche de Solutré.

Rock climbing

Later still, a château was built on the Roche de Solutré, but not a stone now remains of this building. Nowadays, the Roche is used as a training pitch by weekend climbers. There are a number of tourist attractions in the Pouilly-Fuissé district, among them a very interesting museum of prehistory: in limestone caves near Solutré remains of Palaeolithic Man have been found, as well as tools from this era. Solutré also has a cellar where tourists and climbers alike can quench their thirst. The local restaurant, *Relais de*

Louis Tête always manages to produce a Pouilly-Fuissé of great distinction. It is a fresh, distinctive wine with a very strong bouquet and firm, well-balanced taste.

Although I have very little regard for the qualities of the wines of Bouchard Aîné, their Dry Pouilly-Fuissé Réserve is an exception. It is an agreeable wine, despite a certain unripeness, but a little more body would have made it even better.

André Forest owns several acres in Vergisson, the northernmost commune of Pouilly-Fuissé. He produces a wine there which is lighter and rougher than that of the other communes, but still has plenty of character.

Joseph Burrier and his son Jacques export most of their wine to the United States, the United Kingdom, Belgium and the Netherlands. This small château has almost 50 acres in Fuissé and usually produces a distinctive wine with an astonishingly spicy perfume.

Jean and Pierre Troisgros, who run the best restaurant in France — even in the world — at Roanne, offer a wine from Georges Duboeuf on their list under their own name. Their choice of this wine was decided mainly by its bouquet. Duboeuf also produces an excellent wine under his own name.

I have tasted several Pouilly-Vinzelles, including those from Bouchard Père & Fils, Henri de Villamont and Jean Mathias at Chaintré. M. Mathias is one of the few growers who carries out his own vinification and bottling. His wine is often juicy and has nice fruit.

Solutré, serves simple but substantial meals. The largest commune, Prissé, is situated in the centre of an immense natural amphitheatre; the best restaurant of the district *Au Pouilly-Fuissé*, is in Fuissé, where the greatest speciality is the *saucisson bourguignon au vin blanc*. M. Bonnet, the owner, especially recommends his *fromage frais* in summer.

Divided vineyards

Not all the broken terrain of Pouilly-Fuissé is cultivated, nor do all the vines which grow on these rather infertile slopes produce Pouilly-Fuissé. Only after the most minutely detailed analysis of the soil has it been possible to establish which vineyards should have the right to the *appellation contrôlée*. Thus a vineyard may be located in the centre of the region yet produce only an ordinary white wine and not a Pouilly-Fuissé. There is also virtually no scope for extending the *appellation*, since at most another 50 acres could be added to the existing 1,384 acres. There are about 200 growers in the village, so that each small plot of the fragmented vineyard brings in very little to its owner. Tractors are often too expensive; at Vergisson, for example, 20 out of the 50 owners still work with horses. The role of the *négociants* in this area thus assumes very great importance, since they have to build up their stock of Pouilly-Fuissé out of the many individual small quantities sold to them.

Scandal of a poor vintage

It is estimated that 75% of the annual production of 373,300 cases of Pouilly-Fuissé is bought by the *négociants* and especially by Mommessin, Loron and Louis Latour. In 1974, the latter marketed more than 10% of the total harvest. The cooperative of Chaintré takes in 98% of the village harvest and only about a dozen wine growers carry out their own vinification, fermentation and sale. The presence of the independent growers is welcomed by André Forest, the president of the producers' association, since it provides a counterbalance to the strength of the *négociants* and ensures that they observe certain standards of quality. M. Forest may have been thinking of the 1972 vintage, much of which was of mediocre

Pouilly-Fuissé, Pouilly-Vinzelles, Pouilly-Loché   Mâconnais

quality yet allowed to flood the American market, being sold at exorbitant prices and hence damaging the reputation of Pouilly-Fuissé. Even though some good wine was included in the shipments, there was anger and bitter controversy on both sides of the Atlantic.

A wine to mature

A lesson should have been learned from this unfortunate occurrence. Consumers have a right to know that a Pouilly-Fuissé has to be kept for some time so that it loses its acidity and hardness. The majority of the growers insist that Pouilly-Fuissé needs to be kept for at least three years to achieve proper fullness in body and character. I had the proof of this claim in June 1976 in the famous restaurant of Paul Bocuse, where I had chosen a *loup en croûte de la Méditerranée sauce Choron* with a Pouilly-Fuissé 1975 from Georges Duboeuf. Despite its quality, the wine was still too young and far from perfect. However, during a tasting of several vintages, I discovered from Maurice Luquet, owner of the Clos du Bourg at Fuissé, the superior qualities of a really mature Pouilly-Fuissé. I tasted a 1974 (then two years old), a 1973, a 1971, a 1970, a 1969 and a 1966. All the wines were of high quality, but the best and richest was the 1966. The 1974 still had a certain 'greenness', but the 1970 seemed a true masterpiece.

Château Fuissé

I have also tasted a whole range of vintages from Marcel Vincent and his son Jean-Jacques at the Château Fuissé. This was a memorable tasting session: their wines, which are very fine and full of subtleties, are certainly the best of Pouilly-Fuissé. The composition of the soil and the age of the wines are undoubtedly important, but the painstaking care of M. Vincent and his son, who produce their wines according to the old-fashioned methods, help enormously to improve its already exceptional quality.

After a long period of fermentation, the wine is stored in oak casks, which are partially renewed each year. After a rigorous selection procedure only the best 2,800 or so cases are deemed worthy of bearing the name of Château Fuissé. I had the privilege of tasting a number of wines, including Château Fuissé 1975, 1971 and 1961, in the beautiful 15th-century reception room of the château. Each vintage was of extraordinary quality, with plenty of body and delicacy. Neither the 1961 nor the 1971 showed the least sign of fatigue. The 1961 had even kept more freshness than the one ten years younger.

The great 1975 vintage

The most extraordinary Pouilly-Fuissé which I have ever encountered is undoubtedly the Château Fuissé 1975. In spite of its youth, it already had a strong bouquet, a rich taste and a very long aftertaste. The high degree of alcohol, 14.25°, in no way detracted from this beautifully balanced wine, which should reach its peak in years to come. In the opinion of Marcel Vincent, 1975 is one of the great vintages of this century, on the same level as 1945 and 1947. The summer of 1975 was rather rainy, but the autumn was very fine. These weather conditions produced a kind of *pourriture noble*, usual in Sauternes, which made that year's Château Fuissé a wine of unique character.

Something very special

Pouilly-Fuissé is certainly a very special wine. In this region, the Chardonnay (the only grape variety used) produces a wine which is less limpid than Chablis and less yellow than Meursault, being of a beautiful golden colour, tinted with green. The bouquet, full of subtle nuances, suggests the odour of delicate fruit or the scent of fragile blooms; there is occasionally a suggestion of banana, honey or apple, and even sometimes of lemon and wild violets. The taste often has a flavour of nuts, almonds and honey. In short,

this sensual and spirited wine has so many marvellous qualities that the growers of the region sometimes talk, almost wistfully, not of selling their wine, but of being separated from it.

Pouilly-Vinzelles

The producers first asked for legal protection in 1922, long before the official Pouilly-Fuissé *appellation* was created. This protection was initially applied only to Pouilly but the *appellation* became Pouilly-Fuissé in 1931 to avoid confusion with Pouilly-sur-Loire. Around 1930, the mayor of Vinzelles, a small village some two miles from Pouilly, decided that he wanted his own village to have a separate *appellation*, rather than have its wine included in Pouilly-Fuissé. This was how the *appellation* Pouilly-Vinzelles, covering no more than 124 acres, came into being. Production is 20,800 cases. Pouilly-Vinzelles does not, in my opinion, have the quality of Pouilly-Fuissé. Its bouquet is more reserved, its taste flatter. There are few growers making their own wine and most Pouilly-Vinzelles is vinified and marketed by the cooperative of Vinzelles-Loché.
There is a third Pouilly, Pouilly-Loché, produced from 37 acres, which yield, according to official statistics, an average of 13,300 cases which cannot, practically speaking, be found anywhere else. Even Raymond Cullas, the former director of the Comité Interprofessionnel du Mâconnais et du Chalonnais, had never tasted any during his many years in the trade, and with very good reason. Pouilly-Loché is legally permitted to be sold under the *appellation* Pouilly-Vinzelles and, as far as I know, never employs its own name.

Saint-Véran

Mâconnais

The *appellation* Saint-Véran is closely connected to that of Pouilly-Fuissé and both areas have soils of similar composition. The transition from one *appellation* to the other is hardly noticeable and, to complicate the situation even more, Saint-Véran is made up of two separate sub-areas. The larger of the two, located to the south of Pouilly-Fuissé, includes the communes of Saint-Vérand, Chasselas and Chénas and a number of plots in Solutré. The smaller, to the north of Pouilly-Fuissé, includes Prissé and Davayé. The region takes its name from Saint-Vérand (formerly Saint-Véran-des-Vignes); the final 'd' was added later to avoid confusion with Saint-Véran in the Beaujolais. The medieval village of Saint-Vérand is floodlit on summer evenings and well worth a visit. Nowadays a calm and peaceful place, in the 17th century it was the fiefdom of a powerful lord with some 95 serfs lodged on his estate. Even at that period, Saint-Vérand was already known for its wine.

The youngest burgundy

The Saint-Véran area finally obtained its own *appellation* thanks, largely, to the efforts of Louis Dailly (also involved with Saint-Amour in the Beaujolais). In association with the Union des Producteurs (founded in 1947), he began his campaign in 1954 which finally led to the necessary ministerial decree, celebrated with much food and drink in the presence of local dignitaries on 6 January 1971. It is hardly surprising, however, that the Institut National des Appellations d'Origine took such a long time to reach this decision: the list of *appellations* is already too extensive and could do with shortening rather than lengthening. Furthermore, the possible creation of a new *appellation* also requires a long period of practical research; each vineyard has to be carefully surveyed and the soil thoroughly analysed before it can be decided which of them should have the eventual right to use the *appellation*.

Disappointment for the growers

The result of the decision to grant the *appellation* is that wines previously sold as Beaujolais Blanc or Mâcon-Villages are now marketed under their new name of Saint-Véran. Each wine has to be controlled by a special commission and the yield cannot be higher than 45 hectolitres per hectare, whereas the authorized limit in the past was 50 hectolitres. This is not an insurmountable obstacle and the growers hope they can gradually improve the price levels for the wine. So far, their efforts have been rather unsuccessful. Since it is still a relatively unknown wine, it does not always sell easily and the prices are lower than those for Pouilly-Fuissé or, sometimes, even for Beaujolais Blanc.

There is also a feeling that the important *négociants* (with the exception of Georges Duboeuf) have neither supported the new wine sufficiently nor advertised it widely enough, especially in the United States. The *négociants* argue that they already find it hard enough to dispose of their great white wines and that it will be difficult to sell Saint-Véran successfully until it has acquired some reputation. Nevertheless, everyone — growers and *négociants* alike — remains optimistic.

Winner of the inter-crus competition

It only takes a simple tasting to see that Saint-Véran deserves a place of some standing among white burgundies. The annual yield of some 150,000 cases is produced from the Chardonnay, which almost certainly originated in this area. Here it gives a rather perfumed wine, which is also quite fresh, but less firm and greener than Pouilly-Fuissé. If the latter wine is suited to a restaurant of great standing, then Saint-Véran should be drunk in a simple, unpretentious *bistro*. The results of the *inter-crus* competition, in which only wines from the last harvest are tasted, also proves that Saint-Véran can be an excellent wine, if drunk young. Almost every year, a Saint-Véran is chosen to represent the best white Mâcon, indicating that there is no point in waiting for it to improve.

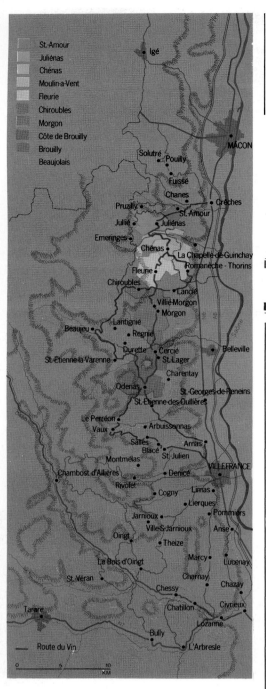

St-Amour
Juliénas
Chénas
Moulin-a-Vent
Fleurie
Chiroubles
Morgon
Côte de Brouilly
Brouilly
Beaujolais

Igé
MÂCON
Solutré
Pouilly
Fuissé
Chanes
Pruzilly
Créches
St-Amour
Julié
Juliénas
Emeringes
Chénas
La Chapelle-de-Guinchay
Fleurie
Romanéche - Thorins
Chiroubles
Lancié
Villié-Morgon
Morgon
Beaujeu
Lantignié
Regnié
Durette
Cercié
St-Lager
Belleville
St-Étienne-la-Varenne
Charentay
Odenas
St-Georges-de-Reneins
St-Étienne-des-Oullières
Le Perréon
Arbuissonnas
Vaux
Sallés
Arnas
Blacé
St-Julien
Montmelas
VILLEFRANCHE
Chambost-d'Allières
Denicé
Rivolet
Cogny
Limas
Lierques
Jarnioux
Pommiers
Ville-s-Jarnioux
Anse
Oingt
Theize
Le Bois-d'Oingt
Marcy
Lucenay
St-Véran
Charnay
Chazay
Chessy
Civrieux
Chatillon
Lozanne
Tararé
Bully
L'Arbresle

Route du Vin

0   5   10
         KM

'Lyon, the capital of French cuisine, is crossed not only by the Saône and the Rhône, but also by a third river, Beaujolais, which never becomes muddy or runs dry.' These words by Léon Daudet show how much the inhabitants of Lyon have always admired Beaujolais. This is hardly surprising, since the vineyards of Beaujolais begin just a few miles south of Mâcon and extend to the suburbs of Lyon. Daudet was hardly guilty of inaccuracy in comparing Beaujolais to a river since there are some 49,420 acres in cultivation which produce well over eleven million cases of wine annually, a quantity greater than that of the total harvest of the other four regions of Burgundy together.

An enchanting countryside

The landscape of the Beaujolais region is enchanting — narrow, twisting roads,

It has been suggested that there should be a tenth cru in Beaujolais; indeed, the commune of Regnié-Durette has already claimed that right. But their wines, for the time being, still come under Beaujolais-Villages, although they are usually more expensive than the others of that appellation. The Regnié-Durette wines are rather hard and relatively robust.

Left:
Map of the Beaujolais. The name 'Bellijocum', which was later to be transformed into 'Beaujolais', first made its appearance in 1031.

Opposite page, above:
One of the direction signs showing the itinerary through the vineyards and villages of Beaujolais.

Opposite page, below:
Harvest in the Beaujolais. The weather is still fine as everyone hurries to bring in the Gamay Noir à jus blanc grapes.

Any foreigner thinking of buying a plot of vines in the Beaujolais will certainly be interested in the following story. Some years ago, 25 acres of the Fleurie appellation were put up for auction. The highest bid came from the Swiss house of Hamel: 2,250,000 French francs. At the last moment, another offer of 2,300,000 francs was made, but not one of the 500 people present would declare himself the buyer and the sale ended in indescribable chaos. The traditional candle had disappeared and the floor was littered with auctioneer's papers. One notable wine grower proclaimed: 'Our region is now going through a period of unprecedented prosperity and we have no wish to see our land bought by a foreign company for its own profit.'

The 18 cooperatives of the region have 4,000 members who cultivate a total of just over 14,000 acres.

A number of other appellations have started promoting their young wine as 'vins nouveaux' or 'vins primeurs' in imitation of Beaujolais; these include Chablis, Muscadet, Roussillon, Côtes du Rhône, Languedoc, and even Bordeaux.

Beaujolais

peaceful valleys, broad wooded hillsides and sleepy old villages. This is a truly romantic country and for a long time 'to go to Beaujolais' had the same magic quality as 'to go on honeymoon'. The whole of the region is now much more obviously crowded with tourists than in the past. The visitors are by no means all French; many come from Switzerland, since Geneva is only 90 or so miles away. During the height of the season, the well signposted Route du Vin through Beaujolais is jammed with cars and coaches which stop at the numerous cellars, where wines can be tasted for virtually nothing, and with no obligation to purchase.

Protective mountains

Geographically, the Beaujolais region is made up of a range of fairly high hills, while the last foothills of the Massif Central can be seen in the distance to the west. It is on these latter slopes that the majority of the vineyards are planted. Even farther to the west is an area of forest which remains almost impenetrable, even today. The fragments of a small English sporting aeroplane were found there in 1960, 10 years after the aircraft had disappeared. The Saint-Rigaud Massif, with a height of 3,350 feet, provides a natural protective barrier against the rains and fresh winds from the west, thus creating relatively mild climatic conditions for the area. In winter the temperature rarely drops below -10°C, but in summer it can rise as high as 40°C. Although these temperatures obviously help the successful cultivation of vines, the broken landscape only too often attracts storms and hail.

Disastrous hail

Hail is the disaster dreaded by every wine grower, since it can wipe out a whole harvest in a few minutes, ruining a year's work and spreading devastation wherever it strikes. Vaux-en-Beaujolais, the original setting of Gabriel Chevallier's famous novel *Clochemerle*, has suffered from hail four times in seven years. I was once caught in the middle of a storm in which the hailstones

were so large and concentrated that in a few seconds the village and its vineyards looked as though they had been buried under a blanket of snow. The seriousness of the problem is further demonstrated by this fact: more than 20 years ago, Bernard Paul, a wine grower of Fleurie, was one of the first in his commune to insure himself against the effects of hail; to this date, the sum of the damages paid substantially exceeds that of the premiums. The constant threat of destruction from hail has forced the growers to try all possible methods to combat it. Some years ago, cannon were even used in an attempt to turn the storms in another direction. This method eventually proved to be ineffective and also dangerous for the air corridor to Lyon. At the present time, the battle against hail is waged by three aircraft, collectively financed, which spray the clouds with silver iodide whenever a storm threatens. But three aircraft are not sufficient to cover the whole of Beaujolais and they are, in any case, unable to operate at night. In 1975, for example, they were powerless against hailstorms which destroyed approximately 5,000 acres. The last defence for the wine growers is a good insurance policy, but two out of three do not believe in them, since they find the premiums too high (8% to 15% of the profit on the harvest). However, the insurance companies are now offering a new form of policy which guarantees a basic income for a premium that is only about a quarter of that for a conventional policy; this method has been more successful.

The métayage system

The Beaujolais wine grower, whose very existence depends so much on the weather and who knows that hail can strike at any time, is both a philosopher and sage. It is sometimes said that the irregular lines of the hills and the narrow, winding roads symbolize the spirit of the region: the grower, who tends to have a rather complex character, still manages to retain his good humour and cheerfulness despite the hard daily grind. The tourist invasion and

Beaujolais

commercial success have probably somewhat hardened his mentality, but the region as a whole still remains very welcoming. During my long tours of the wine-producing areas of Burgundy, I have always been received with greater warmth and kindness in Beaujolais than anywhere else. The reason for this hospitality may be that the majority of estates are small family businesses. In general, the holdings are no larger than 10 acres, too modest to allow great social pretensions. In 50% of cases, too, the wine grower is not the owner of the land he cultivates and is subject to the *métayage* or *vigneronnage* systems of tenancy. According to this, the grower must hand over half the harvest to the owner; in return, the latter provides accommodation and equipment, and shares in the cost of the harvest. A small number of growers work under the *fermage* system, which is the straightforward renting of the land.

Two types of land

Beaujolais can be divided, according to soil type, into two areas along a line running through Villefranche; each area has a characteristic wine. To the north of Villefranche the soils are made up of granite, schists and clay, while to the south they are more calcareous, with elements of marl. Since the only black grape variety allowed in the whole of Beaujolais is the Gamay Noir à jus blanc, the considerable differences between the *crus* of the north and those of the south are above all due to these geographical peculiarities. The élite of the wines of Beaujolais — the nine *crus* with the highest reputations and the Beaujolais-Villages — come from the area north of Villefranche, while the communes of the south produce mainly the simple Beaujolais. The region is composed of several *appellations* and it is useful to look at these in order.

Beaujolais and Beaujolais Supérieur

Beaujolais is considered by many wine drinkers as the very symbol of wine and of France. Indeed, it is known throughout the world, since its very special qualities make it an absolutely unique wine. Even the sound of its name seems to summon up a feeling of youthful joy, of spring, of sunshine. An advertising agency could hardly conjure up a better, yet the name comes quite simply from Beaujeu, formerly the capital of the region. Sometimes called 'a burst of laughter at the table', Beaujolais is recognizable by its fine red colour, its lightness, fruitiness and springtime perfume. It is invigoratingly refreshing (it should be served cool), lively and supple; all these qualities make it an equally acceptable wine at official receptions, business dinners or quite simply by the fire at home or at an intimate meal with friends. It should be drunk young, since it does not improve with age, and therefore needs neither patience nor a cellar. Thanks to all these advantages, and thanks also to its very high volume of production, Beaujolais has conquered the world.

The two most straightforward *appellations* are Beaujolais and Beaujolais Supérieur. The only difference between these two wines is their degree of alcohol: 9° for Beaujolais and 10° for Beaujolais Supérieur. The degree of alcohol for the greater part of the Beaujolais exported often exceeds 10°, so that the wines will travel better. In other words, the Beaujolais which is drunk outside France is almost always Beaujolais Supérieur.

White and rosé Beaujolais

Since the creation of the Saint-Véran *appellation*, the amount of white Beaujolais produced has markedly diminished, but about 59,700 cases are produced annually. The grape variety used is the Chardonnay, and the wine thus produced often gives off such a scent of fruits that you can almost see them by the basketful. I have tasted very good white Beaujolais from Louis Jadot, the Château du Chatelard, Paul Sapin and Mathelin. Some Beaujolais rosé is produced, but the quantity is minimal.

Beaujolais-Villages

'Cru ne puis, Beaujolais ne daigne, Villages suis' ('A *cru* I cannot be, a Beaujolais I would not deign to be, but a Villages I am'). It is with this motto, which is a variation on the old motto of the Château Mouton-Rothschild of Bordeaux ('Premier ne puis, second ne daigne, Mouton suis' — 'First I cannot be, second I would not deign to be, but Mouton I am'), that the Beaujolais-Villages proclaims its pride in being what it is. About 40 villages in the north of Beaujolais have a right to this *appellation*. With good subsoil, a yield of no more than 45

The Château de Saint-Trys, one
of the rare Beaujolais to be sold
under the name of an estate.
Even in mediocre years, this
wine is well perfumed, fruity and
distinctive. It is marketed
exclusively by Henri de
Villamont. Pierre Charmet of Le
Breuil produces an excellent
simple Beaujolais.

White Beaujolais is a speciality
of Louis Jadot in Beaune. The
wines I tasted were of excellent
quality and very fruity.
Mathelin (Domaine de Sandar)
and the Château du Chatelard
also make delicious Beaujolais.

The Château de Loyse belongs
to the Thorin family and is, with
its 15 acres, one of the biggest
producers of white Beaujolais.
The château, dating from 1643,
produces a wine which often has
an aroma of fruit; there is also a
softness and richness about it.

The Château de Corcelles is one
of the most beautiful in the
whole of the Beaujolais. It
makes a light Beaujolais-
Villages, both supple and fine,
which is sold in an attractive
bottle. Unfortunately, this wine
is exorbitantly expensive, a fact
that is not accurately reflected
in the quality. The estate
belongs to the Société des Vins
de France.

Like Georges Duboeuf, Louis
Latour and others, Loron
generally sells a good
Beaujolais-Villages. However,
the quality can vary from one
vintage to another. A good
Beaujolais Villages comes from
the Domaine des Niveaudières,
selected by Dessalle.

Beaujolais

hectolitres per hectare and a minimum of 10°
of alcohol, the Beaujolais-Villages is
generally a better wine than a simple
Beaujolais or Beaujolais Supérieur. This is
usually evident from the moment of first
inhaling the bouquet and tasting.

Beaujolais Primeur

Beaujolais Primeur or Beaujolais Nouveau is
a fairly recent creation which has assumed
increasing importance in the last few years.
It is available on the market a few weeks
after the harvest, usually from 15 November,
which is well before the other *appellations* of
Beaujolais can be drunk. Beaujolais Primeur
is produced by carbonic maceration: the
grapes are not pressed, and fermentation
takes place within the fruit itself before it
bursts. This method produces a very fruity
wine with little tannin, which has to be
drunk very young. It is precisely this fruity
freshness and slightly sparkling quality
which gives Beaujolais Primeur its great
charm and also makes it a wine to be drunk
before Easter, for which little inducement is
normally needed.
It frequently happens that a quarter to a
third of the whole Beaujolais harvest is sold
and drunk as Beaujolais Primeur in the
space of a few months. This wine has to
undergo a compulsory check before being
passed as Beaujolais Primeur, but there
are few controls afterwards and differences
in quality can be considerable. The best
Primeur usually comes from Beaujolais-
Villages, and this is also the most expensive.

The nine crus

The best Beaujolais comes from a group of
nine crus, all in communes in the north of the
region. They must have at least 10° of alcohol
(Côte de Brouilly 10.5°) but if the name of a
vineyard is mentioned on the label, then the
level must be 11°. Geographically, from
north to south, the nine crus are as follows:
Saint-Amour, Juliénas, Chénas, Moulin-à-
Vent, Fleurie, Chiroubles, Morgon, Brouilly
and Côte de Brouilly. The following pages
describe them in greater detail.

One of the most important buyers of Saint-Amour is the Maison Georges Duboeuf. I have tasted several of its wines: very characteristic of Saint-Amour, nicely coloured, with a light bouquet, fruity and stylish.

This wine comes from one of the holdings of the Maison Loron & Fils at Pontanevaux, the Domaine des Billards. Even in mediocre years, this wine was fruity, agreeable and had plenty of body.

The caveau of Saint-Amour makes its own wine. It comes by the glass, in normal bottles or in magnums (1.5 litres). Thousands of litres of this carefully selected wine are sold annually.

The character of the wine produced by Francis Saillant, the wine growers' president, resembles that of its maker: it has the same friendliness. M. Saillant cultivates just over 17 acres and his wine can be appreciated in the best restaurant of Saint-Amour, L'Auberge du Paradis.

The 19th-century Château de Saint-Amour makes a wine which is partly marketed by the British house of Piat. It is an honest wine, though far from being among the best of Saint-Amour. The vineyard of this small château covers 22 acres.

Maurice Delorme, president of the local caveau, makes this Domaine du Paradis. He is the owner of 20 acres and stores an excellent, light and supple wine in a fine cellar.

Saint-Amour

There could hardly be a more aptly named place for a honeymoon than Saint-Amour. Unfortunately, the village has no hotel and any newly-weds would have to seek lodging elsewhere. This may not be such a bad thing, since the still very rural village of Saint-Amour would like nothing better than to be left in its peace and quiet. The commune of Saint-Amour is made up of four hamlets: Le Bourg, Le Platre-Durand, La Ville and Les Thévenins, and it is no doubt this division that has allowed it to retain its old-fashioned atmosphere. There are several stories about the origins of Saint-Amour but the one which the inhabitants of the village prefer goes back to the time of Julius Caesar, when a Roman legionary fell in love with a local girl and married her. Saint-Amour was founded on the spot where they lived happily ever after.

An artistic curé

Although Saint-Amour offers several marvellous views, there are no fine buildings except, as everywhere in France, a church, which has been decorated by one of its *curés* with frescoes painted on the ceiling and on one of the walls. The name of this Leonardo da Vinci of Saint-Amour was Etienne Braqui; his murals could hardly be called optimistic, tracing as they do the various stages of human life from baptism to hell. The *curés* of Saint-Amour, however, were certainly not short of inspiration: they had their own small vineyard just behind the church.

Louis Dailly

Much more than the *curés*, however, the person really responsible for the reputation of Saint-Amour is Louis Dailly. It was only in 1946, much later than the other eight communes, that he managed to obtain the much coveted *appellation d'origine* for Saint-Amour. For many years before that, Louis Dailly had fought to convince the authorities of the quality of the wines from his village. As well as studying the local geology, he searched the archives of Mâcon and Paris, and regularly sent samples of his wine to the necessary influential people, institutions and commissions. His efforts were finally crowned with success and the cellar of Saint-Amour bears the name of Louis Dailly in his memory.

A commune without a cooperative

For a long time the area planted with vines at Saint-Amour was no greater than 435 or so acres. Since 1969, however, this relatively small area has been extended and, according to the latest statistics, the commune now has about 617 acres which yield, on average, about 153,800 cases a year. The majority of the village's 550 inhabitants live from wine growing or one of its related activities. An interesting feature of the village is that it has no cooperative. This does not seem to worry anyone; on the contrary, as Francis Saillant (president of the Saint-Amour wine producers' association) told me, the individual growers make wine of considerably higher quality than one produced collectively. There are, however, certain disadvantages to this situation as well. The sale under a number of different names of a small amount of wine from the same commune helps neither sales,

M. Janin often produces a very characteristic Saint-Amour with a bouquet that is both delicate and very fruity. The taste has a hint of fresh fruit and terroir. Limpid colour.

I recently discovered an excellent Saint-Amour which is produced by wine grower M. Duc at Saint-Amour-Bellevue. The wine usually has a deep colour, pleasant taste and perfect balance.

Saint-Amour has faced a serious problem since 1980. A nearby plastics factory is affecting the taste of some of the wines which have developed an aroma of burnt rubber. This situation was already critical in 1980, but by 1981 perhaps as many as two-thirds of the wines had become affected by the polluted air. Various lawsuits and actions are still continuing and it is hoped that the problem will be solved soon.

Opposite page:
The Château de Saint-Amour. Rebuilt during the last century on 16th-century foundations, the château looks over Saint-Amour-la-Ville.

Below:
Francis Saillant, president of the wine growers, in his cellar which is decorated with inscriptions, such as, 'If you want to stay together, drink Saint-Amour', 'Saint-Amour all the time, bringer of happiness', 'Saint-Amour at midday, sunshine at midnight'.

Right:
Plaques showing the prizes awarded to the wines of Francis Saillant.

One of the legends on the origin of the name of Saint-Amour concerns a Roman legionary named Amore, who had been converted to Christianity and who was martyred on the site of the village in the 4th century.

The Dailly cup is awarded every year to the best Saint-Amour.

Since 1968, Saint-Amour has been twinned with Durbuy-sur-Ourthe in Belgium.

Saint-Amour

reputation nor price. The well-informed *connoisseur*, on the other hand, can certainly profit from such circumstances.

Discreet charm

I found a recipe in Saint-Amour which seemed to define the character of this wine admirably: 'Ferment the Gamay from my lands in a large vat. Add the laughter of a girl, the spring scents of a garden and a good dose of the spirit of Montmartre. After three or four days' fermentation, serve cool.' This seems to sum up the wine of Saint-Amour. It lacks the strength of a Moulin-à-Vent and the robustness of a Juliénas, its neighbour. Accurately, the growers call it a tender wine; with its discreet bouquet, it is agreeable, supple and balanced. It never appears in the slightest bit aggressive, but its fine colour and fruitiness make it a charming wine, which needs to be drunk young, at the latest two years after the harvest.

The considerable quantity of wine produced by the Château de Juliénas is not all sold under its own label; part of the vintage is sometimes bought by the négociants. The quality is good, or even very good.

Georges Duboeuf, the uncrowned king of Beaujolais, offers excellent Juliénas every year. I admire his wines, which are delicately perfumed, full of character and vigour — in every way rather grand.

The Maison Loron produces two Juliénas, one from the Domaine de la Vieille Église and one from the Clos des Poulettes. I found the second very impressive, with its distinctive, fine perfume and strong taste.

The house of Louis Tête manages to find and prepare the finest Juliénas. At its best, the wine has a fine ripe cherry colour and a robust, fruity bouquet. A clean and agreeable taste, with more than a hint of strength underneath.

This Juliénas is served to the visitors to the Château du Bois de la Salle; simple, but good. Although the cooperative markets its wines under its own red label, importers usually sell it with their own individual labels.

Below:
The annual harvest of Juliénas produces about 336,800 cases.

Opposite page, above left:
The Château de Juliénas.

Opposite page, above right:
Presentation bottle packs in the tasting centre which has been set up in the old church.

Opposite page, below centre:
The Domaine des Chers in Juliénas.

Opposite page, far right:
The Château du Bois de la Salle, headquarters of the cooperative.

Juliénas

Though it is not absolutely certain, it is thought that the name of Juliénas — the ancient Julianacas — is derived from Julius Caesar; the same explanation is also offered for the name of Jullié, a neighbouring commune with about 136 acres which belong officially to the Juliénas *appellation*. Whatever the explanation, Juliénas is very old indeed. There is still a 16th-century toll house in the village where the clergy exacted payment for rights of passage. The foundations of the Château de Juliénas are even older, since they were begun in 1308 by the Seigneur de Beaujeu. Nowadays, the magnificently restored château belongs to François Condemine, and its 110 acres of vines make it the largest estate of Juliénas. The cellars of the château are especially large and imposing.

Ancient vineyards

The vineyards of Juliénas are also of considerable age and it has been claimed (as it has at Chénas) that they were the first to be planted in Beaujolais. Whatever the true history, Juliénas has certainly been an important wine-producing commune for a very long time. In 1900, for example, the village already had almost 1,300 acres of vineyards. Today, there are just over 1,350 acres, which cover about half the lands of the commune. Apart from the château and its 110 acres, there are about 10 estates in Juliénas with approximately 25 acres each. Another 300 or so growers cultivate very small holdings which do not allow either vinification or storage; in the majority of these cases, the cooperative takes care of these operations.

A very popular cellar

Most cooperative cellars are housed in simple modern buildings, but the Juliénas cooperative is an exception, for it is installed in a real château — the Château du Bois de la Salle, just outside the village. Modern *chais* and a tasting room have now been fitted out within the 16th-century walls. The

cooperative bought the château in 1960 and today it is one of the most popular tourist attractions of Beaujolais. I visited it one fine, warm Sunday afternoon in summer. A tourist coach and at least a couple of dozen cars in the courtyard indicated numerous visitors. In the tasting room, which has been sensibly stripped of all rare or fragile objects, the wine of the cooperative flowed freely. Outside were scenes that hardly added to the dignity and nobility of the setting: men in vests were playing *pétanque*, while a hot-dog stand did a roaring trade. Not far from the château flows a small river which, in the middle of so much wine, has been unimaginatively named 'La Mauvaise' ('the bad one').

A converted church

The second tasting centre in the village of Juliénas is likewise rather out of the ordinary, for it has been set up in the old 15th-century church. The church had not been used as such for quite some time, since a larger, finer church has taken care of the villagers' spiritual needs from 1868. In 1954, the wine growers decided to use the old church to the greater glory of their wines and so, in these once sacred precincts, the altar has now given way to a tasting bar much frequented by tourists: the House of the Lord has become the Temple of Bacchus. If anyone is troubled by sinful thoughts under the influence of the wine and the gaiety of the scenes painted on the walls, then confession can follow immediately, as the new church is situated just opposite.

The new wine

Juliénas celebrates the new wine of the year on the second Sunday of November. On this occasion, a prize is awarded to the person judged to have been most active in promoting the wines of the commune. This much coveted prize consists of 104 bottles of Juliénas. The winner thus has two bottles for each Sunday of the year, one for himself and

the other for his wife. Juliénas is a fruity, full-bodied, fleshy wine, with a fine colour and often an aroma of cherries and raspberries. It always gives an impression of great fullness and only achieves real maturity after four or five years' keeping. Usually almost two years are required before the bouquet and taste start to take on this fullness without losing anything of their youthful freshness. It needs to be tasted seriously, and its remarkable personality is aptly summed up in the local saying: 'Beware of the person who empties his glass of Juliénas in one go'.

Chénas

One of the past owners of the Château de Chénas was Adrien de la Hante, who advocated reform of the tobacco monopoly during the 19th century. The château now belongs to a group of 250 growers. A good wine.

Louis Champagnon cultivates just over 12 acres in Chénas. He himself only bottles prize wines or wines of exceptional quality. Deeply coloured and strong, they are full of character: Champagnon markets some of them under a black label.

Pierre Perrachon has carried out a brilliant restoration of the old Château Bonnet. His wine is also very successful: full-bodied, distinctive, with a fine deep colour. This is a typical Chénas, which should not be kept more than two or three years after harvesting. It is a more elegant wine than that of Champagnon. There is an illustration of the château on the new label.

Emile Robin owns the largest estate in the Chénas (34½ acres). He makes his wine by natural methods and without even using any sulphur. The results thus obtained are good. The Domaine de la Combe Remont also makes a good Chénas which is bottled by Duboeuf.

Opposite page, above left: There is no use for the little stoves in the cuverie during a fine, sunny autumn.

Opposite page, above centre: Preparing the casks in which the wine will be kept for maturing.

Opposite page, above right: Louis Champagnon, a wine grower, eating with the harvest workers.

Opposite page, below: After a large meal, the workers return to the vineyards.

The Aux Deschamps restaurant, sometimes called 'Robin', is one of the finest in Beaujolais.

The annual harvest of Chénas yields between about 67,000 and 134,000 cases.

The Château Bonnet was the home of one of Napoleon's officers who fought in Prussia and in Spain. The officer retired from the army in 1820, but retained his weapons and his horse, which he later buried on an islet in a small river near the château.

Chénas is a wine found very rarely outside France, the whole area of its vineyards is under 500 acres. This *appellation*, then, is the smallest in volume of production of the nine *crus* of Beaujolais. It should be noted, however, that the greater part of the wines produced from the green slopes surrounding Chénas have the right to the neighbouring *appellation* of Moulin-à-Vent. Chénas itself is produced mainly by the vineyards located in the north of the commune and to the north-west of La Chapelle de Guinchay. The vineyards of the latter village are twice as big as those of Chénas. This rather strange situation tends to make Chénas a puzzling *appellation* for the wine student.

A growing reputation

It is claimed that the owners of Moulin-à-Vent would like to include the whole of Chénas in their *appellation*, but the growers of Chénas are very strongly opposed to anything likely to change the present situation. Louis Champagnon explained their feelings to me: 'Firstly, we are proud of our wine. Secondly, there are more reasons for the owners of Moulin-à-Vent to be jealous of our wine than there are for us to be jealous of theirs, since our vineyards on the side of the slope produce a wine which would improve the quality of Moulin-à-Vent. And finally, Chénas is becoming more widely known.'

The principal forces behind this growing reputation are four estates, the largest of Chénas — the Domaine des Brureaux, the Château Bonnet, the Domaine Champagnon and the Domaine Chassignol, all of which started to bottle their own wine in the 1970s. In addition, the cooperative cellar of the Château de Chénas is very energetic in promoting the wine of the commune, although it still produces more Moulin-à-Vent, Fleurie and Juliénas. In 1975, the growers sold only 20% of their total harvest directly, but since then things have changed considerably.

A hearty snack

It would be quite reasonable to expect Chénas and Moulin-à-Vent to display very similar characteristics, since their lands are alike and they are neighbours. But the wines do taste different. Chénas has a fine, dark colour, a lot of body and plenty of freshness. It lacks the power of a Moulin-à-Vent, but is, with the Juliénas, one of the most substantial wines of the region. I had direct experience of its qualities when, one morning, I was invited by a vineyard worker to share his morning snack at 9 o'clock. The snack proved to be almost a complete meal, with fresh bread, pâté, marbled ham and several varieties of salami sausage, all well washed down with wine. It is perhaps pointless to add that I then spent a very pleasant day.

A bouquet of flowers

A good Chénas can be kept for five or six years without showing the least tiredness. Louis Champagnon, who carries out his vinification according to traditional methods, never enters his wine in a competition without allowing it to age at least three years, and he has often won first prize. The years of ageing allow the wine to get rid of a certain youthful hardness and take on an agreeable suppleness, thus justifying this poetic description: 'Chénas is a bouquet of flowers placed in a velvet basket.'

Oak forests

The Cellier de Chénas, where the wine can be tasted, is proud of its sculpture by Renoir which symbolizes the beginnings of wine-growing in Chénas. It shows woodcutters cutting down an oak tree (chêne), from which the name of the commune is derived, since the region was formerly covered by oak forests. Another statue, in solid oak, of course, is also exhibited in the Cellier; this shows Saint Vincent, the patron of the wine growers. The forests no longer exist and not a single oak seems to have been spared. In the entire area of Chénas, as in the whole of Beaujolais, there is hardly an oak tree to be seen, demonstrating the truth of the local saying: 'The only shade in which the vine is happy is that of the wine grower.'

Wines to note

Jean-Pierre Bloud, owner of the Château du Moulin-à-Vent, produces a wine of brilliant colour and characteristic taste. The wine must be kept for at least four years to allow it to open out.

Georges Duboeuf likes supple, light Beaujolais. There is nothing surprising, then, in the fact that his Moulin-à-Vent, two years after its harvest, seems better than the others. Very fruity.

Chauvet Frères is a small house, but with great Beaujolais. Its Moulin-à-Vent deserves special praise. Full-bodied, fruity, with a quiet strength and long aftertaste. Fine, deep colour.

The Château des Gimarets is marketed exclusively by Henri de Villamont at Savigny-lès-Beaune. Although this Moulin-à-Vent is not one of the strongest, it is still fairly full-bodied and quite distinctive.

It is quite rare for a négociant of Beaune to sell a really good Moulin-à-Vent. Louis Jadot is one exception and I have tasted a full, well-balanced wine from his house, more burgundy than Beaujolais.

The two tasting centres in Romanèche-Thorins usually serve the Moulin-à-Vent of the last vintage but one. Perfect quality. Annual sale of between 25,000 and 30,000 bottles.

Moulin-à-Vent

The king of the nine *crus* of Beaujolais is undoubtedly Moulin-à-Vent, if only because its price is higher than that of the others, including Fleurie, which is not far behind. The reasons for the high price of this wine are immediately evident; the tasting of a single glass of Moulin-à-Vent demonstrates its qualities clearly. It is very virile, with a strength and fullness that make it closer to a burgundy than a Beaujolais. Yet, in spite of its dark colour, rich taste and relatively high level of alcohol, it is in no way a rough wine. As well as its richness and strength, a good Moulin-à-Vent always has that rather joyous quality which is the hallmark of all the wines of Beaujolais. In general, it ages better than the others and the good vintages can be kept for a very long time without losing any of their freshness; a Moulin-à-Vent 1929, as far as I could judge, still preserved all its original qualities intact.

Differences of quality

Not all the Moulin-à-Vent have the same strength or the same capacity for ageing well. A number of *négociants* (Georges Duboeuf, for example) deliberately choose wine that does not have to be kept long. The quality of the Moulin-à-Vent wine is not always constant, due to the fact that this *cru* enjoys such a splendid reputation and commands such a high price that every square yard of land is exploited, even that which is not especially suitable for vine cultivation.

As is the case elsewhere, a number of wine growers prefer quantity to quality, and it can happen that, side by side with the well-balanced, strong wines, will be found rather disagreeable ones, which are too high in alcohol. The 1,605 acres of vineyard produce about 373,700 cases of wine annually. Moulin-à-Vent owes its special character to a rather special subsoil which contains manganese, the hard, brittle metal used in the tempering of steel. In the past, Romanèche-Thorins also had a manganese mine.

The old mill

Romanèche-Thorins was formerly considered a *cru* of Beaujolais, and it was under that name that the wine was sold. But in 1936 the *appellation* was changed to Moulin-à-Vent, thus commemorating the old windmill which

Raymond Siffert lives in a particularly beautiful house where he makes a classic Moulin-à-Vent, strong, full-bodied and needing to be kept for a long time. The 1964 only reached full maturity in 1976. Siffert bottles his best wine himself and sells the rest to the négociants.

The Domaine de Champ-de-Cour, near the mill of Romanèche, is one of several holdings belonging to the house of Mommessin. The wine is not always perfectly agreeable, but it usually has a robust and lively taste.

The Château des Jacques is the largest estate of Moulin-à-Vent (87 acres divided into 15 plots) and belongs to the Thorin family. This wine often has an almost sensual bouquet along with an agreeable taste, although this can be a little too sweet.

The Hospices de Romanèche-Thorins owns almost 20 acres from which the wine is sold to the négociants. The wine usually has a good colour and robust taste and needs to be kept for a long time. It has been sold through the house of Collin and Borisset since 1926.

Opposite page, left:
The standing of the Maison Georges Duboeuf, with its cellars at Romanèche-Thorins, is recognized throughout Beaujolais. M. Duboeuf is a very fine taster and advises on the selection of wines for the personal cellars of the great restaurateurs, such as Paul Bocuse.

Opposite page, right:
The old windmill which gave its name to the appellation.

Below:
Harvest in the Clos du Moulin-à-Vent.

Below right:
The sign of the Caveau du Moulin-à-Vent.

stands in the middle of the vineyard. A classified historical monument, the mill is the last in Beaujolais and lost its sails a very long time ago. It dates from the time when corn was one of the main resources of the region, as is indicated in the name Romanèche, which is derived from 'Romana Esca', a corn depot for the Roman legions.

Well-stocked cellars

This famous windmill is sited on the summit of a hill from which it looks over Romanèche-Thorins, the surrounding villages and a very extensive carpet of vines. The view attracts numerous tourists who can then taste the local wine in a nearby cellar. Along the *route nationale*, in the direction of Lyon, a

miniature of the windmill advertises a second cellar, the *Maison du Moulin-à-Vent* which, along with the local wine, offers a choice of regional specialities, including several varieties of goat cheese. About half the vineyards of Moulin-à-Vent are in Romanèche, while the rest are in the neighbouring area of Chénas. There are about 350 producers of Moulin-à-Vent in the two communes.

The Caveau de Fleurie, established by the wine growers' association, is located close to the church square, which is the main meeting place of the village and a major crossroads. The wine of the Caveau is extremely good.

The artist Yvonne Couibes lives in a house which dates from 1639. I very much enjoyed her rather lively Fleurie. Half the estate (13½ acres) is cultivated under the métayage system; the harvest from the other half is marketed by Jean Matray. Her own wine is sometimes bottled by Loron.

Jean Dutraive owns almost 20 acres of Fleurie, of which nearly 15 acres are enclosed by a wall. He produces a rather firm wine, but nevertheless a typical Fleurie. All his wine is bottled at the Domaine de la Grand' Cour, which belongs to him.

The Château de Fleurie, a solid two-storey building, stands in the middle of the village, close to the church. The estate is owned by the Maison Loron and produces honest wines, typical of the appellation.

Three hundred wine growers belong to the cooperative of Fleurie and, between them, cultivate 740 acres. The annual harvest produces between about 167,000 and 189,000 cases. This abundant harvest is of variable quality, but is generally good.

A prize is awarded each year to the best wines of the nine Beaujolais crus. In 1975, this prize was won by the Fleurie of Bernard Paul. It had a fine, brilliant colour, light bouquet and full taste. An excellent 1978. This is also true of later years.

Fleurie

If Moulin-à-Vent is the king of Beaujolais, then Fleurie could be the queen, since this wine is the very epitome of feminine grace. Its fine colour is especially pleasing to the eye, just as its seductive bouquet is to the nose and its pure and elegant taste to the palate — a taste which kindles only one desire: to have more. In a way, the wine is only paying homage to its name, suggesting, as it does, its flowery aroma in which the perfume of violets and, occasionally, of cocoa are especially noticeable. In my opinion, Fleurie is the quintessence of everything a good Beaujolais should be. As with a woman, a Fleurie is at its most seductive in its youth.

It should never be kept more than two years after its harvest. It goes very well with good meat and I can especially recommend it with the *Charolais vigneronne à la moelle* served in the excellent local restaurant, *L'Auberge du Cep*. It can equally well be drunk as an aperitif; it is served in the village with a touch of *crème de cassis*, a mixture which is referred to locally as a '*communiste*' or, at *L'Auberge du Cep*, a '*communard*.

Two formidable ladies

Perhaps it is not all that surprising that, in a village which produces a wine with such obvious feminine characteristics, I should have met two charming ladies whose daily life is closely linked to that wine. One, Yvonne Couibes, is a talented painter; her ink sketches of the Beaujolais countryside are especially memorable. She also sculpts. Her estate is managed by Jean Matray, with whom she shares the harvest. The second lady, Marguerite Chabert, is known throughout Beaujolais. After the sudden death of her father through illness, she

Georges Duboeuf and his
manager Michel Brun are the
great experts on Fleurie, which
is probably why they are
especially successful in
producing this wine. I remember
very well the intense bouquet of
flowers and the delicious taste of
their Fleurie. A Beaujolais par
excellence.

The Fleurie 1974 from Chauvet
Frères has often surprised
connoisseurs by its dark colour,
its bouquet of ripe fruit and its
full, distinctive taste. A very
good wine, in spite of its slight
femininity.

André Barraud owns the
Domaine de la Presle at Fleurie,
where he makes a delicious wine.
Plenty of body, fruity, supple
and pleasant. Very fruity
bouquet with an aroma of
raspberry; deep colour. A well-
balanced wine.

Opposite page, left:
Marguerite Chabert, president
of the Fleurie cooperative.

Opposite page, right:
Yvonne Couibes, with one of her
paintings, showing the Château
de Juliénas. Mme Couibes lives
at Viviers, the hamlet where
every member of the family of
Cardinal de Fleury, Louis XV's
minister, was once presented
with half an acre of land.

Below:
A pastoral scene in one of the
last meadows of Fleurie.

Other Fleuries not yet
mentioned are produced by:
the house of Chanut Frères; the
house of Mathelin; Château des
Labourons; the house of
Dessalle.

became president of the wine cooperative of
Fleurie in 1946. Under her direction, the
cooperative became the most important of
the whole region. The cellar, with its modern
equipment, produces between 30% and 40%
of Fleurie, excluding the wines of other
communes. The Fleurie of the cooperative is
of very fine quality, as was demonstrated
during a blind tasting, when Jean Troisgros,
obliged to make a choice among a number of
Fleurie 1975s, chose that of the cooperative,
something that has happened frequently
since then.

Celebrating the harvest

The women of the village also play the most
important role in 'La Grappe Fleurie', the
local choral and folk-song group. The group
is 25 strong and has a substantial repertory
of drinking songs, as could hardly be
otherwise in such a region. It is considered
the best in the whole of the Beaujolais and
has also performed abroad.
Each year the new wines are celebrated in
Fleurie on the first Sunday of November.
More than 5,000 people attend this
celebration of the latest Beaujolais and,
between them, they taste about 800 different

wines. During the morning of the Saturday,
before the public arrives, the négociants can
make their unhurried choice in the main hall
of the cooperative. The celebration ends with
an official banquet that lasts until the late
afternoon.

The vine and nothing but the vine

On top of the hill overlooking the village
there is a chapel built in 1875 to
commemorate the halting at Fleurie of the
Prussian invasion in 1870. The statue of the
Virgin was carried to the chapel by the wine
growers in solemn procession. From the hill

Right:
The church of Chiroubles with its easily recognizable tower. The triangle in the foreground is in fact a reference marker for the pilot of the helicopter used for spraying the vines.

Below:
These empty harvest baskets stacked in front of a pile of bottles symbolize the transformation of the grapes into wine.

Opposite page:
Jean-Pierre Desvignes, one of the most notable figures of Chiroubles. He is the manager of the Domaine Cheysson-les-Farges.

There are many houses in Chiroubles made from granite taken from the subsoil of the vineyards; the village is twinned with Marcourt in Belgium.

After first tasting the wine of the region in the chalet at the top of the hill, the tourist can then eat at the nearby La Terrasse du Beaujolais restaurant.

Wine can be tasted at the cooperative of the Chiroubles. The cooperative produces about one-seventh of the total harvest of Chiroubles and also a small quantity of Beaujolais-Villages and Beaujolais.

Fleurie

it is possible to look over the whole of the village and the vineyards; it is easy to see that wine-growing is the only activity of Fleurie and the only source of the village's prosperity. Even the church owes its existence to wine; in 1860, the then mayor, a wine grower, offered to donate 100,000 francs for the construction of a church, on condition that the parish provided the rest. The sum was finally made up by a number of generous donors whose names are listed inside the church. The fact that Fleurie has only one crop (an average annual production of 464,000 cases) causes further problems for each new generation, since successive bequests divide the land up further and further, gradually reducing the size of the holdings. Although this situation benefits the cooperative, it is a loss to the village, since most of the young people are obliged to leave it sooner or later.

Coq au vin de Fleurie

Tourists are very welcome in Fleurie; they can taste the wine either at the Caveau or at the cooperative. The finest local restaurant is *L'Auberge du Cep*, but simpler and cheaper fare can be had at the *Restaurant des Sports*, which serves an excellent *coq au vin de Fleurie*. And, of course, one is always welcome in the cellars of individual wine growers, who will happily give you *un petit verre* of their Fleurie — a glass that is never as small as this French term suggests.

René Bouillard and his father own just over 11 acres of vines and cultivate another 6 acres under the métayage system. In their small but well-equipped cellar I have tasted a marvellously agreeable Chiroubles, with a taste of terroir.

The house of Mathelin — a family business in Chatillon-d'Azergues — usually produces a very good Chiroubles (including the Cuvée Plaforêt). I have also tasted good Chiroubles from Georges Duboeuf and Dessalle (including Les Martins).

When I visited the cellars of Georges Passot in June, it was quite difficult to find a wine to taste: the casks were empty and the wine sold. I finally understood why: his Chiroubles is, quite simply, one of the best. An exquisite wine with a spring-like freshness.

The Château de Raousset is a large estate of 100 acres (all cultivated under the métayage system), with 42 acres in Chiroubles itself. The quality of each vat was very variable. This estate also sells wines under another label with the words 'Grille-Midi'.

Jean-Pierre Desvignes, the manager of the Domaine Cheysson-les-Farges (54 acres), once received a signed photograph from Brigitte Bardot in gratitude for his good wines. Desvignes makes a delicious Chiroubles.

The wine served at the Chalet de Dégustation in Chiroubles is deliberately of only middling quality, since the intention is to show what an average Chiroubles is like.

Chiroubles

Of the nine *crus* of Beaujolais, Chiroubles is both the most remote and on the highest land, since the vineyards stretch over the slopes of a hill at an altitude of 1,314 feet. The hill finally reaches an altitude of 2,493 feet and the summit is marked by a Swiss-style chalet, built by the wine growers of Chiroubles, from which you can survey the countryside while drinking the local wine. Up here, too, is the only farm of the area not concerned with the cultivation of vines, since they cannot be grown at this height. The growing of vines at Chiroubles goes back to the 9th century. Nowadays, Chiroubles produces about 196,400 cases of wine, though this has not always been so. Although there have been vineyards in the commune for about nine centuries, until the middle of the 19th century wine-growing was only of secondary importance. The small quantities then produced were retained for the consumption of the growers themselves who had always known hard times. The accounts of the period are a long chronicle of misery and distress, poverty and infant mortality. It was only when the vineyards began to extend that things got slightly better.

Granite subsoil

The development of wine-growing, however, was not favoured by the composition of the soil. The meagre vegetation grows on a very hard granite soil — so hard that the growers were obliged to dig into the rock to plant the vines. This work obviously had to be done by hand and Jean-Pierre Desvignes, one of the most distinguished wine growers of Chiroubles, remembers being told by his grandfather how he had to make holes in the rock with his bare hands. The hard work has now found compensation in the rising reputation of Chiroubles and the relative well-being and prosperity of the village. Turnips, which were formerly the main speciality of Chiroubles and for which the village was even known in Paris, have now been almost entirely replaced by vines. Even today, stories are still told of the turnip-growing period, when the peasants, it is said, were often compelled to guard their fields, rifle at the ready.

A dynamic mayor

The use of the *métayage* system of tenancy, by which the wine grower pays rent in kind, is widespread in Chiroubles, where more than 400 inhabitants cultivate land that does not belong to them and from which they can only keep half the harvest. But in spite of this, the number of inhabitants has not declined. Young people remain in the village and vineyards are often cultivated by father and son. Chiroubles owes this fortunate state of affairs to its young and active mayor, Paul Geoffroy, who is very energetic in pursuing the interests of his fellow-villagers. The results of his efforts have already been considerable but, when I met him, he was faced with a particular problem: he had to replace the only baker, who had just retired, as quickly as possible. Recruiting a baker is not as simple as might be believed, and Chiroubles cannot really afford, any more than other French villages, to do without its bakery and fresh bread for very long.

Saving the vines

Chiroubles is especially proud of the fact that Victor Pulliat, a self-taught scientist, lived there from 1827 to 1896; his statue is in front of the church. Pulliat, a student of viticulture, possessed a private collection of about 2,000 varieties of vine from all parts of the world. He was the first person to discover the remedy for *Phylloxera*, the terrible parasite which ruined all the vineyards of Europe at the end of the 19th century. He had already experimented with grafting on to American varieties — the effective remedy — when all other experts still pinned their faith in chemical methods. Obviously, no one took any notice of him and, even in his own village, he was considered to be rather eccentric. It was not until 12 years after his death that he was justly honoured and his researches rewarded with a posthumous chair at the university of Lyon.

A light wine

Chiroubles, though highly regarded by the French, is not widely exported. Generally considered as the lightest of the nine *crus*, it has a very individual grace and attractive light consistency. A dazzling red in colour and very fruity, it is often considered as the most '*primeur*' of all the *crus*, since it ought to be drunk — indeed, must be drunk — before the others. From June, therefore, the cellars of Chiroubles are practically empty. The wine, sold long before this, will doubtless already have been served and drunk, since everyone knows that it is at its best when very young.

No wine grower of Villié-Morgon has won as many prizes as Jean Descombes, and his Morgon is indeed of exceptional quality. He sells a certain quantity directly, and the rest is marketed by Duboeuf (under the name Descombes).

This label bears an illustration of the cellars in which the growers of Morgon hold their celebrations and banquets. The wine is that of the cooperative, which sells about 8,800 cases a year to private customers.

The Morgon from Louis Tête is often delicious after only a year. Without being especially heady, it is fruity and full-bodied. Fine colour, characteristic bouquet.

This Morgon Charmes is made by Marcel Vincent of Fuissé. Personally, I think it is one of the best, full-bodied, supple and strong. It is never cheap and should be kept for at least four years.

The 25-acre estate belonging to Paul Collonge is called the Domaine de Ruyère. It produces a fairly light wine, but this is sufficiently firm to be easily recognizable as a typical Morgon and to be a prize-winner.

Each year, Georges Duboeuf produces an extremely good Morgon. I have tasted several vintages, none of which disappointed me. These are not usually wines for keeping.

Morgon

While Chiroubles radiates peace and calm, Morgon, or more exactly Villié-Morgon, is a much more lively place. Two bus routes now meet there, although most of the traffic in the village consists of tourist coaches. During the summer holidays, it is not unusual for the main cellar there to be visited by 125 coaches in a working week. All the tourists are herded into the vast cellars of a château which has foundations dating from the 15th century. These cellars comprise two great vaulted rooms used for banquets or exhibitions, and a tasting room, with a magnificent bar constructed from casks, where more than 80,000 litres of wine are served or sold to half a million visitors. I tasted the Morgon which is usually on sale there but, since I was with the president of the *cru*, Pierre Piron, I also had the good fortune to taste a 12-year-old Morgon, which was a very different experience!

A wine that keeps its youth

M. Piron wanted to prove to me that a Morgon can be kept successfully, as successfully in fact as a Moulin-à-Vent. I am now convinced that this is true, since the 1964 had aged very well. The fine colour, the fullness of the wine and its light but superb bouquet had lost nothing in age. Of all the wines of Beaujolais, it is this, in my opinion, which compares most favourably with a burgundy of the Côte d'Or. Subsequent tastings have confirmed this impression, thus justifying the saying which attributes to the Morgon 'the fruitiness of a Beaujolais, the charm of a burgundy'.

Wild cherries

The soil of Morgon contains a high percentage of sand and gravel which come from a rather unusual geological formation of broken rock; this gives the Morgon a character which is found in no other Beaujolais. In the bouquet, taste and aftertaste, there is a distinct suggestion of wild cherries, as though the wine had been kept in a vat which had contained kirsch.

Pierre Piron, president of the wine growers' association, owns 31 acres of Morgon (Domaine de la Chanaise). His wine is typical of the new-style Morgon: fruity, vigorous and 'warm', but without any heaviness.

The Morgon from Louis Latour is often excellent, with a pleasant, fruity taste and the 'body' which is so characteristic of Morgon. The Beaujolais house of Mathelin also produces a good Morgon.

*Opposite page:
Jean Descombes, one of the best wine growers of Morgon. The walls of one of his cellars are covered with medals and diplomas.*

*Right:
A harvester empties grapes into a vat.*

*Below, left:
Paul Manoa of the Relais des Caveaux. He once cooked for Churchill during World War II.*

*Below:
The cooperative cellar of Morgon. The tiny zoo belonging to the cellar is especially popular with children.*

The annual vintage of Morgon produces 617,300 cases. The population of the commune — about 1,700 — almost doubles during the harvest. Morgon is twinned with Sasbach-Walden in Germany.

The charming Château de Pizay is well known in Morgon. It belonged for a long time to Michel Gaidon, the well-established Beaune broker, was then bought by Seagram and finally purchased in 1978 by a 24-person syndicate for 21,000,000 French francs. F. Barton & Guestier, a Seagram company, still has the exclusive right to market Pizay wines. The vineyard produces Morgon and Beaujolais-Villages.

Morgon

There are aromas of many other kinds of fruit, too, making this wine more supple, warmer and more sensual than the other Beaujolais, which are mainly remarkable for their freshness.

Contrast of styles

The hard, dark, almost dull colour of the Morgon is another of its striking characteristics. Its alcohol content, which is relatively high, is generally 13° or 13.5°, the latter considered by the growers as ideal. Another interesting fact is that there are really two kinds of Morgon: the old-fashioned Morgon, occasionally too heady and too heavy, and the later style, which is lighter and therefore does not need to be kept long. These contrasts are brought about by different methods of vinification and I would not like to give an opinion in favour of one or the other: they both have their distinct qualities. I have tasted excellent bottles in both styles, one of which is perhaps closer to a burgundy and the other to what is usually expected from a Beaujolais.

An extinct volcano

The vineyards of Villié-Morgon extend over the slopes of two valleys, one to the north and the other to the south. The highest hill, the Mont du Py, reaches an altitude of 1,158 feet. Close by is the hamlet of Morgon which has given its name to the *appellation*. Although the Mont du Py is quite picturesque, its vines are not the best of the *cru*; it is generally agreed that this distinction belongs to Les Charmes, although the wines produced by that vineyard are not of consistent quality. The hill of Les Charmes is an area of some 250 acres divided between numerous owners, but the best-quality wines, which command a high price, are only produced by about 30% of the vineyard. Frequently, too, the wine growers own several plots in different vineyards and mix the wine from Les Charmes with the wine produced elsewhere. It is, therefore, rare to come across a pure Morgon-Charmes.

There are now some 2,470 acres of vineyard in the commune, cultivated by about 250 growers, producing a wine of a quality that wholly justifies the local version of the words of Julius Caesar: 'Veni, vidi, bibi.' ('I came, I saw, I drank.')

Brouilly

The presence of a number of great estates, each with their own château, makes Brouilly the only area of Beaujolais with some resemblance to Bordeaux. The Château de Pierreux (175 acres), all *appellation* Brouilly, and the Château de la Chaize (210 acres) are especially worth visiting. The Château de la Chaize was built by Mansart and Lenôtre, the architects of Versailles, and dates from 1676. Inside, the atmosphere of that period has been recreated, since all the furnishings are in the Louis Quatorze style. The vat room and the cellars (one of these, 114 yards long, is the biggest in all Beaujolais) are very impressive. The estate belongs to the Marquis de Roussy de Sales, a director of Dior.

Six villages

Brouilly is remarkable among the nine *crus* in having vineyards in six different villages: Cercié, Odenas and Saint-Lager, as well as various plots in Charentay, Quincié and Saint-Etienne-la-Varenne. Brouilly is not in fact a separate commune; it takes its name from the neighbouring Mont Brouilly, although the wines from the hill area itself have their own *appellation*, Côte de Brouilly. According to the latest statistics available from the Institut National des Appellations d'Origine, Brouilly has more than 2,715 acres which produce an average of well over 744,300 cases annually, a greater amount than any of the other *crus*.

Several kinds of Brouilly

The majority of the châteaux have let either the whole or part of their vineyards, or run them on the *métayage* system. Thus many wine growers work land that does not belong to them. The 175 acres of vineyard of the Château de Pierreux (Odenas), for example, are divided between 13 growers who make their own wine. A portion of the yield is handed over to the owner and the rest is sold by the grower. It is hardly surprising, therefore, that there are considerable differences between the wines. With the

The wines from this château are characterized by their sumptuous bouquet, their fullness without heaviness and their earthy taste. In recent years, however, the wines, sometimes too light, have lost some of their fine qualities.

Georges Duboeuf sells several kinds of Brouilly, notably that of the Domaine de Combillaty (24 ¾ acres owned by Mme de Fréminville) and the Domaine de la Roche. His simple Brouilly is usually excellent, with great fruitiness and a pleasant, rounded taste.

One of the many activities of Paul Bocuse, proprietor of the famous restaurant north of Lyon, is the selection of exceptional wines, especially among the crus of Beaujolais and the Mâconnais. This delicious Brouilly is one of his choices. In this he has been greatly assisted by Georges Duboeuf.

The vineyard of the Hospices de Beaujeu has been recently extended by nearly 25 acres. The total area now covers 148 acres, with the major part producing Beaujolais-Villages. The rest produces Brouilly. The label above is that of the 'Cuvée Pissevieille', an excellent Brouilly.

The Château de Fouilloux is one of three properties belonging to the family of the Maison Pasquier-Desvignes. The wine is memorable for its fine, bright colour, a distinctive bouquet, fruity as is the taste, which also has a hint of terroir. The Château des Tours also makes a very good Brouilly.

Jean Ruet of Cercié has justifiably won many medals for his wines. This has a beautiful, bright colour with a delicious perfume of raspberry and cherry; it is fresh, light, very fruity and supple. The label has now been slightly changed.

manager, Claude Geoffray, I tasted four wines at the Château de Pierreux in succession and each one varied a good deal. They had not been mixed with one another, since a *négociant* of Romanèche-Thorins had already claimed the best casks. As well as the Brouilly of the estates and the Brouilly of the small owners, there is a third Brouilly, produced by the cooperatives, of which there are three in the area: Saint-Étienne-la-Varenne, Quincié and Bel-Air. The quantity produced by the cooperatives is no more than 25% of the total harvest.

Hospices de Beaujeu

The vineyard of Pisse-Vieille produces a wine which could be regarded as a fourth variety of Brouilly. This vineyard belongs to the Hospices de Beaujeu, which, like the Hospices de Beaune, owns extensive areas of vines (148 acres) which have been bequeathed either by patients or by Christians hoping for a place in paradise. As in Beaune, the new wines of the Hospices de Beaujeu are put up for auction midway through December. The best wine of the

Hospices is, without any doubt, the Pisse-Vieille, while the others are hardly better than a Beaujolais-Villages. According to local legend, the vineyard owes its name to a slightly deaf old woman who maintained that, in punishment of her sins, the *curé* had forbidden her to perform the most natural of bodily functions. She suffered to such an extent that her husband went to find out the truth from the *curé* and, on returning, cried out from afar to his wife: 'Pisse, vieille!' ('Piss, old woman!').

'It sings in the mouth!'

Since there are so many different sorts of Brouilly, it is hard to describe the wine in a few words. The least that can be said is that it tends towards a good Beaujolais-Villages. Its fine, bright colour, its seductive bouquet, its fruitiness and strength give it enough character to go very well with game. Some types of Brouilly have a certain earthy flavour, very typical of the wine and very pleasant. Georges Duboeuf gave the best description of the wine, in my opinion, when he exclaimed: 'A good Brouilly? It sings in the mouth!' It is not a wine for keeping more than two years after its harvest, since it can so often be transformed from the good Beaujolais it is into a thin burgundy.

The Domaine du Château Thivin (42 acres in Côte de Brouilly and Brouilly) belongs to Yvonne Geoffray, widow of Claude Geoffray, a well-known local figure and founder of the Maison du Beaujolais. A full-bodied, fleshy wine, with an often sumptuous bouquet.

In 1974, Lucien Verger's wine was chosen as the best Beaujolais of the year. I have tasted other vintages which were all excellent. M. Verger and his son have 28½ acres in cultivation, of which 18½ are exploited under the métayage system.

It is sometimes claimed that a number of négociants boycott Côte de Brouilly because they feel that too many growers sell their own wine. True or false, Alain Chapel did not allow this rumour to influence his choice of a sublime wine from Georges Duboeuf. Another good house for this wine is Mathelin.

The wine grower Jean Sanvers was tragically killed while working as a volunteer fireman. His wife now runs the holding. I tasted a fruity, strong and well-balanced wine in the shadow of her vaulted cellar, with its moisture-covered walls. Recently the label has been changed considerably.

Côte de Brouilly

Once upon a time, in the Beaujolais, there was a giant who, wishing to rest one day, dug a ditch not far from the Saône. The earth which he removed from his ditch was piled in a mound and so, according to legend, Mont Brouilly came into existence. In fact, the mountain is an extinct volcano, as its name indicates, since 'Brouilly' is derived from 'brulé', meaning 'burnt'. The mount dominates the whole area and can be seen from a distance. Although it is right in the middle of the Brouilly region, the vineyards that stretch up the slopes have the right to their own *appellation*, Côte de Brouilly. This *appellation* was created in 1935 at the request of the owners of the vines on the mountain slopes, which produced the original wine of Brouilly. The progressive extension of the vineyards at the foot of the mountain eventually produced a wine that had nothing in common with the Brouilly of the past, and for that reason the wine growers of Mont Brouilly finally requested their own *appellation*.

Warm summers

A comparison of the two wines provides total justification for the existence of two *appellations*: the Côte de Brouilly has more colour, more body, more tannin. Its alcohol level is the highest of all the *crus* since, legally, it cannot be less than 10°5 (instead of 10°), but is often as high as 14°. This unusually high degree of alcohol comes from the location of the vines on steep slopes where they are exposed to the maximum amount of sunshine. It is not uncommon for the temperature on the southern slopes to rise to 40° or 45°C on a summer afternoon. It can happen during very hot, dry years that the grapes are actually burnt by the sun. The action of the sun is intensified by the granitic soil, which retains the heat and then releases it at night, so that the grapes never benefit from nocturnal coolness. In such years, it is better to buy wines that come from the northern slopes of Mont Brouilly, which are less exposed to the heat.

Blue granite

The subsoils of Mont Brouilly are rather special, since the pink granite, so prevalent in the other *crus*, is here replaced by a blue granite, which can be seen used locally in the walls of old houses. This granite gives the Côte de Brouilly a particular perfume in which the scent of flowers, such as the violet and peony, and the aromas of fruits, such as the raspberry, can be distinguished. This bouquet adds a quality of breeding to an otherwise robust, vigorous wine. The annual production of the Côte de Brouilly reaches about 169,000 cases, but any extension of the current 740 acres is practically impossible, since the mount is almost entirely encircled by Brouilly.

An automatic wine-tasting dispenser

Although the two wines of Brouilly are officially separated, the growers work very closely together, for most of them have land both in Brouilly and Côte de Brouilly. The Cuvage of Saint-Lager is a good example of this cooperation and mutual help. This tasting centre, where both *crus* are served, is well worth visiting for its paintings, for its old press which has been turned into a bar, and for its automatic wine-tasting dispenser. Saint-Lager is the business headquarters of the well-known house of Pasquier-Desvignes and itself a charming village, typically Beaujolais, which served as the setting for a television version of Gabriel Chevallier's *Clochemerle*.

Open-air festivities

Each year, the first Sunday of September sees the reunion of all the friends of Brouilly (who are very numerous) in an immense picnic on the summit of Mont Brouilly. The journey to the top begins in the morning and, at the first stop at the chapel of Notre-Dame-du-Raisin, prayers are held for the success of future vintages. Dating from the middle of the 19th century, the chapel was built on top of the mountain to beg the Virgin for help against vine mildew. At that time there was no track up the mountain, and the growers had to carry the stones for the building of the chapel one by one, although this climb was doubtless frequently interrupted for refreshment. After the blessing of the vines, the meal starts and lasts well into the afternoon, enlivened by the appearance of several well-known radio and television stars. One year, there was even a parachute display. Wine is, of course, plentiful and most of the participants bring their own bottles. Both Brouilly and Côte de Brouilly are examined, tasted and compared at great length; on that one day, the two *crus*, normally separated by a mountain, are brought together for a single great festive occasion.

The Négociants

Before World War II, the number of *négociants-éleveurs* in the wine-producing areas of Burgundy was much greater than it is today. There are now no more than about 170, not counting the many subsidiary houses. This chapter simply sets out to be a short survey of about 40 houses in Burgundy. My impressions are obviously strictly personal. The *négociants* are listed in alphabetical order.

Aujoux & Cie
Address: 20 Bld. Emile-Guyot, Saint-Georges-de-Reneins.
A very export conscious house. It owns 54 acres of vineyard mainly in the Beaujolais and for a small part in the Côte d'or. Also markets branded wines and Côtes du Rhône. The wines I have tasted were only average.

Albert Bichot & Cie
Address: 6 Bld. Jacques-Copeau, Beaune.
A very large *négociant* who claimed to be the most important export house in 1975. It is under the control of the Bichot family and owns 24¾ acres on the Côte d'Or and 61¾ acres in the Chablis region. Albert Bichot also has a branch in the Bordeaux region (Chantecaille). This house uses at least 40 different brand names, including those of Jean Bouchard, Paul Bouchard, Caves Syndicales de Bourgogne, Charles Drapier, Labaume Aîné & Fils, Fortier Picard, Rémy Gauthier, Bouchot-Ludot, Léon Rigault and Maurice Dard. Lupé-Cholet also comes under the Bichot group. The quality of the wines is acceptable, although they do tend to be rather uninteresting, lacking character and nuance. Two of the best wines are Château Gris (Nuits-Saint-Georges, sold exclusively through Lupé-Cholet) and the Chablis Grand Cru Moutonne.

Jean-Claude Boisset
Address: 2 Rue des Frères-Montgolfier, Nuits-Saint-Georges.
Since its founding in 1963, this house has become increasingly important, thanks to a range of usually decent burgundies at reasonable prices. Owns vineyards of about 21 acres. Other brands used are Jacques Cortenay, Blanchard de Cordambles, Louis Deschamps and Honoré Lavigne.

Bouchard Aîné
Address: 37 Rue Sainte-Marguerite, Beaune.
A well-known house in Burgundy, with vineyards notably in Mercurey and a large export business to Canada. However, I have not been entirely satisfied with the quality of the wines, which have seemed rather heavy and lacking in character. Subsidiary brand is Audiffred Aîné.

Bouchard Père & Fils
Address: Au Château, Beaune.
Of all the many Bouchards of Burgundy, this house is the most important, as much for its extensive holdings (207 acres of vineyard, of which the majority are Premiers or Grands Crus) as for the fine quality of its wine. The house dates from 1731. The red wine from its own estates is kept first in new casks and bottled early so that it keeps all its body. The Beaune Grèves Vigne de l'Enfant Jésus, the Volnay Caillerets, the Clos de la Roche, the Bonnes-Mares, the Chevalier-Montrachet and Le Montrachet are among the best. There are other good minor wines, such as the Aligoté Bouzeron.

Lionel J. Bruck
Address: 6 Quai Dumorey, Nuits-Saint-Georges.
A medium-size house with very honest wines, which I occasionally find a little hard and severe. Could it be that these characteristics are due to the fact that the director, Henri-François Cruse, comes from the Bordeaux region? The company belongs to the Société des Vins de France. Hasenklever is a subsidiary label.

Champy Père & Cie
Address: 5 Rue du Grenier-à-Sel, Beaune.
A small house, but the oldest of the Côte d'Or, since it dates from 1720. At the entrance is an impressive list of all the names of the companies. The estate has just over 17 acres. The wines age rapidly and generally lack depth. Beaune les Avaux is one of the best.

Chanson Père & Fils
Address: 10 Rue du Collège, Beaune.
Most of the wines of the house of Chanson (founded in 1750) are kept in cellars in the old fortifications of Beaune, but vinification is carried out inside the town in a modern plant. This house owns about 100 acres, divided between Beaune, Savigny-lès-Beaune and Pernand-Vergelesses. Opinions differ about the quality of the wines. The red wines are kept in casks for quite a long time and lose some of their colour and body. In my opinion, this is a disadvantage, but others like this effect. Generally, they keep well and among the best are: the Beaune Clos des Fèves, the Beaune Marconnets and the Savigny Marconnets. Some of the whites can also be very nice (Bourgogne Cuvée Alexis Chanson, Chablis Mont de Milieu, Pernand-Vergelesses).

F. Chauvenet
Address: B.P.4, Nuits-Saint-Georges.
Belongs to a group of owners. Runs La Grande Cave in Vougeot and sells directly to the public, especially in France. Among the good wines are the Château Marguerite de Bourgogne (Bourgogne Blanc), Pouilly-Fuissé and Domaine de Pérignon (Passetoutgrains). The wines are very similar to those of Louis Max (same postal address).

Raoul Clerget
Address: Saint-Aubin.
A small house which sells wines of very high quality, including some from outside Saint-Aubin. One of the better small family-owned firms on the Côte d'Or. Jean Velard is a subsidiary brand.

M. Doudet-Naudin
Address: 1 Rue Henri Cyrot, Savigny-lès-Beaune.
A modest family house with holdings at Savigny itself and in the neighbouring countryside. The wines of the house tend to be heavy, heady, with a deep colour; they can

be kept for a long time and have all the characteristics of what is generally considered — rightly or not — to be the classic burgundy. Do not expect great character. Several subsidiary brands.

Joseph Drouhin
Address: 7 Rue d'Enfer, Beaune.
Well known again for its elegant yet firm wines of very good quality. The red burgundies are nowadays allowed to ferment slowly for about 12 days, a relatively long period. Here, too, the best wines generally come from the house's own estate, which includes 59 acres on the Côte d'Or and 79 in Chablis. The Beaune Clos des Mouches (red and white), the Puligny Clos du Cailleret, the Griotte-Chambertin, the Corton-Charlemagne, the Bonnes Mares, the Chambolle-Musigny Les Amoureuses, the Chablis Vaudésir, the Chablis Les Clos and the Musigny are among the best. Joseph Drouhin also carries out the vinification of Le Montrachet of the Marquis de Laguiche. Fine cellars in Beaune itself and, just outside, a modern vinification plant, where the wine can be matured in oak casks. Drouhin only sells burgundies.

Georges Duboeuf
Address: Romanèche-Thorins.
This company (which has connections with Bass Charrington) possesses a high reputation for outstanding wines from the Beaujolais and Mâconnais. Many French chefs choose their individual range of wines here. Subsidiary makes include Marc Dudet and Jacques Gonard.

Joseph Faiveley
Address: Nuits-Saint-Georges.
Under the management of François Faiveley (born 1951), many things have changed for the better at the house of that name. The red wines have further increased their quality, while the white have now reached a new level of acceptability. The company owns more land than any other house in Burgundy: about 260 acres on the Côte d'Or and in the Chalonnais (especially Mercurey).

Specialities include Nuits Clos de la Maréchale, Mercurey Clos des Myglands, Clos Vougeot and Corton Clos de Cortons.

Geisweiler & Fils
Address: 1 Rue de la Berchère, Nuits-Saint-Georges.
Since 1971, this house has begun working 173 acres in the Hautes-Côtes and 54 acres in the Nuits-Saint-Georges. In general, the wines of Geisweiler, though of good quality, lack character and the most basic *appellations* have often seemed to me the best. Geisweiler markets the wines of A. Roussigneux, Colcombet Frères, Duret, Larbalestier and J. Goubard. The Fondation Geisweiler has republished Dr Lavalle's famous work on the great wines of the Côte d'Or (1855) in facsimile.

Jaboulet-Vercherre
Address: 5 Rue Colbert, Beaune.
This family house, founded in the Côtes-de-Rhône in 1824, established itself in Burgundy in 1920. Perhaps the origins of the house explain why its wines tend to be deep coloured and full-bodied. Though distinctive, they lack personality. For their price, the simplest *appellations* are often the best. They are produced in a modern vinification plant near Beaune. The 34½ acres of the estate produce some very fine wines, such as the Pommard Clos de la Commaraine. Also markets Louis Lesanglier.

Louis Jadot
Address: 5 Rue Samuel-Legay, Beaune.
I consider this medium-sized house, along with that of Louis Latour, to be the best in the whole of Burgundy. All classes of wine, red and white, are frequently magnificent, from the white Beaujolais to the Corton-Charlemagne, from the Moulin-à-Vent to the Clos de Vougeot. The house owns about 50 acres of vineyard. The wines, generally strong but never unsubtle, are either kept in the fine old cellars of the Couvent des Jacobins or in modern cellars. Very high standards in the choice of wines: in 1975, the director of the house, André Gagey, did not

buy one drop of wine from the Côte d'Or. In addition to the wines already mentioned, Jadot also produces other fine wines, such as the Chevalier-Montrachet Les Demoiselles, the Beaune Clos des Ursules, the Corton Pougets and the white Savigny-lès-Beaune.

Jaffelin
Address: 2 Rue Paradis, Beaune.
Owned by Joseph Drouhin since 1969. However, the two houses still choose their own wines separately. Jaffelin owns the magnificent cellars of Le Chapitre and 8½ acres of vineyard. The wines tend to be rather full. They are well made, but sometimes seem to lack personality. A careful selection, however, may yield some very nice wines, both red and white (on different levels of quality), from red Beaujolais Villages Primeur to white Puligny-Montrachet or Corton-Charlemagne.

Labouré-Roi
Address: Rue Thurot, Nuits-Saint-Georges.
A small, traditional and conscientious house offering a large selection of flawless, carefully selected red and white wines. Traditionally buys a lot of Corton Charlemagne, but the Meursaults of the Domaine René Manuel are also very interesting. The owner is Armand Cottin.

Louis Latour
Address: Rue des Tonneliers, Beaune.
A medium-sized house but with a very high reputation. It owns about 120 acres of vineyard, especially at Aloxe-Corton. The wines, both red and white, are full-bodied, occasionally even a little fat. They always have plenty of distinction; the whites are sometimes of even superior quality to the red. This house sells a complete range of white wines, from the great to the modest, like Saint-Romain and Montagny. The most distinguished wines are the Château Corton-Grancey, the Corton-Charlemagne, the Chevalier-Montrachet Les Demoiselles and the Romanée-Saint-Vivant. Hundreds of thousands of bottles age in the old cellars of Aloxe-Corton, but Latour also owns a

modern vinification centre near Beaune.

Leroy
Address: Auxey-Duresses.
A family company famous in France for its reserve of old vintages. In addition to an 11-acre holding, Leroy also owns half of La Romanée-Conti. The wines have a certain grace, but remain closed for a long time and need several years to become more supple. The Auxey-Duresses, of course, is very good.

Loron & Fils
Address: La Chapelle-de-Guinchay.
A very modern house with an extensive choice of wines ranging from the passable to the good. Owner of 235 acres in Beaujolais and the Mâconnais, the house also has some interests in the Côtes-du-Rhône. The best wines, such as the Juliénas Domaine de la Vieille Église and the Saint-Amour Domaine des Billards, come from its own estate. Loron has extensive business with Nicolas.

P. de Marcilly Frères
Address: 22 Rue du 8 Septembre, Beaune.
A small family company, especially active in the British market. Although a bit heavy, their branded red burgundies can be very pleasant. Their other wines seem to be of no more than medium quality, even those of their own estates in Chassagne-Montrachet and Beaune.

Mathelin
Address: Châtillon d'Azergues.
Mathelin is a specialist in Beaujolais, producing elegant wines which are bottled on the premises but vinified elsewhere. The estate (30 acres) produces both red and white Beaujolais. None of the labels of Mathelin have been illustrated in the present book for lack of space, but I have tasted several wines from this *négociant* and the quality varied from good to very good; especially memorable were a Morgon Château Gaillard, a Chiroubles Plafôret and a Brouilly Château Thivin.

Prosper Maufoux
Address: Santenay.
The influence of the owner and managing director, Pierre Maufoux, is very obvious in this small house. He himself looks after customer relations; the white wines, for which he has a marked preference, are his speciality (he also markets a number of Loire wines). His red wines, some of which come from Santenay, where he owns 67 acres, are good. Pierre Maufoux also owns about 12 acres at Chassagne and Puligny. The house of Maufoux also uses the brand Marcel Amance.

Moillard
Address: 5 Rue François-Mignotte, Nuits-Saint-Georges.
This large house, owned by the Thomas family, supplies many other *négociants*. It owns about 45 acres; vinification is carried out by the most modern methods, producing a wine of technically sound quality. A keen promoter of pasteurization, Moillard claims that, far from 'killing' the wine, this technique makes it possible to avoid all kinds of wine ailments. The red wines are almost always highly coloured and full-bodied, although they may sometimes seem a little flat. The white wines are a little disappointing. Moillard also uses the brands of Thomas Frères, Pierre Olivier, Toursier, Javelier-Laurin and Henri de Bahezre. The company supplies other firms in Burgundy; it is the merchants' merchant.

Mommessin
Address: La Grange Saint-Pierre, Mâcon.
One of the biggest turnover figures in Mâconnais-Beaujolais. The quality of the wines is not always especially praiseworthy, but it is generally good and sometimes even better than good. This house owns about 75 acres of vineyard, the most famous being the Clos du Tart. Markets J. Curtil.

Moreau
Address: Chablis.
Not only the largest owner of Chablis, the largest producer of Chablis and the largest *négociant* of Chablis, but also a very important supplier of dry white wines from outside Burgundy and outside France. Range includes the successful branded wine Moreau Blanc. Many subsidiary companies and labels.

Pasquier-Desvignes
Address: Le Marquisat, Saint-Lager.
The history of this house goes back to 1420. Located in Beaujolais, the greater part of the turnover comes from the sale of regional wines. This family company also sells other burgundies, Côtes-du-Rhône and wines from the Midi. Medium to fairly good quality for reasonable prices. Pasquier-Desvignes also markets the brand Henri Gaillard.

Patriarche Père & Fils
Address: Rue du Collège, Beaune.
This house has the highest turnover in Burgundy. Its red wines are somewhat lacking in body and character, but with one exception: the wines from the Château de Meursault (about 100 acres), which is one of the properties of this firm. Excellent Meursault, Volnay, Pommard and Beaune. Wide choice of brand wines, including the sparkling Kriter. Markets Noémie Vernaux, Bocquet.

Piat Père & Fils
Address: 23 Rue de la République, Mâcon.
This house was bought in 1976 by Gilbey, which was itself bought later by International Distillers and Vintners, now Grand Metropolitan. Since then, the Piat family has severed its connection with the firm, which produces wines of a not too exciting quality. A white Piat wine I have often enjoyed is the Mâcon-Viré. This firm also markets branded wines from outside Burgundy.

Right:
The offices of Henri de Villamont (and its numerous companies) at Savigny-lès-Beaune.

Below left:
A few of the treasures from the cellars of Chanson Père & Fils at Beaune.

Below right:
The shop front of Denis Perret in the centre of Beaune. This fine wine shop is used by Bouchard Père & Fils, Chanson Père & Fils, Joseph Drouhin, Louis Jadot and Louis Latour.

Négociants

Pierre Ponnelle
Address: 55 avenue de l'Ague, Beaune.
Old family business dating from 1875, established in the historical abbey of Saint-Martin. This medium-sized house owns vineyards in a number of places, including Musigny, Bonnes Mares, Charmes-Chambertin and Clos de Vougeot. Good but not outstanding quality. This house also sells quite a few wines from outside the Rhône valley.

La Reine Pédauque
Address: Aloxe-Corton.
This house belongs to the Liogier d'Ardhuy family and is one of the most important of the whole region. It specializes in direct sales to individual clients and its tasting centres at Beaune and Aloxe-Corton have already been visited by more than five million people; it also derives a considerable income from exports. La Reine Pédauque owns about 90 acres of vineyards, but even the wines from this estate generally lack class and character. Numerous brand wines of various origin. Other names marketed include P.A. André, Gauthey Cadet, Abel Laporte, Société d'Elevage des Grands Vins.

Remoissenet Père & Fils
Address: 20 Rue E. Spuller, Beaune.
Small *négociant*, whose wines are usually full-bodied, with a certain elegance and a fine colour. Their quality is normally very reliable. Sells Le Montrachet and other wines from the Domaine Thénard.

Antonin Rodet
Address: Mercurey.
Family firm whose wines seem to improve gradually in character and quality. Specializes in simple burgundies. Owns 62 acres in Mercurey: Château de Chamirey (which produces successful wines). Also markets Pierre Desruelles.

Négociants

Ropiteau Frères
Address: Meursault.
Good range of white wines, including those from the Ropiteau estates (about 87 acres, mainly in Meursault). Also offers a number of attractive reds (Monthelie, for instance). Owned by the Chantovent group. Other names marketed include Colomb-Maréchal, Dargent and Battault.

Thorin
Address: La Chapelle Pontaneveaux.
This successful house, which also operates as Henri Bouchard, the Union des Producteurs, the Héritiers Forest, Faye, etc. has about 247 acres in the Beaujolais and Mâconnais.

This land is partly owned and partly leased for the exclusive exploitation by this house. The estate-produced wines range from the acceptable to the good.

Charles Viénot
Address: Prémaux par Nuits-Saint-Georges.
Small family company with vineyards, including some at Richebourg. Produces both good, vigorous wines and some lesser ones.

Henri de Villamont
Address: Rue Henri Guyot, Savigny-lès-Beaune.
Branch of the Swiss company of Schenk. The house owns 25 acres at Savigny and Chambolle-Musigny. The wines are of very variable quality but rarely achieve great breeding. This house also markets wine under a lot of other names. The best known are Arthur Barolet, François Marthenot and Caves de Valclair. Others include Etienney Vergy, Maufort, Louis Serrignon, Paul Rolland, Mesnard and Brocard & Fils.

PLAISIR de BEAUNE
CAVES EXPOSITION
REINE PÉDAUQUE
ENTRÉE de BEAUNE

Bibliography

Many works were consulted in writing this book. For the reader who wants to go further into the subject the following books are recommended:

John Arlott & Christopher Fielden, *Burgundy Vines and Wines*, London 1976
Félix Benoit & Henry Clos-Jouve, *La Bourgogne insolite et gourmande*, Paris 1976
Pierre Forgeot, *Pèlerinage aux sources de Bourgogne*, Colmar 1971
Hugh Johnson, *World Atlas of Wine*, Revised edition, London 1977
Pierre Poupon & Pierre Forgeot, *Les vins de Bourgogne*, 7th edn, Paris 1975
Pierre Poupon, Raymond Dumay et al., *Le vin de Bourgogne*, 1976
Robert Speaight, *The Companion Guide to Burgundy*, London 1975
H. W. Yoxall, *The Wines of Burgundy*, 2nd edn, London 1974

Other sources consulted are:
Gabriel Liogier d'Ardhuy, *Heureuse Bourgogne*
Joseph Balloffet & Léon Foillard, *Petite Histoire du Beaujolais*, Villefranche-sur-Saône 1952
Youngman Carter, *Drinking Burgundy*, London 1966
René Engel, *Propos sur l'art du bien boire*, Nuits-Saint-Georges 1971
Pierre Forgeot, *Origines du vignoble bourguignon*, Paris 1972
Pierre Forgeot, *Beaune*, Colmar 1972
P. Galet, *Cépages et vignobles de France*, Montpellier 1958
M. J. Lavalle, *Histoire et statistique de la vigne et des grands vins de la Côte d'Or*, 1855; reissued Nuits-Saint-Georges 1972
Max Léglise, *Principes de vinification — Elevage et conservation du vin en cave*, Beaune 1974
Alexis Lichine, *Encyclopedia of Wines and Spirits*, 3rd edn, London 1975
Heidemanne Moll, *Siedlungs-, Wirtschafts- und Bevölkerungsgefüge des französischen Weinbauortes Aloxe-Corton*, Aloxe-Corton 1965
E. de Moucheron, *Grands crus de Bourgogne*, Beaune 1955

François Peynard, *Le village de Fixin*, Dijon 1972
Anthony Rhodes, *Princes of the Grape*, London 1975
Camille Rodier, *Le vin de Bourgogne*, Nuits-Saint-Georges 1920
Camille Rodier, *Clos de Vougeot*, Dijon 1959
Georges Rozet, *La Confrérie des Chevaliers du Tastevin*, Nuits-Saint-Georges 1937
Georges Rozet, *La Bourgogne tastevin en main*, Paris 1949
Frank Schoonmaker, *Encyclopedia of Wine*, 3rd edn, London 1967
A. Sloïmovich, *Ethnocuisine de la Bourgogne*, Cormarin 1973
Roland Thévenin, *Saint-Romain mon village*, Saint-Romain 1962
Pamela Vandyke Price, *Eating and Drinking in France Today*, 2nd edn, London 1972

Index

LE PLUS COURT CHEMIN POUR ALLER AU PARADIS C'EST ENCORE L'ESCALIER DE LA CAVE